ɔ|3|œ

Hollywood Genres and Postwar America

C

Cinema and Society series
GENERAL EDITOR: JEFFREY RICHARDS

Best of British: Cinema and Society from 1930 to the Present
      Anthony Aldgate & Jeffrey Richards
Brigadoon, Braveheart and the Scots: Distortions of Scotland in Hollywood Cinema
      Colin McArthur
British Cinema and the Cold War
      Tony Shaw
Children, Cinema and Censorship: From Dracula to the Dead End Kids
      Sarah J. Smith
An Everyday Magic: Cinema and Cultural Memory
      Annette Kuhn
The British at War: Cinema, State and Propaganda, 1939-1945
      James Chapman
The Crowded Prairie: American National Identity in the Hollywood Western
      Michael Coyne
Film and Community in Britain and France: From La Règle du Jeu *to* Room at the Top
      Margaret Butler
Film Propaganda: Soviet Russia and Nazi Germany
      Richard Taylor
From Moscow to Madrid: Postmodern Cities, European Cinema
      Ewa Mazierska & Laura Rascaroli
Hollywood Genres and Postwar America: Masculinity, Family and Nation in Popular Movies and Film Noir
      Mike Chopra-Gant
Hollywood's History Films
      David Eldridge
Hollywood's New Radicalism: From Reagan to George W. Bush
      Ben Dickenson
Licence to Thrill: A Cultural History of the James Bond Films
      James Chapman
Past and Present: National Identity and the British Historical Film
      James Chapman
Powell and Pressburger: A Cinema of Magic Spaces
      Andrew Moor
Propaganda and the German Cinema, 1933-1945
      David Welch
Spaghetti Westerns: Cowboys and Europeans from Karl May to Sergio Leone
      Christopher Frayling
Spectacular Narratives: Hollywood in the Age of the Blockbuster
      Geoff King
Typical Men: The Representation of Masculinity in Popular British Cinema
      Andrew Spicer
The Unknown 1930s: An Alternative History of the British Cinema, 1929-1939
      Edited by Jeffrey Richards

Hollywood Genres and Postwar America:

Masculinity, Family and Nation in Popular Movies and Film Noir

MIKE CHOPRA-GANT

I. B. Tauris *Publishers*
LONDON • NEW YORK

Published in 2006 by I.B. Tauris & Co Ltd
6 Salem Road, London W2 4BU
175 Fifth Avenue, New York NY 10010
www.ibtauris.com

In the United States of America and Canada distributed by
Palgrave Macmillan a division of St. Martin's Press
175 Fifth Avenue, New York NY 10010

HB: ISBN 1 85043 815 3
        EAN 978 1 85043 815 1

PB: ISBN 1 85043 838 2
        EAN 978 1 85043 838 0

A full CIP record for this book is available from the British Library
A full CIP record is available from the Library of Congress

Library of Congress Catalog Card Number: available

Printed and bound in Great Britain by MPG Books Ltd, Bodmin
camera-ready copy edited and supplied by the author

CONTENTS

	Acknowledgements	
	List of tables	
	List of figures	
One	**Introduction: Movies, Genre and Zeitgeist**	**1**
	Film noir and the zeitgeist	*2*
	Intellectualism and middlebrow culture	*7*
	Re-thinking zeitgeist	*11*
	Defining the popular	*11*
	What about the rest of the forties?	*16*
	What's genre got to do with it	*21*
Two	**Re-invigorating the nation: popular films and American national identity**	**26**
	Cinderellas of the services	*28*
	The myth of classlessness	*33*
	Land of opportunity	*46*
	Modernizing the American hero	*55*
	American-ness and immigrant identities	*57*
Three	**The troubled postwar family: "moms" and absent fathers**	**65**
	The absent father	*66*
	The pleasures of fatherhood	*78*
	Momism	*82*
Four	**Performing postwar masculinities**	**95**
	Soldier to civilian: masculinity and performativity	*98*
	Staging masculinities: performativity and genre	*107*
	Stars and performance	*111*
Five	**Military service and male companionship**	**121**
	The all-male group	*122*
	Military service and self "improvement"	*130*
	Buddies	*133*
	Male friendship, mature masculinity and patriarchal continuity	*139*

Six	**Popular films and "tough" movies**	**146**
	Noir and Nation	*149*
	Social status and the veteran experience	*149*
	Class and democracy	*152*
	The noir hero	*156*
	Noir and the melting pot	*158*
	Noir and the family	*160*
	The absent father of film noir	*161*
	"Mom" and the femme fatale	*163*
	Noir masculinities and performance	*164*
	Noir and male companionship	*167*
	The noir male group	*168*
	Noir buddies	*170*
	Noir and patriarchal continuity	*172*
Seven	**Genre and History**	**175**
	Problems with "the popular"	*183*
	Notes	189
	Bibliography	194
	Index	215

LIST OF TABLES

Table 1.1   Popular films in the USA in 1946   13

Table 1.2   Twenty highest revenue-earning films in   18
             America 1946-1950

LIST OF FIGURES

Figure 2.1	Al Stephenson (Fredric March) and Fred Derry (Dana Andrews) in *Best Years of Our Lives* (1946)	34
Figure 3.1	Devlin (Cary Grant) in *Notorious* (1946)	72
Figure 3.2	Madame and Alex Sebastian (Leopoldine Konstantin and Claude Rains) in *Notorious* (1946)	72
Figure 3.3	Madame Sebastian (Leopoldine Konstantin) in *Notorious* (1946)	86
Figure 3.4	Shot sequence from *Notorious* (1946)	88
Figure 3.5	Grandma Leckie (Gladys Cooper) and Robert Shannon (Dean Stockwell) in *The Green Years* (1946)	90
Figure 4.1	Al Stephenson (Fredric March) in *Best Years of Our Lives* (1946)	104
Figure 4.2	Bing Crosby and Bob Hope in *Road to Utopia* (1946)	116
Figure 5.1	Shot from *Blue Skies* (1946)	132
Figure 5.2	Shot sequence from *Road to Utopia* (1946)	137
Figure 5.3	Advertisement for Studebaker cars. *Life Magazine* 18 February 1946	142

General Editor's Introduction

In this illuminating and insightful revisionist study, Mike Chopra-Gant challenges the received scholarly wisdom about the mood in America immediately after the close of the Second World War. Most scholars have taken the *film noir* genre as an index of popular attitudes and consider that these films demonstrate a crisis of masculinity, a perception of widespread corruption in society and a prevailing sense of gloom, pessimism and cynicism. But Chopra-Gant persuasively argues that this is too narrow and one-dimensional an interpretation of the cinematic evidence of the public mood. While not denying the significance of the *film noir* and its attitudes, he suggests that there were alternative outlooks and to discover them he turns to the lists of top box office successes. He finds there films that have been consistently neglected by historians, titles like *Saratoga Trunk*, *Till the Clouds Roll By*, *The Green Years* and *Two Years Before the Mast*. The lists from 1946 to 1950 are dominated by comedies, musicals and 'feel good' movies like *The Bells of St Mary's*, *Life with Father* and *The Yearling*. The *film noir* genre barely figures anywhere in the top popularity lists.

So what do the most popular as opposed to the most studied films tell us about postwar America? Chopra-Gant identifies a whole series of positive values. Many of the films emphasise the triumph of American beliefs – democracy, classlessness and individualism. The biopics of Al Jolson, Cole Porter and Jerome Kern show talented individuals finding success in a land of opportunity. The films indicate not a crisis of masculinity so much as a celebration of the joys of masculine comradeship. Films laud the traditional American family, while recognising the problems that can be created by absent fathers and domineering mothers. Chopra-Gant rightly concludes that the film evidence is more complex and multilayered than previously allowed. He also importantly reminds film historians that it is imperative to study those films popular with the ticket-buying public and not just those popular with critics and academics.

JEFFREY RICHARDS

ACKNOWLEDGEMENTS

The research for much of this book was conducted with the aid of a research studentship, no. 98/3405 for the Arts and Humanities Research Board. My sincere thanks go to Christine Geraghty who provided support of the best kind during the completion of the PhD upon which this book is based and also to Steve Neale and Mark Glancy, whose helpful comments as examiners of my thesis have been of invaluable help in the process of turning the thesis into this book. While completing this book, parts of Chapter 3 have appeared in an article in *Comparative American Studies*, Vol 3 No. 3, September 2005, Sage Publications.

   I would like to thank the following people for their help, support and inspiration of various kinds: Nick Couldry, Jonathan Burston, Caspar Melville, Jonathan Grey, Martha Michailidou, Elizabeth Wilson, Milly Williamson, Bill Osgerby, Paul Cobley, Gholam Khiabany, Jonathan Wright, Gareth Stanton, David Morley and James Curran. The process of completing this book would have been much more arduous but for the assistance provided by the staff of the British Film Institute Reading Room, the New York Public Library, The British Library, The University of London Library, Goldsmiths College Library and the U.S. National Archive and Records Administration. Without the selfless babysitting and other help provided by Mrs. Kamlesh Chopra completing this book would have been unthinkable.

   Thanks also to the bums who nightly drank on the steps of the Riverview Hotel, Jane Street, New York during the summer of 1999 and to the bikers and rodders at the Hotel Congress, Tucson, Arizona in May 2000 for adding colour.

   Most importantly my love and thanks go to Pam Chopra-Gant and our daughters, Keshika and Umika, who have put up with more than anyone has a right to expect while I have been working on this book. I couldn't have got there without you.

CHAPTER 1

Introduction: Movies, Genre and Zeitgeist

It has often been said that every age is dominated by a privileged form, or genre, which seems by its structure the fittest to express its secret truths; or perhaps, if you prefer a more contemporary way of thinking about it, which seems to offer what Sartre would have called the objective neurosis of that particular time and place.

Fredric Jameson 1991: 67

This book is concerned with American popular films and culture in the period immediately following the end of the Second World War. I present here an analysis of a number of the most popular films released within a short period after the war's end. My aim in undertaking this analysis is to examine connections between these films and some of the values, attitudes and anxieties that preoccupied American society as it moved from war to peace, and which found expression in the movies of the period and in key discourses that were reproduced across a wide range of cultural sites including magazines, other periodicals and popular literature—particularly the self-help and rehabilitation literature that proliferated in the period following the war. What I present in this book, then, is a contextualized account of these films: an account that privileges neither the films nor other materials used to establish a cultural context for those films, but rather sees both the movies and the wider cultural context as being involved in a dialogic, discursive relationship and which sees in the dialogue between these different cultural artifacts an expression of the cultural climate of the early postwar period in the United States.

I have two main purposes in undertaking this analysis. First is the straightforward one of providing a contextualized account of the movie culture of the early postwar period in the United States. The second purpose—which follows inevitably from the first—is to challenge the impression of this period cultivated through film scholars' overriding interest in one particular genre among the many genres of films that were produced and enjoyed popular success in the early postwar period: film noir.

Film noir and the Zeitgeist

In the quotation at the start of this chapter, Fredric Jameson identifies one of the major assumptions made by literary and film theory; an assumption that could hardly be better illustrated than by looking at how the movies and culture of the United States in the late 1940s and early 1950s have, more often than not, been approached within film studies. Notwithstanding the existence of numerous different cycles and genres comprising Hollywood's output during the early postwar period, none has attracted as much scholarly attention as film noir. In numerous accounts of the genre,[1] noir is seen as more than a trend in film production; it is regarded as emblematic not only of the cinematic culture, but also of the tone of American culture generally in the period of postwar readjustment. In some respects this may be seen as a revisionist view, forcefully asserted in numerous accounts of the films and culture of the period published years later. However the origin of this image of America in the late forties can be traced to the period itself. In an article published in *Hollywood Quarterly* in 1947, John Houseman argued that Hollywood films were a key location for the articulation of the "shocking spectacle of a nation's most pressing fears and secret desires", and that in the early postwar era these fears and desires found expression in the "tough" movie (1947a: 161). Houseman insisted that the milieu depicted in these tough movies was "no lurid Hollywood invention", but a "fairly accurate reflection of the neurotic personality of the United States of America in the year 1947" (161). Despite the enthusiasm with which later film theorists have embraced this image of America in the late 1940s, it was controversial even at the time of the publication of Houseman's article. In a reply to Houseman in the subsequent edition of *Hollywood Quarterly*, Lester Asheim challenged the validity of Houseman's claim, highlighting the very selective evidence called in support of the argument and criticizing Houseman's tendency to extrapolate generalizations about American films and society from an extremely limited set of examples (1947: 414-416).

In the years since Houseman and Asheim published their articles, it is Houseman's view that has provided the more attractive vision of the period for subsequent generations of film critics and there is now a well established strand of film theory—which Richard Maltby describes as a "zeitgeist theory of film as cultural history" (1992: 41)—which explains the pessimism, cynicism, violence and paranoia that typifies films noirs as a reflection or, more accurately, an articulation of the cultural and social mood of postwar America; a mood that was itself pessimistic, cynical, violent and paranoid. As Pam Cook observes in *The Cinema Book*, "the connection between 'postwar gloom' and the 'meaninglessness', 'depression' and 'angst' of noir became almost *de rigeur* in critical analyses" (1985: 96).

Typifying this approach to film noir, Thomas Schatz suggests that the dark visual style of film noir reflected "progressively darkening cultural attitudes during and after the war" (1981: 113) and in a later book argues that film noir was, "at base a highly stylized treatment of contemporary social and human conditions" (1999: 378). Similarly, Spencer Selby refers to the "historical trends (postwar disillusionment and realism) that helped produce the noir movement" (1984: 2), while Sylvia Harvey argues that:

> film noir captures and magnifies the rumbles that preceded one of those earthquakes in human history that shift the hidden foundations of a society and which begin the displacement of its characteristic and dominant systems of values and beliefs.
>
> (1998: 35)

Numerous other critics have relied on a similar assumption that film noir represented an expression of the unsettled and pessimistic mood of American culture in the early postwar years, but few have looked very far beyond the films themselves for evidence substantiating the existence of this malaise.

Were they to look beyond the limited cultural range of the film noir canon, these writers would be forced to confront the weakness of one of the central assumptions behind the noir and zeitgeist thesis. While the pessimistic social mood proposed by this approach to film noir may have a strong appeal to common sense, there is compelling evidence that the reality of postwar America was more equivocal. Steve Neale casts doubt over the familiar, gloomy image of the mid and late 1940s, citing a number of writers who identify a more upbeat mood as characteristic of the postwar period (2000: 158). Exemplifying the tendency identified by Neale, William L. O'Neill styles the period from 1945 to 1960 the "American High", and refers to the period as "our time of greatest confidence" (1986: 7). Similarly, Joseph C. Goulden described the time as possessing "above the general euphoria, a broad national confidence, both in the future of individuals and in the country's ability to solve any postwar problems that arose" (1976: 9). Providing further evidence of the existence of an optimistic cultural climate after the war, Victor J. Viser refers to a speech given in 1945 by James Webb Young, Chairman of the Advertising Council and Director of the J. Walter Thompson Company, in which Young "talked about an immediate post-war period that was, by most accounts, an exuberant time for an America flushed by a victory that finally marked it as a true global power" (2001: 111).

These accounts of early postwar optimism point to a need to revise our impression of American society at the time, replacing the pessimistic cultural tone familiar in the accounts of film noir with an upbeat mood that is more consonant with the mood of the musicals, comedies and romances that were such significant popular film genres during those years. Simply substituting one unequivocal image of cultural consensus for another is, however, of limited value in understanding the movies of the period and the complicated way contemporary films and genres registered the mood of US society. Although writers who propose a link between film noir and the postwar zeitgeist insist on the downbeat character of the postwar mood, and the writers discussed above talk in more optimistic terms, it is not so much a case of the mood of early postwar America having been either entirely gloomy or totally optimistic: in reality it was a complicated and often contradictory mixture of both.

A number of cultural histories of the period confirm the view that the early postwar years in America were characterized by contradictory intellectual, political and social currents. While insisting on its underlying confidence, O'Neill does acknowledge that "postwar America was less unified and homogenous than in memory it seems", and notes that the period enjoyed its share of "fierce debates, name-calling and finger pointing" (1986: 7). Taking almost the opposite stance to O'Neill—seeing the early postwar years as a period which "produced a culture that was more pessimistic and cynical than before" (1991: 18)—William Graebner argues that these feelings did not coalesce into a "negative cultural consensus" (18), but instead produced a culture that was radically ambivalent, and characterized by its "disparate and conflicting responses to the central problems of forties existence" (18). It is likely, then, that the most accurate image of the intellectual and cultural climate of the early postwar years is one of a culture characterized not by consensus, but by a volatile mixture of contradictory feelings.

One way of conceptualizing the conflictual dynamics of early postwar American society is to regard the opposed images of its mood as being a result of ideological differences between the official image of U.S. culture, which maintained an upbeat tone for political reasons, and an unofficial, dissenting culture of artists and intellectuals who were more critical of the political, economic and social order of postwar America. Exemplifying the latter tendency, Robert Warshow, writing in 1948, recognized compulsory optimism as a characteristic of "official" U. S. culture; "America, as a social and political organization, is committed to a cheerful view of life. It could not be otherwise" (2001: 97). According to Warshow, the fundamental basis for all modern, egalitarian societies such as America was the claim that "they are making life happier" (97). As a result, according to Warshow, the issue of individual happiness became a political one, and discontent could be seen as an expression of political critique since it implied the failure of the political system to achieve its key goal of ensuring individual contentment. Warshow even suggested that this logic demanded the staging of a display of optimism as a patriotic duty:

it becomes an obligation of citizenship to be cheerful; if the authorities find it necessary, the citizen may even be compelled to make a public display of his cheerfulness on important occasions, just as he may be conscripted into the army in time of war.

(2001: 97-98)

The extent to which the optimistic tone that characterizes many of the most popular films released in 1946 is the result of the kind of "compulsory" cheerfulness suggested by Warshow is a moot point. There may be reasons for this other than the pressure of dominant ideologies. So far as the argument I advance in this book is concerned, however, what is significant about the cultural tone suggested by both Warshow and Viser is the fact that it so starkly contradicts the idea that the mood of early postwar U.S. society was unequivocally pessimistic. Even if the upbeat tone described by writers like Viser and O'Neill really amounted to an ersatz display of optimism, promoted by an official culture with a significant ideological investment in encouraging an optimistic vision of the postwar prospects for America, this is a mood that is clearly registered in the most popular films released in the aftermath of the war, and the greater popularity of these more upbeat genres of movies compared with that of contemporary films noirs urges us to reconsider the central position which films noirs have been accorded in our understanding of American culture during those years.

This split between official, optimistic attitudes, registered in the most popular films of the period, and the more critical, pessimistic stance registered in the films noirs of the time suggests a possible explanation for the amount of scholarly attention that has been lavished on the latter at the expense of the former. The critical dimension of films noirs undoubtedly increases their appeal to left-leaning academics, and it is unsurprising that film scholars, with their grounding in literary and psychoanalytic theories, should be attracted to the apparently richer and more complicated texts comprising the film noir canon. Perhaps this explains why, even though some writers have identified the link between film noir and American society proposed by zeitgeist theories of film noir as problematic,[2] film scholars have been slow to adopt a more sociological approach to the film culture of the period and extend their consideration of the connections between movies and society to embrace Hollywood's full generic array.

The implicit hierarchy of cultural value which directs the critical gaze towards certain kinds of film at the expense of others still persists in film scholarship, despite the development in recent years of more historical and anthropological approaches to movies and movie-going as a result of the encounter between film studies and cultural studies. In a recent book, for example, Deborah Thomas claims "not all films are up to close scrutiny", that some movies are too "thin", too "formulaic" to warrant serious scholarly attention (2001: 2). This is a more controversial argument than Thomas's confident statement registers, because it relies on the prioritization of intrinsic textual qualities, that may on their own tell us very little about a film's contextual surround, over the highly revealing intertextual relationships between individual texts. Despite the fact that judgments about aesthetic value may direct critical attention toward one film rather than another, even those films which initially appear to offer few prospects for rewarding critical analysis—on the basis of their intrinsic textual qualities—can reveal much about their historical moment when they are considered within their wider cultural context. And if it is the *significance* of films within the culture of a particular historical moment that interests us then there are good reasons for turning the critical gaze toward those films that possessed the greatest cultural currency in that moment, regardless of how these films might individually be judged for their intrinsic aesthetic qualities. This means looking at the most popular films of the time, those that were seen by the greatest number of cinemagoers.

Intellectualism and middlebrow culture

In his introduction to *Recasting America: Culture and Politics in the Age of the Cold War*, Lary May observes that the mood of anxiety and unease attributed to early postwar America "characterized only a minority of elite intellectuals, far removed from the popular culture of the people" (1989: 7). May supports the suggestion that there was an upbeat tone to the official culture of the time, remarking that the mass media were "characterized by a positive tone that reinforced the affluent consensus" (7), but he also notes the "rise of a large market for dark pessimistic works whose cinematic forms manifested a stark beauty" (7). The split that May identifies, between a pessimistic highbrow culture and a more optimistic popular, middlebrow culture supports the argument that there was a division between an upbeat "official" culture and a gloomier culture of dissent.

In a later book, May identifies a significant number of radical filmmakers working in Hollywood during the late forties who used the crime film as a vehicle for expressions of political criticism (2000: 215-256). This suggests another dimension to the ideological split between the generally affirmative popular postwar culture and a critical faction of film producers, by aligning these two tendencies with populist, middlebrow and more intellectual, highbrow tastes respectively. Within this admittedly schematic dichotomy, film noir seems to fall outside the realm of popular, middlebrow culture and firmly within the minority tastes of the aesthetic elite. It may seem that there is a certain irony in the characterization of film noir as a highbrow, intellectual cultural form, given its indebtedness to antecedents—the gangster movie, hardboiled pulp fiction, the "true story" detective magazine—which were often anything but intellectual. But, as Andrew Sarris has noted, the elevation of lowbrow art to higher aesthetic status as a means of achieving distinction from middlebrow art is a "classic highbrow gambit" (1968: 29). Further evidence of the existence of a tension between intellectual and populist cultural tendencies during the late forties and early fifties—at least as far as entertainment industry personnel were concerned—is provided by the Vice President in charge of television for NBC, Sylvester L. Weaver, in an article published in *Variety* in the early 1950s (3 January 1951: 101). In the article, Weaver attacked "intellectual" critics who belittled the content of much television programming for appealing to the "lowest common denominator", and who attempted to substitute their own (minority) tastes for those of the mass audience who, in turn, demonstrated their approval of the populist content of television by continuing to watch programmes, thereby making them "hits". It is the framing of Weaver's argument in terms of an opposition between intellectualism and populism, rather than his defence of particular types of television programme, which is most instructive, providing further evidence of the existence of a tension between highbrow and middlebrow tendencies in cultural production in America during the early postwar years.

Some of Warshow's writing of the time provides a particularly pertinent demonstration of the functioning of this dichotomy as a structuring opposition within early postwar American culture. In a review originally published in 1948, Warshow noted what he saw as a characteristic error made by what he termed "English intellectuals" commenting on American culture. According to Warshow, these "English intellectuals" advanced a mistaken belief that educating the public in the techniques of "film appreciation" would enable a "progressive refinement of taste [which] will lead almost automatically from bad art to good art" (2001: 286). According to Warshow this error arose because "English intellectuals" occupied a cultural milieu suffused with the values of high culture and, consequently, "have not yet had to face the problem of middlebrow culture squarely" (286). Conversely, in America the "problem" presented by middlebrow culture was at its sharpest and, Warshow argued, film criticism, because of its failure to maintain a clear distinction between the communicative power of film and its intrinsic aesthetic qualities had produced serious errors of judgment precisely because of its failure to "acknowledge the essential *aesthetic* importance of film content" (287, emphasis in original). In this review, Warshow identified *Best Years of Our Lives* (Wyler 1946 USA) as an example of over-rated, middlebrow "trash" (286).[3] In an earlier review of Wyler's film (originally published in 1947), Warshow identified the movie with precisely the kind of "optimistic picture of American life, and of postwar America in particular" (125) I am suggesting typified the popular, middlebrow cultural productions of the early postwar years and which provides the basis for the distinction between these productions and the pessimistic, critical tendency represented by film noir.

The fact that film noir sits on the intellectual, highbrow side of this dichotomy offers another explanation for its appeal to subsequent generations of academic critics. I don't criticize scholars' decisions to turn their attention to intrinsically interesting films, where the claims made about those films are limited to the films themselves. However, the shift from focusing on film noir as an intrinsically interesting object of study to attributing to it a central role in articulating the early postwar mood of American society is one that significantly overstates the evidence when only the films are considered. In his critique of method in cultural studies, Nick Couldry has persuasively argued that the tendency to focus on intrinsically interesting objects—most often cultural forms and sites through which opposition, resistance and dissent are enacted and expressed—has led to a tendency to ignore middlebrow culture and the mundane, everyday world inhabited by the majority within a society (2000: 3). This is a criticism that applies equally to the attempts of film scholars to claim a historiographical dimension to their analysis of films and genres while continuing to ignore those films that were seen, and presumably enjoyed, by the greatest number of people at the time in question. In part this book is an attempt to redress the balance by turning attention to the most popular films released in America just after the Second World War and attempting to relate those films to the wider cultural dynamics of the time.

If the mood of American society immediately after the Second World War was more equivocal than zeitgeist approaches to film noir have suggested, it is necessary to reconsider some of the assumptions that have underpinned this strand of film criticism and some of the questions it asks. R. Barton Palmer suggests that "film noir ... evolved and endured because moviegoers at the time were satisfied by its images and stories, by the world of social relations and values it conjured into existence" (1994: 32) and asks:

> why did viewers at the time approve of and enjoy distressing representations of disturbing social realities? ... Why ... did filmgoers accept and, to some degree welcome anxiety-provoking films from Hollywood?
>
> (33)

If the aim is to obtain a reliable impression of American movies and culture in the early postwar years these questions are misdirected. Instead it is necessary to ask whether contemporary filmgoers did enjoy and approve of these films and, if not, then what films did they enjoy and what can an analysis of these *popular* films reveal about the preoccupations, anxieties, values and "mood" of American society at the time? Where zeitgeist approaches to film noir have focused exclusively on an aspect of elite, highbrow, critical postwar culture, my aim in this book is attempt to answer questions like these by focusing on the hitherto neglected middlebrow movie culture of America immediately after the war, examining the interpenetration of discourses found in the period's most popular films within a range of contemporary, popular (and frequently also middlebrow) cultural forms.

Re-thinking zeitgeist

In the preceding paragraphs I have argued that there is a need to recognize that the cultural climate of early postwar America was not characterized by the uniform cultural consensus that is assumed by zeitgeist theories of film noir, but consisted of diverse and often contradictory currents. The idea of zeitgeist as the *spirit of the age* demands a unanimity that is inconsistent with the fragmentation and contradiction that characterized American society and culture during the early postwar years. The concept of zeitgeist, therefore, is a problematic tool for analysing the films and culture of the period: the idea of the spirit of the age is an impediment to the production of a reliable impression of an age that possessed no singular, dominant spirit. While the early postwar years may have lacked the singular tone which zeitgeist theories of cultural history demand, discourses of the period focused on a distinctive set of concerns, anxieties, values and themes which, while permitting contradictory positions towards these attitudes and values to be taken, provided the era with its distinctive character. In undertaking this analysis of American films and culture in the early postwar moment I, therefore, reject the use of zeitgeist as a central analytical concept. Instead my analysis will focus on the identification of some of these key discourses that register the distinctive concerns of that historical moment.

Although I have questioned the conclusions reached by zeitgeist theories of film noir, some of the themes which film scholars have identified as central issues in film noir remain useful in understanding the preoccupations of American society in the early postwar years. Three of these broad themes—national identity, the family and masculinity—provide the focus for my analysis of a set of the most popular movies in America released shortly after the conclusion of the Second World War.

Defining the popular

In attempting to constitute a reasonably objective set of popular early postwar films it has been necessary to make certain decisions which inevitably shape the study and its conclusions in a particular way. The decision to examine popular films was primarily motivated by a desire to obtain an objective set of movies which was very clearly not chosen by me for the films' consistency with any preconceptions I held about the movies and culture of the period. While there are undoubtedly other ways this could have been achieved, I opted for the simple expedient of using three data sources detailing the rental revenues achieved by films in 1946. Even this was not completely straightforward, however, as different sources of rental revenue data follow different compilation procedures. As a result, some films released late in 1945 are included by some sources in their list of high earners for 1946, while some released late in 1946 appear in the 1947 charts. So, for example, while Lyon (1989) lists *Best Years of Our Lives* as the top revenue earner of 1946, the film appears in the annual list of top-earning movies for 1947 in *Variety* (7 January 1948: 63), while Steinberg—who, up to 1946, draws his data from the records of *Motion Picture Herald*, *Motion Picture Daily* and *Film Daily*, and from 1947 adopts the figures reported by *Variety*—identifies the film as a top earner in his lists for both 1946/7 and 1947 (1982: 19). For the sake of simplicity, Lyon's list for 1946 has been taken as the primary source of box office revenue data and this list has been cross-referenced against Steinberg's lists for 1945 to 1947, and against films listed with a release date of 1945, 1946 or1947 in a chart of "All-Time Top Grossers" published by *Variety* in 1955 (5 January 1955: 59 and 63). The 17 films that appear in all three sources appear in Table 1.1 (listed with their rental revenue according to Lyon 1989: 210-211).

The most notable, and perhaps most surprising feature of this list, given the dominance of zeitgeist theories of film noir in understanding the movie culture of this historical moment, is the almost complete absence of any films noirs from the list of popular films. *Notorious* has been classified as noir by Borde and Chaumeton (2002) as well as other writers, but none of the remaining films possesses the stylistic and thematic characteristics associated with film noir. Even the classification of *Notorious* as film noir seems to owe more to what Rick Altman (1999) terms "re-genrification" by subsequent generations of scholars than to the way the film was likely to have been understood by forties audiences. The pressbook for the movie promoted two main generic identifications for the film: suspense movie and romance. While the former may be consistent with the film's later assimilation into the noir canon, the identification of the movie as a romance is problematic both in relation to the later re-definition of the film as noir, and in terms of what the fact of the film's popularity implies about the mood of the surrounding culture. Eleven of the remaining sixteen popular films of 1946 can also be classified as romances, comedies or musicals. These popular films, then, provide a contextual surround for *Notorious* which suggests that it is more likely that the movie would have been understood as a romance by contemporary audiences, rather than a "tough" movie—to use John Houseman's contemporary phrase for what film scholars would later understand as film noir. Reviews of the film at the time of its release support this view. *Variety* called the film a "romantic drama of topnotch caliber" (24 July 1946); the *New York Times*, in its review of the Ten Best movies of the year, referred to the film as a "romantic melodrama" (29 December 1946); Bosley Crowther, also reviewing the film for the *New York Times*, described the movie both as a "romantic melodrama" and a "remarkable blend of love story with expert thriller" (16 August 1946).

Table 1.1 Popular Films in the USA in 1946

Best Years of Our Lives (Wyler 1946 USA)	$11.4m
The Jolson Story (Green 1946 USA)	$7.7m
Blue Skies (Heisler 1946 USA)	$5.9m
The Yearling (Brown 1946 USA)	$5.5m
Saratoga Trunk (Wood 1945 USA)	$5.1m
Notorious (Hitchcock 1946 USA)	$4.9m
Road to Utopia (Walker 1946 USA)	$4.8m
The Harvey Girls (Sidney 1946 USA)	$4.7m
The Razor's Edge (Goulding 1946 USA)	$4.7m
Till the Clouds Roll By (Whorf 1946 USA)	$4.6m
Night and Day (Curtiz 1946 USA)	$4.5m
Two Years Before the Mast (Farrow 1946 USA)	$4.4m
Easy to Wed (Buzzell 1946 USA)	$4.2m
The Green Years (Saville 1946 USA)	$4.2m
Margie (King 1946 USA)	$4.1m
The Kid from Brooklyn (McLeod 1946 USA)	$4.0m
Ziegfeld Follies (Minnelli 1946 USA)	$3.7m[4]

The significance of this debate about the generic identity of the movie does not rest on whether the later re-classification of *Notorious* as a film noir can be justified. The important point is that, at the time of its release, the available evidence—the pressbooks, reviews and the contextual surround provided by the other popular films—suggests that the film was more likely to have been understood as a romance rather than one of the other genres—thriller, suspense—with which the film was also identified, and which would be more compatible with the later redefinition of the movie as a film noir. This is an important historical point since it implies the existence of a stronger leaning toward the lighter, more optimistic genres within early postwar American culture, than toward the downbeat pessimism of noir. This in turn supports my argument that it is vital to look at the films which achieved the greatest success at the box office in order to gain a reliable insight into the culture of the period: if the one film in this list of popular films that has subsequently been classified as a film noir was understood to be a romance by audiences at the time of its release; if audiences went to see this film because of its romantic elements rather than its "noir" dimension, then this strongly suggests that it is the other films from the more optimistic genres—the musicals, comedies and romances which dominate this set of popular films—rather than film noir that had a particular resonance with the American mood after the war.

Another notable feature of this list is that it contains a number of films which are not now well known and which have featured little in film scholarship relating to the period. *Saratoga Trunk*, *Two Years Before the Mast*, *The Green Years*, *Easy to Wed*, *Margie* and *The Kid From Brooklyn*—all among the biggest earners at the American box office in 1946—have now all but disappeared from film studies' historical consciousness of the period. And while other films, such as *The Harvey Girls*, *Till the Clouds Roll By*, *Night and Day* and *Ziegfeld Follies*, have established a limited profile in film scholarship, academic interest in these films has largely been premised on their generic qualities—on their status as musicals—not on their ability to express something about the early postwar mood. It is films such as *It's a Wonderful Life* (Capra 1946 USA) and some of 1946's films noirs—*Gilda* (Vidor 1946 USA), *The Strange Love of Martha Ivers* (Milestone 1946 USA), *The Postman Always Rings Twice* (Garnett 1946 USA), *The Big Sleep* (Hawks 1946 USA), *The Blue Dahlia* (Marshall 1946 USA), *Scarlet Street* (Lang

1945 USA) and *The Killers* (Siodmak 1946 USA)—which film scholars have tended to regard as being particularly attuned to the mood of the historical moment. Among the popular films listed in Table 1.1, only *Best Years of Our Lives* has been considered by film scholars for its articulation of some of the defining themes of the time. It is not my argument that this list of popular films should simply be substituted for these more familiar films in attempting to produce a reliable account of the films and culture of the period. Although *It's a Wonderful Life* was less popular than any of the films in the above list, attracting revenues of $3.5 million,[5] other contemporary indices of the importance of the film support the view that the movie was an significant one: the film was nominated for Academy Awards in five categories,[6] only to lose out to *Best Years of Our Lives* in all but one and to *The Jolson Story* in the other. Several of the major films noirs released in 1946 also achieved markedly lower revenues than any of the popular films—*The Big Sleep* ($3.5m), *The Blue Dahlia* ($3.0m), *Scarlet Street* ($2.6m), *The Killers* ($2.4m).[7] Of these films, only two received any Academy Award nominations: *The Killers* was nominated in four categories[8] in all of which it too was beaten by *Best Years of Our Lives*, while *The Blue Dahlia* received one nomination.[9] Several films noirs released in 1946 achieved higher revenues, closer to the amounts achieved by the lower earning movies listed in table 1.1 (and sometimes exceeding them, according to some sources). In relation to these films the line dividing them from the lower earning popular films is less easy to draw. According to Lyon, *Gilda* and *The Strange Love of Martha Ivers*[10] each earned $4.1million while *The Postman Always Rings Twice* earned $3.9 million.[11] In financial terms, then, these films appear to have achieved a level of popularity approximately equal to that of the lower earning popular movies listed in table 1.1.

As these examples indicate, revenue figures prove to be a rather rough-and-ready guide to which films were most significant in cultural and social terms. The use of rental revenue figures does not produce a clear and unambiguous list of films that had a particular resonance with America's popular consciousness in 1946, and certainly not one that would entirely exclude film noir from consideration. This difficulty in identifying a set of films (let alone a particular film genre) that achieved a popularity demonstrably exceeding that of other groups of films or other genres highlights one of the major problem inherent in the zeitgeist approach to film noir. This approach is premised on the existence of a pessimistic postwar mood in American society, which is registered in the tone of the films. But not only does the character of many of the most popular films directly contradict that downbeat mood, but the ambiguities that arise in attempting to produce a list of the most significant films of the time—and the diverse generic character of the films in that list—suggests that the mood of the period was considerably less univocal than zeitgeist theories of film noir suggest. To gain a reliable insight into the films and culture of the period it is necessary, therefore, to consider a broader range of popular films, unconstrained by preconceived generic boundaries.

This was, in fact, the view Lester Asheim advanced in his response to John Houseman. Asheim argued for a "careful study of the whole universe of the popular film" (1947: 416) in place of the selective approach adopted by Houseman. The problem with the zeitgeist theory of film noir is not that it attributes a historico-cultural significance to film noir, but that it does so by excluding other kinds of film that were demonstrably popular in America at the time; films that suggest an image of early postwar American society that is in direct conflict with that promoted by the film noir and zeitgeist thesis. Films such as *Easy to Wed* may not be obvious candidates for scholarly analysis; they may be, as Deborah Thomas puts it "thin and merely formulaic" (2001: 2), but their demonstrable popularity at the time makes it imperative that film scholars should pay attention to them if the opportunity to gain reliable historical insights into the period is not to be lost.

What about the rest of the forties?

Of course the set of popular films identified above is taken from 1946 alone and might indicate nothing about which types of films were popular throughout the remainder of the decade. There might have been a pessimistic turn in the most popular films of 1947 that would entirely vindicate the impression of the forties promoted by the film noir and zeitgeist thesis. Firstly let me make it clear that, because my project in looking at these films was initially motivated by an interest in how movies contributed to discourses relating to the postwar readjustment, and particularly to the figure of the returning veteran, movies of the pre-war and the war years have necessarily been excluded from consideration. However, the question of how representative the popular films of 1946 are of the postwar forties as a whole is highly pertinent. Two factors motivated the decision to look at popular films in 1946, one theoretical the other practical. In embarking on this study, my desire to examine the treatment of issues relating to masculinity, the family and national identity originated in a belief that the films released immediately after the end of the war would register the distinctive cultural dynamics of that brief moment when America began to demobilize its forces and attempt to readjust to peacetime living, and before the distinctive discursive currents of the immediate postwar moment were diluted by other, newly emerging, factors—the cold war; the revival of HUAC; the impact of the Paramount Decree, which compelled the Hollywood studios to divest themselves of their chains of movie theatres; the 1948 Presidential election campaign and so on. My aim is to provide a synchronic snapshot of the film culture during that immediate postwar moment, and 1946 seemed to provide the best opportunity for that. From a purely practical standpoint, the publication of annual lists of top grossing films in industry publications such as *Variety* made it both easier and less susceptible to suggestions of personal bias to focus on a single year rather than attempt to construct a list of the most popular films released in the postwar forties.

Nevertheless, if this study is to be more than a synchronic curiosity, its conclusions ought to be valid in relation to the early postwar period in a wider sense. While I have produced my set of popular films by triangulating three sources of box office figures for 1946, another way of approaching the problem of identifying the most culturally significant films of the early postwar years would involve taking the box office returns from 1946 through 1950 and compiling a list of, say, the twenty highest earning films of that period. Using the annual summaries of rental revenues published each year by *Variety* a list of the highest earning films of the postwar forties has been constructed—table 1.2 (films are listed with the year in which the film appeared in *Variety*'s list and the revenue figure published by *Variety*).

The most striking feature of this list is the fact that with only two exceptions—*Samson and Delilah* (De Mille 1949 USA) and *Jolson Sings Again* (Levin 1949 USA)—all of the films appeared in *Variety*'s charts for either 1946 or 1947. In fact, taking *Variety*'s lists from 1946 to the end of the decade as a whole, there is a marked disparity between the revenues gained by films released in 1946 and 1947 and those released later in the decade. *Variety's* chart for 1946 indicates that 19 films achieved revenues of $4 million or more. Fifteen movies met or exceeded this figure in 1947. In 1948 this fell dramatically to 7 movies, while in 1949 the number was down to 5. In 1950, 7 films again achieved or exceeded revenues of $4 million. In other words, from 1948 and 1950 the number of movies achieving revenues of $4m or more is equal to the number that achieved this figure in 1946 alone. Even this does not adequately indicate the extent of the dramatic downturn in cinema-going after 1947. Sixteen films earned $5m or more in 1946 and 1947. From 1948 to 1950 only *Samson and Delilah* and *Jolson Sings Again* exceeded $5m.

Table 1.2 Twenty highest revenue-earning films in America 1946-1950

Best Years of Our Lives	1947	$11.5m
Samson and Delilah	1950	$11m
Duel in the Sun	1947	$10.75m
The Jolson Story	1947	$8m
Forever Amber	1947	$8m
The Bells of St. Mary's	1946	$8m
Unconquered	1947	$7.5m
Life With Father	1947	$6.25m
Welcome Stranger	1947	$6.1m
Leave Her to Heaven	1946	$5.75m
The Egg and I	1947	$5.75m
Jolson Sings Again	1949	$5.5m
The Yearling	1947	$5.25m
Green Dolphin Street	1947	$5m
The Razor's Edge	1947	$5m
Blue Skies	1946	$5m
Road to Utopia	1946	$5m
Spellbound	1946	$5m
The Green Years	1946	$4.75m
The Hucksters	1947	$4.7m

The total rental revenues earned by the five highest-earning films in 1946 and 1947 amounted to $74.5m. In comparison, the figure for the top five films in 1948 and1949 was only $53.05. Adding this to the figure for the top five films of 1950 brings the total to $71.525m, still less than the combined revenues earned by the top five films in the two years immediately after the war. This rapid decline in revenues gives some sense of the sharp fall in cinema attendance from its peak in 1946. More speculatively, this fall suggests that the significance of film as a cultural form may also have declined as the decade progressed, and this supports the rationale behind the decision to confine this research to 1946 alone.

Another important feature of table 1.2 is that it clearly indicates that there was not a dramatic change in the generic character of the most popular films released after 1946 and that, throughout the postwar part of the forties, a similar mix of genres, dominated by musicals, comedies and romances, continued to characterize the movies that attracted the highest box-office revenues. Only two of the films listed in table 1.2 might now be defined as films noirs—*Leave Her to Heaven* (Stahl 1945 USA) and *Spellbound* (Hitchcock 1945 USA)—both principally because of their explicit concern with psychology and psychoanalysis. As in the case of *Notorious*, understanding these two movies as films noirs is not entirely inconsistent with contemporary conceptions of their generic character, but neither does this way of classifying the films exhaust the possibilities available to 1940s audiences for understanding the generic affinities of these movies. The pressbook for *Spellbound*—like that for *Notorious*—offers a hybrid generic identity for the movie, at once emphasizing the elements of "drama", "mystery" and "suspense" while also foregrounding elements of romance, whether explicitly, in the publicity copy, or implicitly through the preponderance of images of the film's stars, Ingrid Bergman and Gregory Peck, embracing or about to kiss. Contemporary reviews of the film placed roughly equal emphasis on the film's identity as both thriller and a romance. *Variety* noted the success of the director in handling the "players and action in suspenseful manner", while also commenting on Bergman's performance as "the scientist who discovers her heart really rules her" (31 October 1945). Bosley Crowther, in the *New York Times*, displayed a similar ambivalence about the film's genre, noting the director's status as "the old master of dramatic suspense" while also remarking that "his real success is in creating the illusion of love" (2 November 1945: 22).

In similar fashion, *Leave Her to Heaven* is explicitly referred to as a "psychological drama" throughout its pressbook, but the use of images of the film's stars, Gene Tierney and Cornel Wilde, locked in passionate embrace conveys a strong impression of the romantic elements in the film. Romantic elements are reinforced in the advertising copy: "20th Century-Fox maintains moviegoers haven't had their biggest romantic thrill until they see the mountaintop kiss of Wilde and Tierney in 'Leave Her to Heaven' ". The possibility that the film was equally likely to be understood by viewers as a romance and a psychological thriller receives further support from contemporary reviews. Although *Variety* does refer to the plot's many murders, it is clear that the reviewer saw the film more as a romance, commenting that the film "offers heavy magnet for the femme trade" and that it is "essentially [a] woman's story" (2 January 1946). On the other hand, Bosley Crowther, in the *New York Times*, foregrounded the more noirish elements of the film, describing the movie as a "moody, morbid film" (26 December 1945: 15).

It is not my aim to try to settle definitively the question of the generic identity of these films. I do not believe that such a foreclosure on the possibilities for reinterpreting the generic identities of movies is either possible or desirable, although this is, in effect, precisely what zeitgeist approaches to film noir have attempted to achieve by imposing a singular generic frame around a set of films which may have been understood in rather different ways by their original audiences. The contemporary documents identified above show that, in relation to these films, there were ways for 1940s audiences to understand what kind of film they were watching other than as precursors of what we now understand as film noir. While this potential to apprehend the generic identity of a movie in different ways does not amount to an ability to reverse the mood of a film, transforming a gloomy movie into an upbeat one, different understandings of a film's generic character do inflect the meanings of a film in subtly different ways: *Notorious* becomes a slightly different film depending on whether attention is focused on its noirish elements—the obsessive controlling relationship between a mother and son—or its romantic components—a tale of ultimately requited love.

What's genre got to do with it?

While Fredric Jameson may be correct to observe that the idea that every age produces a genre which best captures the focal concerns of the era is a belief that is commonly held, it should be apparent from the arguments I have advanced so far that I question the validity of that belief itself. While film scholarship has promoted film noir as the privileged genre of the late forties and early fifties, analysis of the generic character of the most popular movies of the time reveals that these high-earning films consisted of a broad range of Hollywood's genres, with no single type of film clearly dominating. The only clear trend that is suggested by the box office figures is that films noirs were relatively marginal compared to a corpus of popular films which is dominated by romances, musicals, comedies or hybrids of several of these genres. An important factor contributing to this erroneous belief in the existence of historically privileged genres has been the way film studies has traditionally approached the study of genre.

Conventional approaches to film genre have relied on the existence of a number of relatively stable and readily definable classes to which individual films can be said to "belong". However, the processes through which these taxonomies of film types are constructed involve the application of subjective selection criteria, and this casts doubt over the validity of the categories themselves. Particularly problematic in this respect is the fact that conventional film genre theory evades the question of how it is possible to objectively select the core group of films which is then used to establish the characteristics subsequently understood to define the genre. It may seem perfectly obvious to the viewer today that *Duel in the Sun* (Vidor 1946 USA) is a western, but this apparent obviousness conceals the fact that the category, "the western" is not an objective, natural one, but is the product of a selective refinement of the category through a process of inclusion and exclusion to produce that seemingly obvious movie genre. Rick Altman has noted that film genre has been understood to cover multiple aspects of film production, texts and reception (1999: 14) and argues that film genre theory has avoided potential conflicts between these different aspects of film genre "by regularly choosing examples from genres where all definitions ... neatly line up" (15). Thus the apparent naturalness of a generic class is maintained by focusing attention on genres in which there are no conflicts between producers', exhibitors', audiences' and critics' understandings of the films which make up the generic corpus (although, as Altman demonstrates, the coherence of even these classes tends to disintegrate when probed sufficiently deeply: 30-48).

While film genre theory has traditionally understood genres as organic categories with their origins in both the practices of film producers and in the audiences' ability to recognize and appreciate the features of particular genres, recent interventions by Altman (1999) and Steve Neale (2000) have challenged this understanding by demonstrating the centrality of retrospective processes to the formation of genres. Both Neale and Altman criticize the artificial coherence of the generic corpuses produced by these selective processes, and the lack of attention to the historical realities of film production and reception that results from this approach to genre criticism. Both argue that historical analysis of movies needs to attend to generic hybrids and to the full range of Hollywood's output rather than the highly selective samples which have characterized conventional approaches to film genre (Altman 1999: 16; Neale 2000: 252-3).

The selectivity of traditional approaches to film genre would be less problematic if studies based on these approaches confined themselves to consideration of a particular genre, and the films which comprise it, in isolation from the wider cultural context. However, genre theory has consistently asserted the existence of the privileged relationship of which Jameson writes, between particular genres and the wider historico-social context within which they develop. This leads, as Neale points out, to the belief that "socio-cultural issues can be parcelled out among and between genres" (2000: 224). This belief in the existence of a privileged relationship between particular genres and particular issues (and, therefore, also the particular historical moments at which those issues come to prominence) is pervasive in what Altman identifies as "ritual" and "ideological" approaches to genre (1999: 26-28) and is, therefore, a cornerstone of conventional approaches to film genre. Despite the pervasiveness of this truism, the belief that genre offers the opportunity to gain insights into the connections between Hollywood's films and American society has, as Neale remarks, "in practice nearly always used the concept of genre as a way of avoiding detailed study of anything other than selective samples of Hollywood's art" (2000: 252). This is very clearly the case in relation to the attribution of particular historico-social significance to film noir in the early postwar moment. Not only is noir a retrospectively constructed critical category which bears little relation to the way the films may have been understood by their producers or their original audiences, but it also fails the economic test central to the ritual approach to film genre, which suggests that genres which engage particularly well with the concerns of audiences become a form of cultural expression for the audience who, through their support of the genre at the box office, influence the production of further examples of the genre (see Neale 2000: 224-5). As I have shown in this chapter, throughout what is now regarded as the classic noir period, films noirs were routinely out-performed at the box office by a range of Hollywood's other genres; genres which display none of the bleakness, pessimism and anxiety that characterizes film noir. The centrality film noir has attained in the historical account of postwar American culture presented by zeitgeist theories of film noir is not supported by the available evidence relating to which movies in particular—and which types of movies in general—1940s audiences were more inclined to see. Richard Maltby has observed that the film noir and zeitgeist thesis owes more to its "critical ingenuity" than any real ability to locate noir movies in their historical context (1992: 41) and this is amply borne out by the example provided by the highest earning films of 1946, and by each subsequent year until the end of the decade.

Genre theory has, then, been central to the production of an incomplete picture of the films and culture of early postwar America. However, just as I do not advocate entirely excluding film noir from our understanding of the period, I also argue that a revised approach to genre itself continues to provide a useful framework for understanding the complicated relationships between films and their socio-historical context. Steve Neale and Rick Altman both advocate approaches to genre which abandon the inflexible, critically-derived taxonomies which have characterized genre theory in the past, and which instead focus on the generic hybridity of Hollywood's productions and on the way films were understood by their producers and audiences. Altman's shifting of the terrain of genre study away from the production of taxonomies and towards the study of genre as a discursive activity offers a way of tracing the interpenetration of textual meanings through different cultural forms—films, popular literature, magazines, advertising—within the same historical moment, and so offers the prospect of using genre to produce a more reliable historical account of the films and culture of the past.

This book is structured around key themes that have been identified by film critics as being focal concerns of the films noirs of the late 1940s and early 1950s: the family, masculinity and American national identity. Chapter 3 considers the treatment of the family in the popular films, focusing in particular on two discourses about family life that gained currency during the war and remained important elements of public discourse in the postwar period. The first of these discourses registered concern about the effect that the compulsory removal of men from their families in order to engage in military service would have when these men returned to their families after the war. The second, related in some respects to the first, articulated anxieties about the domination of men by their mothers. In the movies these discourses were embodied in two allegorical figures—the "absent father" and the "mom"—who together represented a distillation of some of the anxieties that developed in postwar America, relating to the organization of family life after the war.

Chapters 4 and 5 consider different aspects of masculinity in the popular films. Some of the most recent work on masculinities in film has employed Judith Butler's (1990) conception of gender as a performance of identity as a way of moving beyond the limitations of feminist psychoanalytic accounts of gendered representation (see especially Cohan 1997). In Chapter 4 I use Butler's conception of performative gender to examine the use of explicitly performative masculinities in several of the popular films released in 1946. My argument in Chapter 4 is that, by foregrounding the performativity of masculinities these films functioned to allay keenly felt anxieties about the readjustment of ex-servicemen to civilian life. Chapter 5 examines the popular films in relation to the representation of men's relationships with other men. Contemporary discourses concerning all-male relationships tended to focus on anxieties about men's sexualities, which were fuelled by the homosocial environment of military life, and the close male friendships which inevitably developed within that setting. The popular films of the period, however, display few of these anxieties and provided a cultural space in which the pleasures of male friendships could be examined.

Chapter 6 takes a different approach to those that precede it. In Chapter 6 I revisit the themes discussed in Chapters 2, 3, 4, and 5 in relation to some of the most popular "tough" movies released between 1945 and 1947. This analysis reveals the consistencies and contrasts between the popular films and these "tough" films (or films noirs, if you prefer) in their treatment of these themes. The contradictions that exist between these different groups of films suggest that contradictory currents—rather than the uniformly gloomy consensus suggested by the film noir and zeitgeist thesis—also characterized the wider cultural context within which the movies, and the discourses they register, originally circulated. The contradictions between these two groups of contemporary films also reveal that the pervasive impression of the early postwar period cultivated by the zeitgeist thesis is unsustainable when the artificial, critically derived generic boundaries are breached and a wider range of Hollywood's popular postwar movies is taken into consideration. Finally, in chapter 7, I review some of the major conclusions of this study and suggest areas in which further research is needed.

In the following chapter I focus on the treatment of American national identity in the big box-office successes of 1946. The zeitgeist approach to film noir has presented an image of the early postwar period as a time of crisis in which confidence in the myths which sustained American national identity was undermined by the uncertainties of the postwar readjustment. Within film studies this is an extremely influential understanding of the movies and culture of the time, but this view is only sustainable through a highly selective examination of the films released as America began to adjust to the postwar world. In contrast to this vision of a time in which bleak movies reflected a general mood of pessimism about the American dream, some of the most popular films represent an effort to reinvigorate those myths and reinstate the cornerstones of American national identity through the nation's popular cultural productions.

CHAPTER 2

Re-invigorating the nation: popular films and American national identity

One of the fundamental assumptions of the zeitgeist approach to film noir is that the end of the Second World War ushered in a period in which Americans lost faith in some of the key myths upon which the American sense of national identity was founded. The zeitgeist theory understands film noir as a reflection of the mood of Americans during a period of, as John Belton phrases it, "national identity in crisis" (1994: 201) or, as Bruce Crowther puts it, the "climate of dislocation and disillusionment" (1988: 157) that characterized American society after the war. As I have indicated in the preceding chapter, I am suspicious of this explanation of film noir for several reasons. First, it attributes a cultural significance to film noir which is clearly questionable, given that only a relatively small number of films noirs were produced, measured against Hollywood's total output in the period. Second, the rental revenues achieved by those films noirs compared with revenues achieved by other contemporary film genres, suggests that films noirs had less appeal to contemporary audiences than these other genres. Finally, critics making this sort of claim tend to base their conclusion that the mood of American society after the war was pessimistic on their reading of a limited body of films noirs alone, seldom troubling to look beyond the film noir canon for corroborating evidence of the supposed malaise.

In this chapter I examine how some of the key myths, attitudes and values that sustained the American sense of national identity were treated in some of the more popular films released shortly after the war. I will be arguing that, unlike the films noirs, the most popular films of the time celebrate traditional American values and provide an impression of the mood of American culture in the immediate aftermath of the Second World War which is better characterized as optimistic about the future of America than as anxious and paranoid. The impression of the cultural tone gained from these popular movies is confirmed by the range of other materials—articles published in contemporary books and magazines—which I also examine in order to illustrate the concrete connection between these popular films and the wider culture of early postwar America.

In advancing this argument it is not my aim to refute absolutely the suggestion that there were anxieties about American national identity in the early postwar period. The revival of the House of Representatives Committee on Un-American Activities (HUAC) after the war and the commencement of its investigation into the Hollywood movie industry in 1947[1] provides a clear indication of the existence of concern that distinctly un-American tendencies lay concealed beneath the surface of ostensibly American institutions and threatened to undermine the core values of the American way of life. Furthermore, social shifts resulting from America's involvement in the war had foregrounded the contradictions which lay behind the idea of America as a classless society—as a land of opportunity in which any person was able to achieve success and status through hard work—and had exposed the real class stratification of American society, thereby destabilizing one of America's key myths. While film noir may register the anxieties of Americans, which were provoked by the exposure of this myth as a myth, my argument is that it is considerably over-simplifying the matter to conclude that the anxiety undoubtedly evident in numerous films noirs was Hollywood's—and, indeed, American society's—only response to this situation.

Hollywood's response to the destabilization of the myth of classlessness was by no means uniform and this chapter is, therefore, divided into a number of sections, each of which covers a particular aspect of its response. In the first section I discuss the treatment in popular films of the shifts and inversions in status which men experienced as a result of the move from the military back into civilian life. In this section two films in particular, *Best Years of Our Lives* and *Blue Skies*, serve to illustrate some of the concerns that were provoked by this status inversion. In the second section I examine more generalized efforts the films make to reassert the myth of America as a classless, democratic society; taking examples from *Two Years Before the Mast*, *Saratoga Trunk* and *The Razor's Edge*. In the third section, I discuss one particular aspect of this myth, concentrating on three films; *The Jolson Story*, *Till the Clouds Roll By* and *Night and Day*. Each of these films presents a story of individual success—a central element of American mythology—and all three of these films operate to reassert the idea of "self-made" individualism as a key American value. In the final section of the chapter I discuss the deployment of the myth of America as a cultural "melting pot" as a way of projecting a unified sense of "American-ness"; a national identity forged from the wide range of different ethnic and cultural identities that comprised the nation's population. *The Jolson Story* is, again, of key importance in this section, providing the clearest example of a narrative centrally concerned with the assimilation of ethnic identities into a unified "American-ness", but a similar theme can also be observed in *Saratoga Trunk*, *Till the Clouds Roll By* and *The Green Years*.

Cinderellas of the services

America's entry into the Second World War, and the resultant induction of millions of men into military service, produced reverberations throughout American society that would continue to echo long after the war had ended. As John Belton argues, one of the key myths structuring American national identity had been the myth of Jeffersonian democracy; of social equality guaranteed by universal ownership of property (1994: 200-201). By the time America entered the war, however, this myth had been under pressure for some time. The closure of the frontier at the end of the Nineteenth century had curtailed dreams of unlimited expansion and the accompanying promise of free land, which was a pre-requisite of the Jeffersonian vision of a nation characterized by agrarian self-sufficiency. The progress of modernity and urbanization in the early part of the twentieth century further challenged the image of rural idyll in this vision of America. Later still, the hardships of life for many Americans during the great depression widened the cracks in this vision of America as an egalitarian, classless society. In economic terms, the immediate impact of the war was to end the depression almost at a stroke, producing a massive boom in the American economy as it geared up for war production. As Frederick Lewis Allen noted of the time:

> by 1944 the signs of prosperity were everywhere. It was hard to get a hotel room in any city. Restaurants in which it had always been easy to find a table for lunch were now crammed by a few minutes after twelve. Sales of fur coats and jewelry ... were jumping
>
> (1952: 147)

Along with this economic boom, the war also produced shifts in social status that would become particularly significant after the war. One of the key shifts in this respect was the elevation of men from working-class backgrounds to positions of high status within the military hierarchy as a result of their appointment as officers, or to branches of the services that attracted high prestige. A major concern, which arose as a result of these moves, was the question of what would happen to these men at the conclusion of the war. A cartoon that appeared in *Life* magazine shortly after the war (15 April 1946: 14-15) made light of this situation. In the cartoon, an ex-sergeant is taken on as an employee after the war by two of his former subordinates. His new employers exploit the situation to exact revenge for hardships suffered under their sergeant's command in the army, before eventually relenting and reaching a new equilibrium, based on mutual respect, with their former superior. This pattern is repeated in a song and dance routine in *Blue Skies*, which exploits the humorous potential of this situation. Johnny (Bing Crosby) and Tony (Billy De Wolfe) perform the routine, *I've Got My Captain Working For Me Now*, which echoes the tone of the *Life* cartoon. In the song, Johnny sings of the satisfaction of the ordinary private who, in postwar civilian life, finds himself employing his former commander:

> I've got the guy who used to be my captain
> working for me.
> He wanted work

So I made him a clerk
in my father's beanery.
And by and by I'm gonna keep him wrapped in work
up to his brow.
I make him open the office every morning at eight
(Tony) He comes around about four hours late.
(Johnny, laughing) It's great!
Everything comes to those who wait,
I've got my captain working for me now.

While both the song and the *Life* cartoon take a light-hearted approach to this situation, indulging in a harmless fantasy of the ordinary soldier's retaliation for the indignities and discomforts of military life against those seen to be directly responsible, this situation was treated by a number of writers as a considerably more serious problem for ordinary men who had achieved officer rank but were unlikely to be able to maintain this elevated status on their return to civilian life. In his book, *Back to Life: The Emotional Adjustment of Our Veterans*, H. I. Kupper referred to these men as "Cinderellas" of the services, "young men who have been officers ... who must now return to menial and very boring civilian tasks" (1945: 74) and for whom "the return to civilian life is the clang of midnight that marks the end of the enchanted ball" (127). In a similar vein, Stanley Lebergott, writing in *Harpers* magazine, discussed the problems faced by employers who would have to help "Captain Joe, who commanded a bomber on fifty combat missions, to make the delicate adjustment back to a humdrum stock clerk's job", and the difficult economic adjustment required of ex-servicemen who were accustomed to an income "considerably higher than the average real income of single men in peacetime" (1945: 195).

In his book, *The Veteran Comes Back*, Willard Waller took a different approach to this problem, emphasizing the lack of utility of the skills acquired during military service in civilian life. Noting that "discharged veterans often display a grandiose conception of their own abilities" (1944: 178), Waller recognized that military service may have equipped men with a high level of skills, which may in turn have raised certain expectations about the kind of job they could expect after the war, only to find that their military skills were of no value in civilian employment. Waller suggested that such men may prove to be "unwilling to accept the sort of job and the level of pay to which their skills entitle them" (178). Similarly, N. A. Pelcovits' account of the expectations of returning veterans, published by *Harpers* magazine, suggested that a combination of new skills and broadened horizons of experience produced in ex-servicemen an expectation that on their return to civilian life they would be able to avail themselves of "more promising opportunities than those they left behind" (1946: 158). However, Pelcovits recognized that these expectations were often founded on unrealistic evaluations of the usefulness of these new skills in civilian life, and that many men would have to come to terms with returning to low status occupations similar to those they possessed before the war (158).

While all of these writers recognized the potential for reversals in status in the move from soldier to civilian, only Waller identified this reversal specifically as a matter of adjustment to the different class economy of civilian society. The problems of adjustment which Waller discussed in his book are the familiar ones of movement from high to low status accompanying the move from military to civilian life, and problems of adjustment relating to the lack of utility of high level military skills in civilian employment, but Waller's particular insight was his framing of these problems in terms of class structure (1944: 147). The resurrection of problems associated with class was also recognized as a key postwar issue by Neal Stanford in a pair of articles published in consecutive editions of the *Christian Science Monitor*. As Stanford observed:

> Whatever side of the tracks they originally came from they have crossed and recrossed those tracks many times in their service experience. Those tracks have come to mean only a quick means of transportation. Now they come back to their
> civilian life and those tracks suddenly assume their old role of social barrier
>
> (1944a: 3)

The inversions of status and shifts in class position experienced by these "Cinderellas" of the services are articulated in *Best Years of Our Lives* through the narrative trajectory of the character of Fred Derry (Dana Andrews). Fred personifies the military "Cinderella" identified by Kupper. A captain in the Air Force, Fred served as a bombardier, flying numerous missions over enemy territory, and was highly decorated for his service. Early in the film, however, Fred reveals that in pre-war civilian life he had been employed at the local drugstore as a "soda jerk". The disparity between Fred's high status within the military and that which he enjoys on his return to civilian life is graphically portrayed in a scene in which Fred arrives back at his father's home. A number of signifiers are deployed in this scene to indicate the gulf in status. The cliche which Stanford referred to, of railway tracks as a signifier of social division, separating those on the "right" side from those on the "wrong" side of the tracks is a key motif in the scene. Fred's father's home is shown to be located right next to the town's railway line and although Fred is not shown literally crossing the railway tracks in the scene, the symbolic crossing of a social divide is made clear by the juxtaposition of this scene with that showing Al Stephenson's (Frederick March) arrival home, in the preceding scene, at a "swanky" apartment which is the antithesis of the dingy shack to which Fred returns. The clanging of trains' bells periodically throughout the scene provides a constant reminder of the presence of the tracks, and their symbolic function, marking the social divide that has been crossed in moving from Al's home to Fred's. The two men's relative status within the military—sergeant and captain respectively—intensifies the sense of status inversion involved in the return to civilian life.

This scene goes further than merely identifying Fred as working class; it denies him respectability or dignity as a member of the working class, using the characters of his "blowsy stepmother" and his alcoholic father who "lives in frowzy gin-reeking existence" (*Variety*, review of *Best Years of Our Lives*, 27 November 1946) to convey a strong impression of Fred's family as morally delinquent members of that class, largely responsible for their own impoverished condition because of their personal weaknesses.

Despite Fred's determination not to return to his pre-war occupation, the lack of alternative opportunities eventually forces him to approach his old employer. The neighbourhood drugstore where Fred used to work has been taken over by a large corporation and Fred is introduced to the new manager, who seems to derive some pleasure from pointing out the lack of utility of Fred's wartime skills in civilian employment. Nevertheless, he does offer Fred what is effectively his old job. After initially resisting this offer, Fred is ultimately driven by economic necessity to return to this job. While he does not encounter precisely the situation referred to earlier of having one of his military subordinates as his manager a broadly analogous situation arises in that Fred's former assistant at the drugstore, "Sticky" Merkle (Norman Phillips Jr.), has been promoted to the position of supervisor while Fred has been away and takes pleasure in reinforcing the status reversal this change of roles involves by insisting that Fred should address him as "<u>Mr</u>. Merkle".

The myth of classlessness

If *Best Years of Our Lives* only registered the status reversals experienced by ex-servicemen on their return to civilian life it would not conflict with the suggestion that the disintegration of the American myth of classless democracy was a key feature of the films of the period. However, as well as registering these inversions the film also symbolically restores the vision of America as an egalitarian society by reinvigorating the myth of classlessness. In deploying this myth to resolve the disequilibrium created by the status inversion experienced by Fred, the film reveals a connection between this specific social problem of status inversion after the war and the maintenance of a vision of America as a classless democracy that was a feature of a number of the popular films released after the war.

The key to *Best Years of Our Lives'* reinscription of the mythical possibility of a universal middle-class—effectively a classless society—is the way it resolves the binary opposition formed by the different classes. In the film this opposition is embodied in the characters of Fred and Al. In civilian life, Al represents the upper reaches of the class hierarchy: the affluent, professional, family man. Homer Parrish (Harold Russell) represents the other end of a spectrum of middle-class-ness, the respectable lower middle-class. Fred is excluded from the continuum between Al and Homer, being constructed as neither professionally successful nor morally respectable. What ultimately enables Fred to gain access to middle-class status, and thereby enables the film to promulgate the myth of classlessness, is the development of a relationship between Fred and Al's daughter, Peggy (Teresa Wright). Although the pursuit of this relationship involves breaking up Fred's marriage, and so risks Fred's continued exclusion from a position of middle-class respectability, great care is taken in the film to construct Peggy's character as thoroughly respectable and to strike a contrast between her character and Fred's sexually promiscuous wife, Marie (Virginia Mayo). Respectable in herself and clearly middle-class by virtue of the metonymy between her character and that of her father, Peggy functions as a bridge between the class positions occupied by Fred and Al, creating an equivalence between the two men, through her relationships with both, which effaces the reality of the men's class differences and promotes an impression of a classless civilian order.

Figure 2.1 Visual symmetry as equivalence. Al Stephenson (Fredric March) and Fred Derry (Dana Andrews) in *Best Years of Our Lives*

A scene late in the film captures particularly well the tension between the appearance of classlessness and the real class differences between the men. Fred and Al meet in a bar. The two men sit face-to-face, talking to each other in a booth and the scene is filmed using a long take with the camera positioned to the side of the booth, precisely mid-distance between the men (fig. 2.1). The symmetry of the shot creates a strong visual impression of equality between the men. However this visual impression is contradicted by the narrative function of the scene: Al has called the meeting in order to compel Fred to end his relationship with Peggy. The scene presages the termination (albeit only temporarily) of the relationship that offers Fred the opportunity to rise to a higher status level in civilian society, and amounts to a claim by Al to a moral authority that further reinforces the sense of Fred's social inferiority. The inherent tension in this contradiction between visual signification and narrative function is apparent throughout the scene, for example in the awkwardness between the two men (who had previously been close, warm and friendly towards one another) which Fred attempts to defuse by making a joke about Al wanting to borrow money from him. But this joke itself highlights the class differences between the men, foregrounding the enormous economic differences between them and the fact that the idea that Al might want to borrow money from Fred could only ever be a joke.

The film goes further than simply highlighting the contradiction between the superficial appearance of classlessness and the social reality of class divisions, however, to suggest that the ideal of the classless society was a realistic possibility. This is achieved by ultimately allowing the romance between Fred and Peggy to flourish. Fred's postwar experiences have changed him and it is evident in Fred's speech to Peggy, in the final scene of the film—"it may take us years to get anywhere. We'll have no money, no decent place to live. We'll have to work, get kicked around"—that he has internalized the middle-class values of hard work, determination and resilience that will enable him to transcend his prior class position and allow him to take his place within the new middle class.

Fred's eventual ascent into the middle class may present the positive dimension of class mobility, but *Best Years of Our Lives* also hints at the fragility of this class structure and the inevitable corollary of this upward class mobility: the danger of moving to a position of lower status. Throughout the film, Al's excessive drinking is a key element in the construction of his character. As the film progresses, it becomes increasingly clear that his drinking is problematic, and this reveals a parallel between his character and that of Fred's alcoholic father. The resonance between these two characters signals a danger of a loss of respectability and social position for Al. Al does indeed court social humiliation when, while very drunk, he gives a speech criticizing the cautious conservatism of his superiors at the bank. At points the speech veers dangerously close to an expression of disillusionment with America itself, but ultimately affirms Al's rediscovery of faith in the nation and its values, and the worth of persevering to uphold a traditional vision of America: "people are going to think we're gambling with depositors' money. And we will be: we'll be gambling on the future of this country".

Al's drinking also strengthens the symbolic relationship between Al and Fred. In a later scene, which echoes the rediscovery of faith in American values expressed in Al's speech, Fred's father discovers his son's citations for bravery during the war and, as he reads these, even this most hopeless and disillusioned of characters re-awakens to the possibilities for individual achievement in the land of opportunity, and he weeps with pride at his son's accomplishments. In creating this parallel between Al and Fred's father, the film positions Al as a symbolic father to Fred. In this way the film prepares the way for Fred's ultimate attainment of middle-class status (something which the film does not actually show but does set up as an inevitable outcome) as a kind of inheritance passed from father to son.

Al's character also functions to link the supposed classlessness of the postwar order to the levelling of social class that would have been an important aspect of the military experience, which inevitably drew together men from all strata of society into a bounded group in which the civilian class structure was superseded by the military hierarchy and in which the development of group solidarity between men from different backgrounds could overcome civilian class differences. Al's experiences as an army sergeant have given him a strong feeling of solidarity with the ordinary working man, and this continues to exert an influence over his professional judgment after the war. So when an ex-serviceman who approaches the bank for a loan is referred to Al, he refuses to adopt a superior position in relation to the applicant: "don't 'Sir' me. I'm a sergeant". Al's embrace of the egalitarian rhetoric of the myth of classlessness is also evident in his decision to grant a loan to this veteran, despite the latter's inability to provide any collateral for the loan. The benign paternalism of Al's character goes beyond the symbolic father/son relationship with Fred, then, to become a metaphor for the relationship between the nation and its people, with Al's character embodying all of the ideological values of democracy and classlessness that characterized one of the key tropes of the postwar social order.

The reassertion of the American value of democratic classlessness in *Best Years of Our Lives* registers the fragility of the class structure of American society, the susceptibility of positions within the structure to being dislodged and of individuals occupying those positions to ascend (Fred) and descend (hinted at by the similarities between Al and Fred's father) to other positions within the hierarchy. In acknowledging this possibility of movement in both directions, the film offers a cautionary picture of class in postwar America. Other popular films, however, offered less ambiguous images of America as a classless society.

In *Two Years Before the Mast*, the pressganging of Charles Stewart (Alan Ladd) into service aboard the *Pilgrim*, a merchant ship owned by his father, raises the issue of class by bringing opposite poles of the class spectrum into direct contact with one another. Removed from the civilian class structure, Charles becomes subject to the hierarchical order of the bounded society that exists aboard the ship. Refusing to recognize Charles's claim to a privileged position aboard the ship, Captain Thompson (Howard Da Silva) forces Charles to take up a position as an ordinary member of the crew.

Initially Charles's relationship with other members of the crew is highly antagonistic. Significantly this antagonism is presented as a general friction between social classes rather than a specific resentment towards Charles although, as the ship owner's son, the crew might quite reasonably be expected to hold Charles responsible for the brutality and deprivation they suffer aboard the ship. At the outset Charles holds himself apart from the crew, and it is this sense of his own superiority, rather than his relationship to the ship's owner, that is resented by the crew. On his side, Charles freely expresses his evaluation of the rest of the crew as a "rabble" and remains aloof from the group. Tensions between Charles and the rest of the crew reach their peak when Charles refuses to confess to his theft of food, intended for one of the ship's mates, from the ship's galley. Charles's action and his subsequent silence result in the punishment of the entire crew for the theft, by being placed on rations of "hard tack and water". Despite his lack of solidarity with the crew, the crew's own code of honour and their resentment of the Captain's authority protect Charles from having his theft reported to the Captain. This does, however, put Charles at risk of retribution from the crew members themselves, and he is only rescued from this by the intervention of another member of the crew, Richard Dana (Brian Donlevy).

Although he is an ordinary member of the crew and an experienced seaman—and so has much in common with the other regular sailors—Dana's high level of literacy and articulacy places him in a different class position from the rest of the crew. In a move that blurs the boundary between the film's fiction and the real existence of a well-known work of American literature bearing the same title as the film and authored by Richard H. Dana, the film incorporates the writing of the book into its narrative.[2] This device allows Dana's character to function as an authenticating presence within the film as well as differentiating his character from the rest of the crew in terms of social class. Dana occupies a unique position within the film's class economy, between Charles and the remainder of the crew, and this allows Dana to mediate Charles's eventual integration into the crew through his relationships with both.

Charles's friendship with Dana and the shared hardships of the voyage ultimately produce a convergence between Charles's interests and those of the rest of the crew, leading to a gradual effacement of the class differences that initially characterized their relationship. Charles's integration into the crew does not, however, erase all traces of his former, superior class status. The romantic relationship that develops between Charles and Maria (Esther Fernandez), an aristocratic passenger taken aboard the ship in the course of its voyage, allows the preservation of a sense of Charles's earlier class position once he becomes more integrated into the crew. This romance is a rather odd element in the film; it fits uneasily into the adventure narrative of the movie and it ends very abruptly, suggesting little narrative commitment to this aspect of the film.[3] Despite the way it disrupts the verisimilitude of the narrative, this relationship performs the important ideological function of allowing the film to position Charles as the embodiment of the interests of all social classes, by enabling Charles's character to retain traces of his superior class position while his immediate interests converge with those of the working class crew. This construction of a dual class affiliation for Charles situates his character in a position that is truly class-less, in the sense that it abolishes all contradictions between the interests of the different classes that Charles represents; his character's interests become the interests of society as a whole.

Charles's relationship with Maria also provides the film with an opportunity to establish a link between classlessness and masculinity. The murder of Captain Thompson paves the way for the establishment of a more humane and democratic regime aboard the ship. At this point Charles insists that Maria should leave the ship, and only after her departure does the milieu aboard the ship become truly classless, with the last representative of an unambiguously superior class position removed from the diegesis (her character does not reappear). The scene that follows Maria's departure shows the operation of the newly established democracy of the now all-male group. In this scene the entire crew stands on the ship's deck to decide on their course of action in the wake of Captain Thompson's killing. One crewmember forcefully argues that they should take the ship and sail to "the Orient" to avoid punishment for mutiny. Dana opposes this course of action and argues that they should return to Boston to face trial for the mutiny, in the belief that the publicity generated by the trial and the publication of his account of the voyage will lead to the acquittal of the men and will gain improvements in the conditions of service for merchant seamen. Given that he is the son of the ship's owner, it is perhaps surprising that Charles does not claim authority over the ship. Instead he remains silent throughout the early part of the scene, contemplating the different positions in the debate between the men. When he does interject, he does so as an equal of the men rather than their social superior, and in this way the film indicates the extent of the shift in Charles's class position. Supporting Dana's argument, Charles responds to the objection of another crew member, that Charles might expect preferential treatment on the ship's return to port, with a clear statement of his commitment to the ideal of classlessness: "I may be a ship owner's son but I'm a seaman now". This phrase registers Charles's shift in position without erasing his earlier class identity, thereby reinforcing the sense of his character functioning as an embodiment of the interests of all social classes. Mirroring the shift in Charles's class position, a shift in the locus of power aboard the ship is also registered in this scene. While decisions had previously been made by the captain, usually against the interests of the crew, they are now made by the crew itself in its own interests: a shift from autocracy to democracy that is amply demonstrated by the fact that the decision to return to Boston is reached following a free vote among the all the men.

This decision is a clear indication of the belief that this ideal of democratic classlessness can persist beyond the bounded, all-male society of the ship and can be carried ashore into American society. On the ship's return to Boston, the old class order attempts to reassert itself. Charles's father visits him in his cell and promises to get him the best lawyers available in order to get him released the following day. Charles refuses, however, choosing instead to stand trial with his shipmates; rejecting the class privilege of the old order in favour of the democracy of the new.

The trial of the crewmen and the publication of Dana's account of the voyage do provoke a national debate, as predicted by Dana, and this eventually results in the passing of legislation guaranteeing more humane conditions of service for merchant seamen. In this way the film confirms that the men's faith in the willingness of the American establishment to adapt to the demands of classless democracy was justified. The adaptation of America's legislative institutions to the demands of a just cause in the name of classlessness reproduces the shifts in Charles's attitude through the film. In this respect Charles's character can be seen as metaphor for the character of the nation: classless, democratic and resolutely masculine.

Saratoga Trunk also features a central male character that functions as a metaphor for the national character. Although the film is not a western it shares thematic concerns and binary structure with the genre, but the link with the western is clearest in the iconography employed in constructing the central male character, Clint Maroon (Gary Cooper). Clint is every inch the western hero. Dressed in cowboy boots, white pants, fancy tie and ten gallon hat, Clint's visual signification draws heavily on the familiar iconography of the western gambler or hustler; a frontier hero who makes his living not on the range but through his wits at the card table and speed on the draw in the small towns of the mythical west. Reinforcing this strong visual impression, Clint's first appearance in the film is accompanied by a distinctive musical theme that, again, references the western movie genre. Finally, completing the heavily over-determined construction of his character as a western hero, Clint speaks using an idiom that reinforces the association of his character with stereotypes of rural American-ness. This distinctive characteristic of Clint's speech is more in evidence in the early parts of the film where, set against the backdrop of a representation of New Orleans as a place in which the cultural influences of Europe and Africa dominate, Clint's speech aggressively asserts his American-ness. When he is presented with a menu written in French in one restaurant, Clint protests to the waiter; "what's all this stuff sonny? Where I come from we write our menus in American". Later, while listening to Clio Dulaine (Ingrid Bergman) singing in "Gombo ... New Orleans French flavoured with African", Clint demands; "what does that say in American". Later still he mocks Clio's accented pronunciation of his name; "Cleent, Cleent. Why don't you talk American?" In addition to these explicit assertions of American-ness, Clint's speech employs a number of rustic colloquialisms which identify him with the mythical western hero: "they say everything here is lickin' good"; "I haven't laughed so much in a coon's age"; "you're darn tootin"; "those two nags a-pullin' it".

In *Two Years Before the Mast* the arrival of a truly classless, democratic milieu presents the men with a choice between returning to Boston to face the consequences of their actions and fleeing to "the Orient" to avoid them. The binary opposition so constructed between America and "the Orient" is key to structuring the sense of "American-ness" in that film. In *Saratoga Trunk,* a similar opposition is developed, in this case between America and Europe. The precise identity of the opposite pole of this binary pair is less important than its ability to structure a representation of America in these films by signifying "not-America". The "Orient" and "Europe" are collapsed together in the key binary opposition between America and not-America that is crucial to the assertion of American-ness and American values in both these films.

There are two main elements in the signification of Europe/not-America in *Saratoga Trunk.* First, the New Orleans setting of the film's early scenes is constructed as a highly un-American milieu. The image of New Orleans constructed in *Saratoga Trunk* seems more European than American, but elements of African cultures—while diluting its specifically European character—also contribute to the elaboration of a setting that projects a strong sense of being "not-America". Notwithstanding the complication introduced by the incorporation of elements of African cultures into the film's construction of the New Orleans setting, there is still an overwhelming quality of European-ness to the city. The French language dominates the life of the city and, at a deeper level, its class structure is founded on decidedly "Old World" concepts such as aristocracy and noble birth, which function as determinants of an immutable class position. This contrasts starkly with the values of merit, enterprise and industry that characterize the class structure of the more American setting of Saratoga Springs in the later parts of the film.

The class-stratified society of New Orleans provides a key motivation for the film's narrative in its early parts. The disparity in class position between Clio's father and mother had led the father's close relatives to prohibit their relationship, anxious that he should not bring shame on the family name by marrying beneath himself. In turn, this prohibition had led to the death of Clio's father, who was accidentally killed when he intervened to prevent the mother's attempted suicide; the result of her being informed of the prohibition on their relationship. When Clio returns to New Orleans from Paris—where her mother had been living in an exile forced and financed by her father's family in their attempt to avoid a scandal—she does so with the intention of provoking precisely the kind of scandal involving her father's upper-class family that her mother's exile had been engineered to avoid.

Clio's character provides a second dimension to the film's signification of Europe/not-America. Clio is strongly associated with the European milieu. She has been raised in Paris and is comfortable in the world of European manners she finds in New Orleans, using her intimate understanding of the mores of European high society to maximize the embarrassment her actions cause to her father's relatives. Additionally, Clio's adoption of the ersatz title, Comtesse de Trenaunay de Chanfret, on her arrival in America reinforces her association with a highly class stratified, Europeanized setting. Finally it is important not to overlook the importance of casting in the establishment of the binary opposition between America/not-America. Ingrid Bergman's own European origins and her heavily accented speech are key elements contributing to the establishment of an aura of exotic otherness for Clio's character. Conversely Gary Cooper's well-known star character, and particularly his association with the western genre, could hardly be better suited to the task of establishing Clint's American-ness.

In the early parts of the film Clint's immersion in the Europeanized milieu of New Orleans and his relationship with Clio threaten both his sense of American-ness and his masculinity. From their first meeting, Clio makes plans to dress Clint differently, replacing his westerner's outfit with fine linen shirts embroidered with his initials; she imagines him carrying linen handkerchiefs, similarly adorned. The film associates Europe with femininity and America with masculinity through its linking of Clio with the former and Clint with the latter. Clio's actions in divesting Clint of his western garb and dressing him in this more European manner threatens to both de-Americanize and feminize Clint. Responding to this threat, Clint begins to express concern about the effect of his relationship with Clio. He openly questions what he is doing, living "in a house like this, la-di-da-ing it around" and makes clear his feeling that it is "too soft and pretty 'round here for me". His new clothing is the most obvious manifestation of the threat to his masculinity—"you got me roped tied and branded ... I'll be wearing ruffles in my pants next"—and it also removes the visible signifiers that mark Clint as a western hero and which are crucial to the maintenance of his sense of American-ness.

In the second part of the film the location shifts to the more securely American setting of Saratoga Springs. Saratoga society is also class stratified, but with significant differences from New Orleans. Here class status is based on wealth rather than birth, so that it is possible for individuals to gain access to the highest reaches of the class stratum through the acquisition of wealth, through success in business. So although it is class stratified, Saratoga society, with the possibilities it provides for upward class mobility, is more democratic than that of New Orleans. Saratoga Springs presents a more modern vision of a class stratified society, based on entrepreneurial or commercial success rather than outmoded notions of aristocracy, and this again reinforces its sense of American-ness. In Saratoga Springs, the Europeanization and feminization of Clint's character that threatened his masculinity in New Orleans are reversed and instead it is Clio who now begins to change. Significantly, on her arrival at Saratoga Springs, Clio insists on dropping her "title" (albeit very publicly and in a manner guaranteed to ensure that everyone is aware of it) and on being known as simply Mrs. De Chanfret, claiming that she wishes to "live in America quietly and democratically"—an indication of her increasing acceptance of American values. Clio's threatened feminization of Clint is also reversed in the film's closing moments, when Clio accepts her subordination to Clint within a patriarchally structured couple as the price of their relationship, finally agreeing that Clint will "wear the pants".

The variety of terms employed to construct the opposition between America and its Other in *Saratoga Trunk* and *Two Years Before the Mast*—Europe, Africa, "the Orient"—illustrates the importance of the binary opposition, America/not-America in constructing American-ness: this abstract binary is repeatedly brought to the fore in the films through these different textual manifestations. *The Razor's Edge* also employs this binary to articulate a sense of American-ness. Two characters are key to the film's articulation of class and the association of America with the ideal of democratic classlessness. At the start of the film Elliot Templeton (Clifton Webb) and Larry Darrell (Tyrone Power) occupy similar class positions. Both belong to the higher reaches of the class order, able to enjoy lives of gentlemanly leisure. However, the two men possess very different attitudes towards their class status and the privileges it affords them. While Elliot revels in the advantages provided by his superior position in a highly class stratified society, Larry is haunted by uncertainties about the meaning of his life. His search for answers to these questions provides the film's central narrative strand. Significantly, given the postwar context in which the film was released, the event that provoked these uncertainties was the death of Larry's closest friend, while he saved Larry's life during their military service in the First World War.

Both men travel to Europe early in the film. However, while Larry pursues his quest for meaning in his life by journeying through the lower reaches of society—mixing with rough-hewn working men in Paris; working in a coal mine; living an ascetic existence as the student of an Indian guru (a move from Europe to the Orient which illustrates the interchangeability of America's Others)—Elliot spends his time in Paris, enjoying an endless round of elegant social engagements. The contrast between the two men's activities delimits the extremes of the class structure within the European (or at least not-American) setting they occupy. The contrast between these two extremes is clearly articulated in a section of the film that uses a montage of short scenes to depict Larry's journey to, and activities in Europe. In this montage sequence non-diegetic voiceover is used to sever the visual images from the soundtrack, the latter being used to communicate Elliot's vision of Larry's European travels. Not only do the visual images and aural information directly contradict each other—Elliot's description of Larry sharing the captain's table aboard the *Aquitania* is juxtaposed with the image of Larry, bare torsoed, sitting on the deck of a tramp steamer sharing a joke with its crew; Elliot's reference to the elegant parties he plans to host on Larry's behalf is accompanied by an image of Larry playing chess in a working-class Parisian bar—but the very fact of the severance of the visual from the aural serves to heighten the sense of contradiction.

Up to this point in the film the opposition between America and Europe/not-America has not fully come into play in the articulation of America's vision of itself as a classless democracy. Although the distinction between the extremes of the class order is presented through Elliot and Larry's characters, there is no clear alignment between the individual characters and either Europe or America. Indeed, both characters have a strong affinity for Europe as a place in which each of them can pursue their chosen lifestyle, Elliot by moving among the highest reaches of European nobility and Larry by pursuing his personal quest for some meaning in life through what the film presents as the more authentic experience of life of the working classes. Later, during his pilgrimage to the Himalayas, Larry is advised by his guru to abandon his quest for meaning, which separates him from society, and to "live in the world and … love the objects in the world for what there is in them of God". Larry decides to return to America and from this point of the film on a much stronger connection develops between his character and the ideals and values of American-ness. This is accompanied by a complementary shift creating a much stronger alignment between Elliot's character and the European milieu. Having traced an obscure European title to which he apparently has some entitlement, Elliot has taken to having his tailor embroider his heraldic crest on his underwear. The visual traces of this title, this claim to superior class position, are concealed beneath "the modest pinstripe of an American gentleman", so that although his outward appearance remains American, beneath the surface Elliot is firmly committed to the class stratification which is now more clearly constructed as a European/un-American characteristic.

On his return to America, Larry rejects Isabel's (Gene Tierney) plea to resume their relationship. Throughout the film, Isabel has been associated with a class-stratified vision of America. When Larry first indicated his wish to travel to Europe, Isabel tried to convince him of the importance of remaining to participate in the economic life of the nation—"this is a young country and it's a man's duty to take part in its activities"—in order to achieve the national goal of making America "the greatest and richest country in the whole world". Later, while visiting Larry in Paris, Isabel articulates more clearly the opposition between America and Europe: "how can you bear to sit in *a backwash* when *America* is living through the most glorious adventure the world has ever known?" (my emphasis). Despite a downturn in her fortunes following the Wall Street Crash of 1929, it is clear at the film's end that Isabel's experiences have not taught her humility or led her to embrace the vision of America as a classless society. Her attitude is very clear in her reference to "little people" when discussing the investors who had entrusted their savings to her husband, and lost them in the crash. In contrast, Larry's ambitions on his return to America are modest—to work in a factory or buy a taxi to run as a small business—tempered by his experience of living among the different levels of the class order.

Through the characters of Isabel and Larry, *The Razor's Edge* presents two visions of America; one materialistic and class stratified, the other of more egalitarian and democratic ambitions. It is Larry's vision that is preferred by the film. As well as the contrast created by the selfish and unsympathetic construction of Isabel's character and the high idealism and spiritualism of Larry's, the film also uses the authority of the narrational voice of the character of Somerset Maugham (Herbert Marshall) to frame the actions of the characters, thereby pre-empting the possible value judgments of the audience with its own evaluation of Larry's character and, by extension, of American democracy itself:

I don't think anyone can fail to be better and nobler, kinder for knowing him. You see, my dear, goodness is after all the greatest force in the world, and he's got it.

Land of opportunity

Three of the films already discussed in this chapter hint at another pillar of the American sense of national identity that features in a larger number of the popular films: a vision of America as a land of opportunity, in which any person can achieve success in their chosen occupation through determination and individual effort. In *Best Years of Our Lives* this vision is strongly implied in the final speech Fred makes to Peggy (quoted earlier in this chapter) and in the opportunity which Al allows the ex-serviceman by granting him the bank loan he seeks to purchase a property in order to develop his farming business. In *Saratoga Trunk*, Clint moves from being a professional gambler to owner of a substantial stockholding in a valuable railway by assisting the existing stockholders to wrest control of the line from their business rivals. Finally, in *The Razor's Edge*, although the film is not entirely sympathetic in its portrayal of the ruthless ambition of Isabel's character, its disapproval of her hardly detracts from the force of the vision of American economic dynamism she expresses throughout the movie. While it is Larry's vision of the future of America as a classless democracy—indicated in his intention to work his way up from the bottom to a position of success in business—which provides the main ideological direction of the film, the character of Somerset Maugham (the authoritative narrational voice in the movie) also expresses his deep affection and regard for Isabel near the end of the film.

Three more of the popular films released in 1946 also take occupational opportunity and economic success as a central theme. These films, *The Jolson Story*, *Till the Clouds Roll By* and *Night and Day*, are based on the biographies of three famous and well-loved figures from the entertainment industry; Al Jolson, Jerome Kern and Cole Porter respectively. As Thomas Schatz implies (1999: 374), these films form a significant part of a distinct, if short-lived, postwar cycle of musical biopics which also included *Jolson Sings Again* (Levin, 1949 USA), and *Words and Music* (Taurog, 1948 USA), a biopic about Rogers and Hart.

While none of the films explicitly presents a "rags to riches" story, two films, *Till the Clouds Roll By* and particularly *The Jolson Story*, feature central characters who are initially positioned on the margins of American society but who, by achieving success as entertainers, come to occupy positions at the heart of American popular culture. *Night and Day* differs from these other films in that the film makes it clear that Cole Porter (Cary Grant) comes from a very comfortable middle-class WASP background. However, he does marginalize himself by neglecting his studies at Yale and refusing to comply with his grandfather's wish that he should become a lawyer, choosing instead to pursue his dream of becoming a successful composer. All three of these films, then, present narratives involving the central character's passage from marginality to mainstream success.

In *The Jolson Story* this passage from the margins to the mainstream has two distinct dimensions. First, this shift is presented as a process of Americanization of an immigrant identity and, second, as a success story which moves the protagonist from obscurity and poverty to fame and wealth. The first of these dimensions is discussed later in this chapter but, without wishing to pre-empt that discussion, it is important to recognize here the distinction between these two aspects of the film in order to avoid an over-simplifying conflation of immigrant Jewish identity with economic poverty. The early parts of the film foreground Jolson's Jewishness: shown as a youth, Jolson is still known by his real name, Asa Yoelson, and he sings in the choir at the synagogue. Jolson's background is not, however, portrayed as one of particular poverty. Indeed, Al's father is the Cantor at the synagogue and the Yoelson family consequently occupy a position of some prestige within the community. Their manner of dress and the appearance of their home reinforce an impression of respectable middle-classness. In an early scene, Cantor Yoelson's express distaste on discovering that Asa has been spending his time at the burlesque house serves to further secure the impression of the respectability of the Yoelson family. It also sets up an opposition between the middle-class and respectable family, and the disreputable and socially marginal theatrical milieu.

While Jolson's Jewishness does not mark his character as marginal in terms of either class or economic standing, the film does emphasize the un-American-ness of the Yoelsons in order to create a sense of ethnic marginality that works against the suggestion of their position in the social mainstream that follows from its construction of the family as respectable and middle-class. The casting of European actors in the roles of the Cantor (Ludwig Donath was born in Vienna) and Mrs. Yoelson (Tamara Shayne was born in Perm, Russia) contributes greatly to the sense of the characters as un-American. Additionally, the characters themselves are revealed to lack much knowledge about America, and this intensifies the impression of their "foreignness". In a scene that is key to establishing their Otherness, the Cantor and his wife are shown reading a postcard sent by Al, who is on tour. After reading the card Mrs. Yoelson places it on a screen.

This is followed by an edit to a shot of the same screen, now covered in cards. The camera pans across the cards, showing the different places visited by Al, while the image of Al singing is superimposed over these cards. The soundtrack during this sequence consists both of the sound of the song Al is singing and the commentary of Cantor and Mrs. Yoelson on the places he has visited. These comments reinforce the sense of the couple's foreignness by revealing their lack of familiarity with the places visited by Al and their naive preconceptions about the America that exists beyond the major cities of the Eastern seaboard:

Mrs. Yoelson:	Indianapolis.
Cantor:	Indians! He'll come home scalped yet!
Cantor:	Kickabock.
Mrs. Yoelson:	Is this in the United States papa?
Cantor:	Ah! Don't be foolish.

So while in certain respects, notably in relation to their class status, Jolson's family can be seen to represent the mainstream of American society—conceptualized as a classless, or more accurately as a universally middle-class society—their foreignness, which is reiterated throughout the film, also marks them as Other, or marginal within that society. The film utilizes this dual aspect of the construction of Jolson's family to make the family a mobile signifier, capable of possessing different and sometimes contradictory meanings in the various contexts the film presents.

As the film moves through its narration of Jolson's life story it employs a number of similar mobile signifiers to articulate the relationship between margin and mainstream. In different contexts, Jolson's family is used to signify both poles of this opposition: although Jolson's parents are positioned as ethnically marginal, when the family is juxtaposed with the theatre it becomes more clearly aligned with the social mainstream with the theatre being constructed as a marginal place. Like the family, however, the theatre is not a static signifier: it is also characterized by an internal dichotomy between mainstream and margins. Viewed as a bounded society in its own right, the theatre possesses its own establishment, its own mainstream in which entertainers working within well-established entertainment genres earn a "living", plying their trade before a reliable audience. In the film, this theatrical mainstream is represented by characters such as Jolson's mentor, Steve Martin (William Demarest)—a thirty-year veteran of the burlesque who resists Jolson's attempts to change his well-established act—and by institutions such as Dockstader's minstrels, which provides a reliable if unoriginal entertainment and an institutional setting which possesses something resembling a career structure for entertainment workers. In this structure, entertainers begin in the chorus and progress through various ranks of quartets, trios and duets before reaching the pinnacle of the structure as solo performers. However, despite their relatively prestigious position, even these soloists remain constrained by the generic conventions of the minstrel show and are restrained from expressing their individual creativity. This theatrical mainstream constructs entertainment as labour rather than an expression of the individual talent of the performer as an artist.

While Jolson's potential as a worker within this theatrical system of labour is recognized and he is afforded the opportunity to progress to the highest reaches of this entertainment mainstream, the film depicts Jolson's early theatrical career as a period of increasing, self-willed marginalization. As he progresses up the career structure offered by the minstrel show, Jolson becomes increasingly dissatisfied with the staid, unvarying entertainment offered by the show. Dockstader (John Alexander), the show's leader, resists the changes Jolson desires. The combination of dissatisfaction and the desire to pursue a more exciting and authentic form of entertainment further marginalizes Jolson. One evening he misses a show, having become transfixed by a performance by black musicians in a jazz club; an event that can be seen as a rejection of the ritualized expression of mainstream (white America's) perceptions of racial marginality in the minstrel show in favour of the *real* racial marginality of the black community within America and the authentic musical forms of that group.

As a result of this incident Jolson moves to his most marginal position in the film. Dismissed from Dockstader's minstrels for missing the show and because of his expressions of dissatisfaction with this inflexible genre, Jolson disappears for a time, his postcards to his parents becoming less frequent. Jolson's marginality is evident on his return home, when his mother remarks that he appears not to have been eating properly, an observation that registers Jolson's movement from his initial position of economically secure middle-class respectability to one of marginality and poverty. Jolson has rejected middle-class respectability by choosing the theatre rather than the synagogue, and he is even marginalized in the theatrical context as a result of his insistence on pursuing his own vision of entertainment rather than the safer option of work within the theatrical mainstream. As a result he has ended up in a position of irregular and unreliable work , and consequent economic impoverishment.

The passage of the main character through a period of economic impoverishment is a common factor in all three of the musical biopics. In *Night and Day*, Cole Porter rejects the upper middle-class position of his family and the career in law, which is expected of him, in order to pursue a less secure future as a composer. In the early parts of *Till the Clouds Roll By*, Jerome Kern (Robert Walker) is established as an economically marginal figure, repeated references to his emaciated appearance signalling his poverty.

As well as the economic hardships endured by the struggling composer, Kern is also marginalized from the theatrical mainstream by a peculiarity of Broadway show-business at the time. While Kern is attempting to interest producers in his material, he finds it impossible to get an interview because he is an American and the producers are only interested in English composers. When Kern eventually does get a song included in a show, he only achieves this by travelling to London and pretending to be English in order to interest a visiting American producer in his material. Kern is doubly marginalized, then: excluded from the American theatre because he is American and then compelled to feign a non-American identity in order to gain access to that theatre, but thereby denying his true nationality and so alienating himself from the society to which he belongs.

The central characters in all three of these musical biopics are marked as marginal in various ways in the early parts of the films and the association of these characters with the theatre is key to their marginal status. Similarly, in all three films the achievement of outstanding success within the entertainment business redeems these characters and restores them to a position of mainstream respectability at the same time as providing them with high economic status. *The Jolson Story* provides the clearest articulation of this movement from margin to mainstream and, in doing so, it presents Jolson as the agent of his own success. This endows the film with a particularly strong sense of the narrative's articulation of a distinctively American vision of individual success in the face of obstacles presented by the dominant forces of the milieu within which the individual exercises his agency.

In a key scene Jolson is shown enjoying a meal with the family he has just returned to, having reached the extreme extent of his marginality. During the meal he receives a telephone call from Tom Baron (Bill Goodwin). In an earlier scene Jolson secretly took the place of Baron, performing the latter's blackface minstrel act when Baron was too drunk to do so himself. Jolson's version of Baron's act was so successful that it led to Baron gaining a contract to perform in a prestigious Oscar Hammerstein show. In this later scene, Baron recounts how his performance in that show had been so poor that Hammerstein had eventually paid him off. However, influential contacts he made while performing in the show had enabled him to gain a position as manager of a Broadway theatre. In offering Jolson a slot in his new show, and agreeing to allow Jolson to develop his own material for the show, Baron effectively acts as the instrument of Jolson's own agency, since he would never have been in a position to make this offer if Jolson's earlier actions had not given this new direction to Baron's own career. The slot offered by Baron is the turning point in Jolson's career, since it finally allows him the opportunity to perform his own choice of material, freed from the constraints imposed by traditional theatrical forms. On the opening night of the show, Jolson's individual agency is foregrounded once again when he forces his way onto the stage to perform despite the stage manager having cut his act from the show due to the overrunning of other acts.

Following the success of this performance, Jolson's progressive rise in status within the theatrical hierarchy is registered in a montage sequence in which a soundtrack consisting of a medley of Jolson's songs is accompanied by images of a succession of billboards for shows in which Jolson appeared, and which depict his ascent from unbilled performer to top-billed star. The last stage in Jolson's movement from the margins to a central position in a reconfigured entertainment establishment is marked by his first performance without blackface makeup; Jolson now finally appearing as himself—without the marker of racial marginality signified by the makeup—and performing on his own terms, without the generic frame of reference connecting his act to the traditions of the minstrel show, such as the wearing of blackface makeup, the adoption of particular gestures and the performance of a limited musical repertoire. The other significant move in this respect is Jolson's decision to take one of his successful Broadway shows on a tour of the USA, taking a relatively marginal entertainment form (in national terms) with a necessarily limited audience resulting from its normally fixed geographical location in the major cities and particularly on Broadway, into the heart of the American nation, thereby democratizing and nationalizing this hitherto privileged cultural form.

The narratives of these three films tell a distinctively American kind of success story; a story that centres on the individual who possesses unusual talent but who, as a result of the limited horizons of existing institutions, is positioned as an outsider, a marginal figure sustained only by his own self-belief, and ultimately vindicated in that belief. It is this thematic concentration on success and the individual that marks these narratives as peculiarly American. Although these preoccupations are not unique to the early postwar period and are a key diachronic dimension of American culture, the clustering of the release of these rather unusual films around the early postwar years does invite explanation, particularly when set against the background of the degree of academic attention that has been given to films noirs, which articulate a strong sense of disillusionment with the very values celebrated in these musical biopics. The relative popularity of these biopics, compared with that of their film noir contemporaries, does suggest that a more upbeat and optimistic culture existed in America in the early postwar years than has hitherto been widely acknowledged in film studies.

There is, of course, an argument against seeing the emphasis on individual enterprise as the motor of success evident in these films as something peculiar to the early postwar moment. A belief in the value of individualistic entrepreneurialism is a deeply ingrained feature of American culture and is not necessarily specifically linked to the early postwar moment. However, looking at other cultural artefacts of the period, it is possible to identify a distinctive postwar discourse linking individual agency to the promotion of the general social good, and this does suggest that the stories of extraordinary individual success presented by these musical biopics were peculiarly attuned to the postwar mood.

Former governor of Minnesota and ex-naval officer, Harold E. Stassen employed this rhetoric of individual enterprise in an article published in *The Atlantic*. Stassen urged that a key factor in the postwar reconstruction of the American economy would be the leadership of the federal government in "vigorous support of the free-enterprise system" (1946: 48). Furthermore, the "over-all objective of the American system" in the years after the war should be the promotion of "individual freedom of thought and action" (48). Americans should "champion, implement, and stimulate an expanding competitive American economic system of private capital, individual enterprise, and free workmen" (48). Stassen argued that this required "that we must encourage and applaud the pioneer, the originator, the inventor, the risk taker" in order that America could become "a nation of originality, of boldness, and of imagination" (48). In another article published by *The Atlantic*, Sumner H. Slichter concluded a cautious assessment of the postwar economic prospects for America on a similar note:

> Let us keep clearly before us these great potentialities of our economy. Awareness of them will help us keep our sights high; it will stimulate our confidence in our power to achieve; it will help us retain and strengthen the spirit of pioneering and innovation
> (1944: 91)

Not all commentators were as optimistic about the postwar economy. Gunnar Myrdal (1944), also writing in *The Atlantic* (part of the same series, entitled *The Future of Free Enterprise in America*, as Slichter's article) expressed reservations about the economic basis of this boosterism, but perhaps it is not surprising that Myrdal, a Swedish sociologist looking at America from the outside, would be less easily seduced by a rhetoric which is so deeply implicated in the distinctively American sense of national identity.

There is a clear resonance between this rhetoric of pioneering individualism and the three musical biopics I have been discussing in this chapter. So although an emphasis on individualism and enterprise might well be a characteristic of American cultural productions at almost any time in the nation's history, the specific historical context within which these films were made and viewed endows their treatment of these themes with a particular relevance to these discourses concerning the postwar economic reconstruction. These films can be seen to be embedded within the specificity of their historical moment and perhaps this offers an explanation why this unusual and short-lived cycle of films should have emerged at this particular time and have disappeared so rapidly, despite the exceptional success of the films.

Modernizing the American hero

Before moving on from these musical biopics there is one further aspect of the films to consider. As I have observed, the central characters in all three of these films are constructed as marginal figures, occupying a place outside mainstream society and even outside the mainstream of the theatrical milieu, which is the site of their chosen occupation. Jolson, Porter and Kern are thus established as maverick figures whose self-belief and pursuit of their individual visions, against the mainstream currents of both society at large, and the more localized social microcosm represented by the theatrical milieu, is finally vindicated by the unexpected degree of their success and the extent to which the agency of these characters transforms the mainstream against which they were initially positioned as marginal. Their success produces, in each instance, a paradigm shift that establishes these performers as the central figures in a new mainstream. In this construction of the hero as a maverick figure there are some striking and unexpected parallels between these icons of the entertainment industry and another figure that occupies a central place in one of the myths that structures the American sense of self: the western hero.

These parallels operate at a deeper structural level than that of purely superficial similarities between individual non-conformists. While it would be going too far to suggest that the narratives of these musical biopics conform precisely to the pattern of western narratives, there are some striking similarities between the narrative structures of these biopics and the model of the classical western plot suggested by Will Wright (1977: 48-49). Wright's model consists of sixteen functions that "describe the narrative structure of the classical Western" (49). The functions enumerated by Wright do not exactly correspond to the narrative structure of the musical biopics. However, eliminating those functions in Wright's model that relate to the activities of villains (perhaps replacing them with functions that concern the overcoming of adversity) it becomes possible to see Wright's model as providing a summary of the narrative pattern of these three biopics.

Wright's first five functions offer a clear outline of the narrative movement of the early parts of the musical biopics:

1. The hero enters a social group (in this case the theatre)
2. The hero is unknown to the society (taken here to refer both to society at large and that particular microcosm represented by the theatre)
3. The hero is revealed to have an exceptional ability (in the biopics, a unique talent)
4. The society recognizes a difference between themselves and the hero; the hero is given special status (in relation to the biopics several different functions are collapsed together in this statement. Initially the difference between the society and the hero results in further marginalization of the hero, who later receives special status when the genius of the hero's vision is more widely recognized)
5. The society does not completely accept the hero (marginalization)

The final two functions describe the late stages of the biopics:

15. The society accepts the hero (his genius is recognized)
16. The hero loses or gives up his special status (no longer marginalized, the hero establishes a new mainstream with himself at its centre)

The structural similarities between the narratives of the biopics and Wright's model of the classic western suggest a way of seeing the protagonists of these biopics as a new kind of modern American hero within a mutated form of the western myth which has traditionally been such a key element in the development of the American sense of national identity. The modernity of this heroic figure is most clearly signified in the shift from the classic western's preoccupation with the violent defeat of those whose actions threaten society to the theme of overcoming difficult obstructions to the realization of the hero's vision, through sheer hard work and single-minded determination.

Another of the most popular films released after the war—*The Harvey Girls*—deals more explicitly with this transformation of the traditional western hero into a more modern kind of hero. This transformation is articulated through gradual shifts in the values of the character, Ned Trent (John Hodiak), as the narrative progresses. In the film's early scenes, Ned is clearly linked to the conception of the west as an uncivilized, lawless wilderness. He is the owner of the local saloon and brothel and, as such, has a vested interest in maintaining the lawlessness of the frontier town. He actively resists the establishment of a Harvey restaurant in the town and the promise of increasing civilization that it brings. However, as the film progresses, Ned falls in love with Susan Bradley (Judy Garland), one of the Harvey waitresses, and becomes increasingly resistant to the violent means employed by Judge Purvis (Preston Foster) in his efforts to drive the Harvey Girls out of town. In this transformation of Ned's character it is possible to detect a shift in the ideal of American heroism, away from the violence of the classic western hero and toward the modern hero's embrace of civilized values. The fact that the film employs a western setting and iconography but has a greater generic affinity with the musical than the western strengthens the feeling that the film articulates a shift in the conception of American heroism from a frontier mode to a more modern, more civilized mode. Considered in this way, *The Harvey Girls*, *Till the Clouds Roll By*, *Night and Day* and *The Jolson Story* can all be seen to update the conception of the American hero, providing a distinctively modern mode of heroism, with an emphasis on qualities of hard work and determination, in place of the violence of the western hero (a shift in emphasis which would have been particularly appropriate for a society moving from a period of war into peacetime), but without departing from the familiar structure of narratives of frontier heroism.

American-ness and immigrant identities: the cultural 'melting pot'

In his study of the American character, Geoffrey Gorer observed that America could be distinguished from the rest of the world because American national identity amounted to "an act of will, rather than the result of chance or destiny" (1948: 146). This voluntary dimension to American national identity may be intimately related to America's long history of immigration, and the assimilation of immigrants into American society that this inevitably involves. The conception of American national identity as an "act of will", or more accurately as a performance of identity which mutates from an ethnically marked immigrant identity into a performance of American-ness which retains few traces of this ethnic inscription, is very clearly mobilized in *The Jolson Story*. In the early parts of the film Jolson's Jewishness is emphasized. Indeed, it is fair to observe that "Al Jolson"—the highly performative, theatrical identity that evolves in such a way as to efface all traces of Jewishness, initially through the adoption of blackface and later through an accomplished performance of white American-ness—does not exist in the early stages of the film. The character who will become "Al Jolson" possesses, in early scenes, a more obviously Jewish identity as Asa Yoelson, the only child (a fiction of the film, in reality Jolson had siblings) in a family of Jewish immigrants to America from a location in Eastern Europe which is not specified in the film (Srednicke, Lithuania in reality, according to Freedland, 1995). Although Asa is less obviously marked as Jewish than his parents—lacking their "foreign" accents—his position as a Jewish immigrant is established by virtue of his family background. Asa's move into the theatre under the mentorship of Steve Martin initiates the process of transforming Asa/Al's identity from immigrant Other to American.

Steve is instrumental in this process of transformation, not only because he separates Asa from his immigrant family background by taking him into the theatre and into his care, but also because it is Steve who identifies the need for Asa to take a more American sounding name and so initiates Asa's adoption of the name "Al Jolson". In the sense that this renaming represents a significant stage in the transformation of Asa/Al's identity from Jewish immigrant to American, it is appropriate to view this as a symbolic "christening": not that it effects an actual religious conversion, but it does begin a process of removing the most obvious signs of Jewishness as part of the process of Asa/Al's Americanization.

The next stage in this process of transformation begins with Al's adoption of blackface makeup when he substitutes himself onstage for the inebriated Tom Baron. While the use of blackface might seem to invite a conclusion that this marked its wearer as more visibly Other than Al's Jewishness had done, the use of this makeup actually functions to affirm Al's increasingly secure American-ness. Initially, Al's wearing of this makeup enables him to pass himself off as Tom—a non-immigrant American—and fool a large audience with this masquerade of American-ness. Later, when Al performs in blackface in his own right, he does so within the context of a highly ritualized, white American entertainment tradition. In this context, despite the superficial markers of racial Otherness employed in blackface entertainment, by participating in this entertainment Al engages in a distinctly *white* American performance of black identity. An observation made by Bernard Wolfe in relation the performance of black American entertainers is also pertinent to white entertainers using blackface. Wolfe's observations reinforce this understanding of the white blackface performer as the participant in a performance of whiteness enacted through a ritualized performance of a conception of blackness constructed by and for whites:

> The truth about the Negro performer is that he is required to be a *Negro impersonator*. This truth has been hauled out into the open and even made into a public joke in our popular culture: for more than a century, whenever an occasional Negro *was* allowed to perform in a minstrel show, he too had to blacken his face with burnt cork and whiten his lips with cornstarch … The very same idea has long been codified in Southern caste etiquette, which requires each individual Negro to personify the white man's image of the composite Negro.
>
> (1955: 61, emphasis in original)[4]

Al only abandons blackface makeup as the mainstay of his theatrical performances after he has achieved considerable success and gained widespread recognition. Now fully Americanized, Al is free to dispense with the ritualized performance of white American-ness involved in his blackface act and instead just "be himself" (although this is, of course, just as much a performance, but one which effaces the means of its construction rather than foregrounding them in the same way as the blackface act). It is worth noting that Al's early post-blackface performances in the film also have him playing ethnically marked characters such as the "Spaniard" he plays in his first non-blackface show and his role in "Sinbad", indexed by a brief shot of a billboard within one of the film's montage sequences, thereby retaining some sense of Al's immigrant Otherness. On the whole, however, from this point in the movie the construction of Al's identity is characterized more by American-ness than ethnic Otherness. This mixing of residual elements of ethnic difference within an overall sense of American-ness foregrounds the reality of the construction of American national identity from the assimilation of a disparate range of immigrant identities to a unified American-ness. This has the effect of referencing yet another myth that is central to American society's sense of itself, presenting a vision of America as a cultural "melting pot".

Like *The Jolson Story*, *Saratoga Trunk* also employs signifiers of racial Otherness as elements in its presentation of an American national identity that incorporates a diverse range of immigrant identities. The impression of America as a cultural "melting pot" is strongly suggested by the mise-en-scène of the New Orleans location in which the early parts of the film are set. I have argued earlier in this chapter that New Orleans represents a highly Europeanized milieu in contrast to the more obviously American setting of Saratoga Springs later in the film. While this specific Europeanization of the setting is crucial to the film's articulation of class relations, the New Orleans setting also functions, in a more general sense, as an Other to the image of America presented in the film. Mixed together in this setting are not only the American and European characters who are foregrounded by virtue of their roles within the narrative, but also a host of minor characters ("figures", as Thumim would style them, 1992: 88) who, although having no narrative role, populate the mise-en-scène and contribute a sense of realism to the film and who, by virtue of their wide range of cultural backgrounds—predominantly European and African—also project a clear image of America as a cultural "melting pot". Early scenes, such as one in which a black chimney sweep and his assistant ply their trade outside Clio's home while a number of other black characters assist with the cleaning and renovation of the house, and particularly another scene in which Clio and her two servants, Angelique (Flora Robson[5]) and Cupidon (Jerry Austin) promenade through the French market, peopled by figures representing this diverse range of cultures, reinforce this impression. At the market Clio samples some jambalaya—a Cajun meal derived from a traditional Provençal dish but given a distinctive American regional identity through the influence of the other cultures that meet in Louisiana. This meal serves as a particularly potent metaphor for the mixing of cultures, especially with its literal use of a large cooking pot, the significance of which as a metaphor for the cultural "melting pot" is hard to ignore.

Clio herself embodies some of the ambiguities inherent in a national identity formed within a cultural "melting pot". While at one level *Saratoga Trunk* is almost entirely concerned with the process of Americanizing the European Clio, this process of Americanization leaves unresolved key questions concerning her character's racial identity, which the film raises in its early scenes. These questions are, however, couched in such vague terms that even the issue of whether there is ambiguity concerning Clio's racial background itself becomes highly ambiguous. The film provides enough information to hint that there is something questionable there, but not enough to allow the viewer to gain sufficient purchase on what precisely the issue is. Although Clio's statement of her desire for revenge on "these pasty-faced aristocrats" and Clint's remark to Clio, "you look kinda funny yourself with all that white stuff on your face", suggest that Clio may be of a mixed racial background, these "flickers of meaning" (Barthes 1990) are as elusive in *Saratoga Trunk* as the flickering light of a candle suggested by Barthes' metaphor, illuminating an apparently important feature momentarily before cloaking it in darkness once more, leaving the observer wondering what precisely they had glimpsed in that momentary light.

Saratoga Trunk taunts the viewer with these veiled suggestions of Clio's ambiguous ethnicity but fails to resolve the question it raises. The issue concerning Clio's racial background raised in the early parts of the film simply disappears in the later parts. This disappearance indicates a paradox in the presentation of America as a cultural "melting pot", stemming from the disparity between the image of harmonious multi-cultural co-existence that this representational figure implies, and the experiential reality of a racially divided and unequal society. This is a contradiction which the film is incapable of containing or resolving and so the question of Clio's racial background simply disappears from the film leaving the narrative to negotiate only the process of Americanizing the now purely European Clio.

As well as the articulation of the relationship between American-ness and immigrant identities in *The Jolson Story* and *Saratoga Trunk*, the conglomerated vision of American national identity presented in these films is also hinted at in some of the other films: for example, in Jerome Kern's performance of Englishness as a way of gaining acceptance as an American composer in *Till the Clouds Roll By*, and in the situation, which motivates the narrative of *The Green Years*, in which an orphaned Irish Catholic boy, Robert Shannon (Dean Stockwell/Tom Drake), comes to live with his late mother's Scottish, Protestant family. The film captures a clear sense of the complicated interplay of likeness and Otherness inherent in an American nationality comprised of a variety of different immigrant identities. While familial bonds connect Robert to his new family in a relationship of likeness, his religious and national background mark him as Other. In this way the film indirectly highlights one of the paradoxes of the idea of American nationality, in the sense that the coherence and unity implied by the concept of nationhood is contradicted at every turn by the differences between the various immigrant identities that constitute that supposedly coherent national self. Despite this contradiction foregrounded by *The Green Years*, the overall presentation of American-ness in these films glosses over contradiction in favour of an image of American-ness that encompasses a set of core American values—democracy, classlessness, equality, enterprise, opportunity—while also acknowledging the culturally enriching qualities brought by the disparate range of immigrant cultures of which American society is comprised.

As the Second World War came to an end and America turned to face its postwar future, undoubtedly certain anxieties about what that future held rose to the surface. By the time the war ended, traditional patterns of American life had been disturbed for some time; the disruptions of the war itself compounding those of the Great Depression that immediately preceded it. In these circumstances, it would be hard to deny that the pessimism and cynicism towards traditional American beliefs and values evident in numerous postwar films noirs registered these anxieties. But, as the analysis of some of the more popular films of the time demonstrates, this was by no means Hollywood's only response to the postwar situation. The treatment of components of key myths that structure America's sense of itself in Hollywood's most popular early postwar films reveals a far stronger imperative to celebrate and reinvigorate traditional attitudes and values, traditional myths, than to problematize them. The first two of these components considered in this chapter, concern over "Cinderellas" of the services and the reassertion of the myth of classless democracy are both aspects of the same issue, the former being a historically specific concern arising from the potential destabilization of the latter in the wake of the social disruptions flowing from America's involvement in the Second World War. While the myth of classless democracy is probably an element that could be identified in American cultural productions at any historical moment, the intertextual discursivity between the films that re-assert this myth and other contemporary cultural artefacts illustrates the particular relevance of this issue in the early postwar period and how important it was that these traditional American values should be confidently asserted in popular cultural forms at this time.

Another key area of American mythology, the myth of America as a land of opportunity, is also a significant presence in a distinct (and peculiarly limited) cycle of musical biopics that were among the most popular films after the war. The three of these films released in 1946 have a clear function as "success stories", which promote this vision of America. Additionally, by constructing their central characters as maverick heroes these films appropriate significant elements of the structure of the classic western. This endows these characters with the quality of being modern versions of the western heroes. In this way, these films offer the prospect for revitalizing the western myth, updating the hero's mode of signification while still retaining traces of the traditional themes of the frontier, the pioneering spirit and the primacy of the individual.

Finally, the articulation of American national identity in relation to the immigrant identities that are crucial components of that nationality was also a distinctive element in popular postwar films. This is an area in which the films often struggle to contain the contradictions which inevitably follow from the effort to forge a unified national character from a disparate range of pre-American national identities, all of which contribute to the American sense of self but also retain a strong sense of prior national or ethnic affiliation. This results in a certain awkwardness in some of the films and leads to the introduction of questions which the films are unable to resolve. These are then simply left unanswered—the question of the racial identity of Clio in *Saratoga Trunk* being the key example. Despite the difficulties the films have in resolving these problematic issues, the films ultimately gloss over contradictions, so allowing the development of a vibrant and optimistic image of America as a cultural "melting pot".

A similar sense of optimism characterizes the presentation of all of the different aspects of American mythology discussed in this chapter. In this respect there is a marked difference between the most popular films released in the early postwar period and the impression of the period presented in studies of postwar films noirs. I explore this apparent contradiction further in chapter 6. The following chapter examines the treatment in the popular films of two key figures—the absent father and the "mom"—figures that were of central importance to the representation of family relationships in popular early postwar films.

CHAPTER 3

The troubled postwar family: "moms" and absent fathers

The publication, immediately after the war, of the first edition of Dr. Benjamin Spock's *Baby and Child Care*—a book that would not only become enormously popular and influential itself, but would also establish the pattern for a new non-fiction genre of infant care guides—provides some indication of the degree to which family life became a focal point of public concern in post-war America. The timing of the appearance of the first edition of Spock's volume was undoubtedly coincidental, and it would be misleading to interpret the publication of the book at that time as part of a concerted ideological project to normalize a particular vision of family life following the disruptions that resulted from the war. Given its extraordinary influence, however, the book does provide a sense of prevailing attitudes towards the family in early postwar America.

Spock's book maintains a delicate balance between a progressive view of family relations—allowing that women who wished to work should not be censured for this desire, and recognizing the need for fathers to take an active role in child rearing—and acknowledgement of the persistence of a deeply ingrained division of roles between the sexes. While the more progressive ideas in Spock's book register shifting American attitudes towards childcare after the war, other contemporary publications about the family pursued an unambiguously conservative moral agenda, directed towards returning men and women to traditional familial roles. These more conservative commentators (see, for example, Overton 1945; Lundberg and Farnham 1947) advocated the restoration of an ideal of family relations premised on female domesticity and the man's role as breadwinner. The stability of these traditional roles had been disturbed for some time, even before the war, and American involvement in the war was merely the final phase of a period of disruption of normative, traditional gender roles that had arguably begun during the Great Depression, when women were forced to seek paid work because their husbands became unemployed (see Filene 1998: 166). Against this already unsettled background, the Second World War had boosted female employment to unprecedented levels (177) and brought women into areas of work that were previously the exclusive preserve of men.

These disruptions to the traditional structures of the family and gender were a source of anxiety that can be detected in a number of countervailing tendencies in the films of the early postwar period, from the restoration of traditional patterns of family life presented through images of cosy small-town domesticity in films such as *It's a Wonderful Life*, to the almost total absence of the family in film noir and the centrality of the figure of the sexually predatory femme fatale in many of those dark movies. In this chapter I am going to look at two of the manifestations of these anxieties in popular films, by examining two key figures—the "absent father" and the "mom".

The absent father

While not making an explicit connection between paternal absence from the family and America's involvement in the war, Spock did devote two sections of a chapter dealing with special child care problems to "The Fatherless Child" (1946: 481-484). Given the proximity of the end of the war to the first appearance of this volume and the fact that Spock devoted a separate section of the same chapter to parents who had separated because of problems within their marriage (473-475), it seems likely that Spock's concerns about fatherless children were implicitly directed toward the problems of children whose fathers were absent due to their involvement in the war. Spock's concerns fell into two broad categories: first the need to maintain the absent father's feeling of involvement with the family; second, the impact of the father's absence on children. The first of these concerns addressed very specifically the situation of men posted overseas on military service, and stressed the need for mothers to provide those men with detailed accounts of the development of their children. The latter reflected concerns about the damaging effect of the absence of fathers on children; particularly boys who were thought to be at risk of becoming "precocious and effeminate" (484) if deprived of contact with appropriate male role models.

Numerous other writers were also concerned about the effect of paternal absence on children's development and behaviour. Noting that "war forces a change in the entire peace-time system of family living" (1944: 83), Willard Waller expressed concern over the "great damage to the pattern of family life" (83) caused by the need for the family to "give up members to the army, to war work" (83), as a result of which, the family "loses its hold on the minds of the young" (83). The absence of fathers on military service (and mothers engaged in war work) destabilized the family, leading to a "relaxation of sexual morality" (83) and to "neglect of children and so to a rise in juvenile delinquency" (84).

A contemporary article in *Life* magazine also linked juvenile delinquency (which it characterized as sexual rather than criminal delinquency in the case of young women) to the absence of fathers. Paternal absence might mean the father's actual, physical removal from the family—"Alvin's father died ... 18 years ago" but was also understood as including less tangible absences, caused by the father's failure or inability to exercise patriarchal authority as a result of a moral character flaw such a drunkenness—"Joe's parents have been separated 14 years. His father was a no-good drunk" (8 April 1946: 83-93).

Another article, "Marriage and the Family After the War", published in the *Annals of the American Academy of Political and Social Science* also predicted a difficult period of destabilized family life after the war and linked this instability to a high rate of juvenile delinquency and lapsed sexual morality:

> The family is in for a hard time ahead ... Individual families will be so broken that they can never be mended, but new ones will spring up to replace them. Divorce will increase after the war.

> Juvenile delinquency will remain high for a time, and in many
> homes family discipline and parental authority will not be re-
> established. Sex standards, already lowered, will be extremely
> hard to raise.
>
> (Baber 1943: 175)

Similarly, Grace Sloan Overton, in her book, *Marriage in War and Peace*
(1945), envisioned the post Second World War readjustment as a time
of advancing promiscuity by resurrecting an image of the 1920s as a
highly eroticized and sexual period. Overton made an explicit link
between the war and the rise of promiscuity arguing that the situation
in the 1920s had been caused by a failure to manage properly the
readjustment after the First World War. This acute concern about
delinquency, and particularly the linkage between the absence of
fathers and an expected increase in promiscuous behaviour among
young women, is a marked feature of early postwar publications
concerned with fatherhood and family life. Similar concerns can also
be detected in the popular films of the period, *Notorious* and *Saratoga
Trunk* being particularly good examples.

The opening scenes of *Notorious* show Alicia Hubermann's (Ingrid
Bergman) father being convicted of treason, as a result of his political
activities as a member of a cell of Nazi activists operating in America.
Herr Hubermann's imprisonment and subsequent suicide definitively
absent the father from the diegesis, but the film makes it clear that a
rift had developed between father and daughter some years before. In
the sense that paternal authority had already evaporated and mutual
respect between father and daughter had broken down, the father had
been absent for some time before his definitive removal. During her
time in America, Alicia has developed an intense patriotism towards
her adopted country and regards her father's conspiracy against
America as a personal betrayal:

> I know what you stand for, you and your murdering swine. I've
> hated you ever since I found out ... I hate you and I love this
> country ... I love it. I'll see you all hang before I raise a finger
> against it.

Alicia's discovery of her father's activities represents a decisive
moment in the formation of her character: the moment at which her

father became an "absent father". Later she reveals to Devlin (Cary Grant) that everything in her life "went to pot" after she discovered her father's Nazi sympathies. Since then, her life has been characterized by excess and moral abandon.[1] In a scene near the beginning of the film, following her father's conviction, Alicia hosts a party for a number of friends. All of the guests are very drunk, but none more so than Alicia herself, who finally forces her other guests to leave (at least those still capable of standing), while she continues drinking and flirting with a mysterious stranger who remains (whom the viewer now discovers to be Devlin). Numerous references throughout the film to Alicia's "conquests" and "playmates" hint at the aggressive sexuality that is a key element of her character. At the end of their extended drinking session, Alicia insists on taking Devlin for a high-speed drive. Her reaction when pulled over by a highway patrol officer reveals how close Alicia's delinquency comes to outright criminality: "drunken driving. My second offence, now I go to jail. Whole family in jail, who cares". Significantly it is Devlin's intervention that saves Alicia from prosecution on this occasion, just as it will be the containment of Alicia's sexuality within a normative heterosexual couple with Devlin that will ultimately redeem her character.

Devlin secures Alicia's participation on a mission for the American secret service that requires her to infiltrate a cell of Nazi activists in Brazil by seducing its leader, Alex Sebastian (Claude Rains), a former associate of her father who had been infatuated with Alicia in the past. This task seems entirely suitable for a woman of Alicia's blatant promiscuity. However, by the time the precise nature of the mission is revealed, Alicia's relationship with Devlin has started to transform her character, and she has begun to conform to a more sober, chaste and domesticated feminine norm. When Devlin meets Alicia at a café a few days after their arrival in Rio, he is surprised by her decision to decline a second drink and by her claim that she has been sober and has made no new "conquests" since their arrival in Brazil. The reforming quality of their nascent romance, and the increasing conformity of Alicia's character to norms of female domestication, is clearest in a scene in which she offers to cook for Devlin despite having previously indicated that cooking was a chore she found especially disagreeable.

However, if romantic involvement with Devlin promises to redeem Alicia's character, his lack of faith in her ability to reform and his unwillingness to put his feelings towards her before his patriotic duty (an attribute he shares with her father) impedes her movement towards a more conformist femininity. At their meeting at the café, after Alicia informs Devlin of her new sobriety and chastity and declines his offer of another drink, Devlin expresses extreme scepticism about the ability of her character to reform:

| Alicia: | ... I'm pretending I'm a nice unspoiled child whose heart is full of daisies and buttercups. |
| Devlin: | (Coldly) Nice daydream. Then what? |

Visibly hurt by Devlin's remark and disappointed by his lack of faith, Alicia recants and decides to order another drink after all, prompting Devlin's response, "I thought you'd get around to it".

A later scene reinforces the sense of contradiction between the potential of Devlin's relationship with Alicia to act as a normalizing influence, and the impediment to her restoration to norms of femininity that Devlin's lack of faith in Alicia's ability to change represents. Devlin returns to Alicia's apartment after learning the exact nature of her mission. Alicia is cooking when he returns and so has reached the point in the film where she is at her most domesticated, as is apparent from her comment, "marriage must be wonderful with this sort of thing going on every day". Alicia's fantasy of domestic normalcy collapses, however, when Devlin reveals that her mission involves acting as a "Mata Hari", becoming involved in a fraudulent romance with Alex Sebastian in order to gather information about the activities of his group. It is not so much the nature of the mission itself as it is Devlin's unwillingness to prioritize their romance above his patriotic duty that breaks the romantic spell. In the conversation that follows, Alicia is palpably desperate for some sign that her love of Devlin is reciprocated, hoping that their nascent romance might have led Devlin to decline the mission on her behalf. For Devlin, however, patriotic duty takes precedence over their romance, and he reveals that he raised no objection to the mission:

| Devlin: | I didn't say anything. |

Alicia:	Not a word for that little lovesick lady you left an hour ago.
Devlin:	(Coldly) I told you, that's the assignment.
Alicia:	Now don't get sore Dev. I'm only fishing for a little birdcall from my dream man.

Two further elements in the scene—Alicia's comment that the food she had prepared for them has gone "all cold" and Devlin's recollection that he has left behind the bottle of champagne he was bringing to celebrate their new romance—signal the breaking of the romantic spell between the pair. For Alicia, the end of this romantic interlude presages a return to sexual delinquency: she agrees to the mission and begins to seduce Sebastian.

The scenes that follow the start of Alicia's attempt to seduce Sebastian transgress the film's ideology of romantic love: Alicia makes herself sexually available to a man she does not love. However, the fact that Alicia pursues this relationship out of an intense sense of patriotic duty militates against reading this as a simple relapse into delinquency. It is clear that Alicia's ability to pursue a mission which involves sexual intimacy with, and eventually marriage to, a man she not only does not love but, in view of the opinion of Nazis she expressed earlier in the film, must actively hate, is founded on a combination of patriotism and disillusionment at the failure of Devlin to put their romance before his own patriotic duty.

Although it is directed towards a different set of circumstances from those elaborated in *Notorious*, Spock's discussion of the problems of paternal absence and his strategies for minimizing the impact of these has a resonance with the film's positioning of Devlin not only as Alicia's lover but also as a kind of surrogate father. Spock stresses the need for the children of absent fathers to maintain contact with "agreeable men" such as "a friendly grocer or milkman" and other men who can serve as "substitute fathers". These men "will influence his conception of his father, will make his father mean more to him" (1946: 483). While Devlin's character functions, at one level, to uphold an ideology of romantic love, of the heterosexual couple as the socially sanctioned institution for the expression of female sexuality, there is another dimension to his character, which positions Devlin as a kind of substitute father, linking his character to that of Alicia's father by foregrounding the failure of both men to prioritize their relationship with Alicia over their patriotic duty. Devlin's failure in this respect hinders the development of his relationship with Alicia and the formation of the romantic couple that will ultimately redeem her from delinquency.

Figure 3.1 Devlin (Cary Grant) administers a hangover cure. *Notorious* (1946).

Figure 3.2 Madame and Alex Sebastian (Leopoldine Konstantin and Claude Rains) administer poison. *Notorious* (1946).

Two scenes, one early and the other late in the film, linked by the use of expressionist visual devices in both, convey a strong sense of the redemptive qualities of Devlin for Alicia's delinquent character. In the first scene Devlin administers a hangover remedy to Alicia; in the later scene Alicia realizes that Sebastian and his mother are poisoning her. The visual devices in each scene are slightly different—a skewed camera angle designed to depict Alicia's point of view while lying flat on the bed, as Devlin enters the room and moves around the bed to stand beside her in the earlier scene (fig 3.1); the use of blurred and distorted silhouettes of Sebastian and his mother to capture a sense of the effects of the poison on Alicia's perception in the later scene (fig 3.2)—but the fact that the use of such expressionist devices in the film is limited to these two scenes, together with the fact that both scenes offer sustained shots from Alicia's point of view provide good reasons for considering the two scenes to be linked to each other. These linked scenes describe the two poles of an opposition, between cure (the administration of a remedy in the earlier scene) and destruction (the poisoning in the later scene), which circumscribes the narrative options for Alicia's character. Late in the film, Devlin realizes that what he had taken to be signs of alcohol abuse during his last meeting with Alicia are actually symptoms of poisoning and he enters Alicia's bedroom for a second time to "rescue" her from her predicament. This time the "cure" he brings is not a hangover treatment nor even an antidote to the poison she has been receiving (which the narrative logic would seem to demand), but is just himself, and the promise he offers to redeem Alicia's character, to "cure" once and for all her sexual delinquency through their union in a normative, heterosexual romantic couple.

The absent father is also a key figure in *Saratoga Trunk*. The father's death precedes the commencement of the film's narrative and a strong sense of his absence inhabits the early parts of the film. This is particularly marked in early scenes showing Clio's return to her late mother's house. Like the young children of absent fathers of whom Spock wrote (1946: 483), Clio has a mental image of her father, built up over the years through the accounts provided by her mother and her two servants, but this image needs to be given substance. So while her servant, Cupidon, reacts with fear at the creaking of the front door to her mother's old, long abandoned house—"ghost in there"—Clio looks forward to the opportunity to finally encounter this hitherto absent figure; "if there is, it's my father and I'd like to see him". As Clio and her two servants move through the cobwebbed rooms of the old house, the location evokes memories of incidents from Clio's parents' doomed romance, particularly when the group discovers the sofa on which Clio's mother sat while a lawyer informed her of the father's marriage to another woman. Angelique's description of this earlier episode is notable for the father's absence even at this stage, sending the family lawyer in his place. Finally, Cupidon finds the dried remains of a pool of the father's blood, which provides Clio with the sense of her father's corporeal presence that she seeks; "my father's blood, my blood, they are the same".

Like Alicia in *Notorious*, Clio is characterized by her deviation from conventional moral norms and she possesses an aggressive sexuality. Clio's major concern on her arrival in New Orleans is to take revenge on her father's family for their prohibition of the father's relationship with her mother, which resulted in the father's death and the mother's life-long exile in Paris. Clio's very presence in New Orleans is itself the scandal that the mother's exile, financed by the father's family, was engineered to avoid, but Clio compounds the insult of her mere presence by her outrageous behaviour, always ensuring that her connection to the Dulaine family is well known.

Clio's aggressive sexuality is a key element in establishing her character as disruptive and transgressive of norms of femininity. The first meeting between Clio and Clint provides a clear example of this. While Clio enjoys a plate of jambalaya from a street vendor, Clint leans against the counter of an adjacent coffee shop. As Clio finishes the plate, Clint catches her and she turns her head to look directly at him, firstly at his face, but her eyes soon scan down his body and there is a cut to an eyeline match shot scanning Clint's body from head to toe. Clint returns her gaze, but his attention is fixed firmly on her face and he is not afforded the same opportunity to gaze at the whole of her body. The merest twitch of Clint's eyes downwards to glance momentarily at the rest of her body, signals his sexual interest in Clio. Her response is one of initial surprise (signalled by her averting her eyes) turning rapidly to pleasure and interest in pursuing the relationship (indicated by her repeated attempts to gaze at him again). Clio's prolonged and objectifying look at Clint's body is repeated in a later scene in which Clio, having invited Clint to share her table at a restaurant, once again takes the opportunity to look up and down his body from head to toe. A still later scene hints that the couple's evident sexual interest in one another has developed into a sexual relationship. In this early morning scene, Clio sits brushing her hair at her dressing table, still dressed in her nightwear, while Clint also sits in her bedroom. While the scene is inexplicit about the development of a sexual relationship, it does convey a strong sense of the couple preparing to start their day after spending the night together.

While Clio's relationship with Clint might be thought to redeem her character by containing her sexuality within the context of a heterosexual couple, the fact that Clio not only has no intention of marrying Clint, at this point in the movie, but is also quite open about her intention to seek a man to marry purely for his wealth, works against any suggestion of containment. Furthermore the constant presence of Clint as the real object of Clio's sexual desire throughout her later attempts to woo the millionaire, Bartholomew Van Steed (John Warburton), negates the possibility that marriage to Van Steed could redeem Clio's sexuality. Only toward the end of the film, after Clint acquires a substantial stockholding in a railroad company are the conditions created for Clio's redemption through their relationship. Clio loves Clint but is determined to marry a wealthy man. His new wealth allows Clio to marry Clint and thereby comply with the ideological prescription of the film by marrying for love rather than money. Conclusive evidence of her new-found compliance with feminine norms is found in the closing moments of the film, Clio accepts her subordination to Clint's patriarchal will, and so the traditional, normative feminine position, conceding that, contrary to the view she had previously expressed, he will "wear the pants" in their relationship.

In *Saratoga Trunk*, as in *Notorious*, the central female character is constructed as delinquent, by virtue of her failure to comply with feminine norms, particularly in relation to her sexual conduct. In both films the source of this delinquency is located in the removal of the father from the family. And in both films the female protagonist's sexuality is ultimately made safe through her involvement in a relationship with another man who replaces the absent father as the source of patriarchal authority.

A similar pattern exists in *Margie*, although this film lacks the overt sexual element in its construction of the eponymous heroine's character. The absence of Margie's father immediately strikes an odd chord, since it lacks a sufficient narrative motivation. Margie's (Jeanne Crain) father has not been killed or imprisoned but has simply passed responsibility for his daughter's upbringing to her maternal grandmother, after the death of the child's mother. Margie's resultant delinquency is not manifested through criminal behaviour, sexual aggressiveness or other moral lapses. In *Margie*, the young woman's deviation from feminine norms takes the form of the threat of female incursion into a public sphere conceptualized as masculine. This threat originates in the influence of Margie's grandmother (Esther Dale), a former suffragette who proudly displays above her fireplace the chain with which she once bound herself to the railings of the White House. She has political ambitions for Margie, to become the first woman president of America, and she encourages Margie's nascent political engagement through her membership of the high school debating team. Margie herself seems to share few of her grandmother's ambitions. Although she does participate in the debating team, her real interest lies in attracting the romantic attention of the school's latest heartthrob, the new French teacher, Mr. Fontayne (Glen Langan). The fact that a romance does develop between Margie and this obvious figure of masculine authority provides a clear example of the same narrative strategy of replacing the absent father with a romantic partner that also characterizes *Notorious* and *Saratoga Trunk*.

A key function of the male partner in all of these films is to substitute for the father as a source of patriarchal authority, regulating the conduct of the female protagonist and restoring her to conformity with traditional norms of femininity. In *Margie*, the sense of restoration of normative equilibrium between the sexes is clearest in the opening and closing scenes. These are the only scenes in the film that are set in the diegetic present, the remainder of the film being depicted as an extended flashback. In the opening scene Margie, now a married woman, and her teenage daughter sort through a trunk in their attic. Several items in the trunk—a pair of bloomers, a heavy chain and a photograph album—serve as a cue for the film's flashback section in which the significance of these items is revealed. In its final scene the film returns to Margie and her daughter in the attic, now replacing the items in the trunk and awaiting the imminent arrival of Margie's husband. His arrival confirms that Margie has married Mr. Fontayne (her husband's identity having been withheld up to this point).

Significantly the husband's return coincides with the replacement of items with connotations of transgression against feminine norms—the chain is that with which Margie's grandmother had attached herself to the White House railings, the bloomers those which at moments of impending romantic engagement in the film's flashback section would fall around Margie's ankles and undermine any impression of graceful femininity—into the trunk where they are safely contained, just as the transgressive potential of Margie's character is contained by her marriage to an obvious figure of authority, and the film's own account of this transgressive potential is consigned to the past by the flashback structure of its narrative.

The elimination of Margie's transgressive potential is confirmed in this closing scene by a newspaper article, which Mr. Fontayne shows to Margie. This report relates to the appointment of Margie's father as U. S. ambassador to Nicaragua. In an earlier scene Margie's father's opposition to American military intervention in Nicaragua had been catalysed by an argument that Margie had put forward during a high school debating competition. In several scenes after the debate, Margie's father repeats the arguments she put forward, in a rather comical and uncomprehending manner. In one register, his appointment as ambassador may simply work as a joke concerning the competence of politicians. At another level, however, it marks the restoration of normative gender roles; Margie as a housewife in the domestic sphere, her father having gained an important role in the public sphere by appropriating a political stance which was originated by his now domesticated, depoliticized daughter.

Although *Notorious*, *Saratoga Trunk* and *Margie* are all very different films, with a diverse range of generic affinities, each relies on the figure of the absent father as a key element of its narrative. All three films construct femininity as problematic, and in each case the problematic status of femininity is causatively linked to the absence of fathers and is resolved by the woman becoming involved in a heterosexual romantic couple that functions to normalize the woman's character both through the dynamics of the couple itself and by constructing the woman's male counterpart as a sort of substitute father figure who assumes the mantle of patriarchal authority. In this way the films all handle the problem of transgressive femininities by proposing a restoration of traditional relations between men and women and the re-establishment of clearly demarcated gendered spheres of activity.

The pleasures of fatherhood

In addition to its centrality to discourses concerning juvenile delinquency, the figure of the absent father reappears in another emergent postwar discourse concerning the pleasures of fatherhood. The absence of fathers from the family was not solely a result of the war, but was also part of the institutionalized segregation of parenting roles, which began at the moment of a child's birth. Spock provides a vivid account of the exclusion of fathers from the birth of their children, which was, at the time, standard practice in maternity units:

> the poor father is a complete outsider. He has to wait around alone for hours while the baby is being born, feeling useless and miserable
>
> (1946: 13)

Spock also noted that some fathers had an ingrained belief that they had no active role to play in childcare: "some fathers have been brought up to think that the care of babies and children is the mother's job entirely" (15). Spock also observed that some fathers "would get goose flesh at the very idea of helping to take care of a baby" (15). Spock argued against these attitudes towards parental roles in childcare, advocating greater involvement by the father, although he did concede that "there's no good to be gained by trying to force them" (15).

Male detachment from parenting may have been the norm in pre-war America but, in the early postwar period, Spock was not alone in emphasizing the benefits of paternal involvement in parenting, and the views expressed in Spock's writing at this time signal a shift in these entrenched attitudes, away from the tradition of a low level of paternal involvement in child rearing, and toward the ideal of a more domesticated type of masculinity that would become increasingly important in American culture as the decade following the war progressed.[2]

In an article published in the *New York Times Magazine* in 1944, Juliet Danziger gave an account of the experiences of her family following her husband's departure for the war. Danziger's account did not suggest that fatherless families would fall apart, the children turning to lives of criminal and sexual delinquency in the absence of a paternal authority figure. On the contrary, Danziger emphasized how well her family coped without a father and how the need to continue everyday life as normally as possible led her to the discovery of new skills and abilities as she was forced to take on tasks which would usually have been undertaken by her husband. Danziger even noted distinct advantages to family life without a male partner: "from a cold and calculating point of view, there are definitely points on the credit side of this wartime ledger" (1944a: 16). She concluded that "after a year of life without father, I have discovered that we can make things go, that I can live alone, and—well almost—like it" (47).

Despite the perceived advantages of the situation, Danziger nevertheless emphasized the importance for the children of maintaining a sense of their father's presence in the home:

> leaving things where they've always been makes the children feel strongly that they still have a Daddy ... It preserves some of the masculinity in the household ... They don't have that insecure sense of "Daddy's gone. He may never come back." Daddy isn't gone. He's away for a while.
>
> (16)

In another article, published in *Parents* magazine later in the year, Danziger's emphasis had shifted to restoring a sense of the need for fathers in the home: "everyday living with no man about the house is essentially an unnatural way of living" (1944b: 78). In the later article, Danziger also emphasized the importance to the family that the father should play an active role in parenting: "Daddy should take an active part in the going-to-bed rites. He can read to them before they go to sleep, or tell them something about what he does on his field or in his camp or on his ship" (78). In this later article Danziger echoes the call for greater paternal involvement in childcare to be found in Spock's writing.

This emergent discourse concerning male participation in childcare is less frequently an element in popular early postwar movies than the concerns about juvenile delinquency in fatherless families already discussed in this chapter. The central ideological push of this discourse—the promotion of an ideal of active paternal involvement in family life—does, however, figure in one of the most affecting scenes in *Blue Skies*. So far as it is relevant to the use of the figure of the absent father in the film, the narrative tells of the development of a romance, and eventually a marriage between Johnny and Mary (Joan Caulfield). The marriage is no equal partnership, and is marred by Johnny's constant failure to involve Mary in making important decisions affecting the family. In particular his repeated buying and selling of nightclubs—which each time involves uprooting the family and relocating to another city—without ever mentioning his intentions to Mary, is a source of considerable conflict. Even before the marriage finally breaks up, then, Johnny displays considerable remove from his family. However, he really becomes an absent father when Mary, who can no longer bear the continual upheavals, finally leaves Johnny, taking their daughter with her. Johnny's status as an absent father is clearest in a scene in which he pays a night-time visit to see his daughter, Mary Elizabeth (Karolyn Kay Grines). As he enters her bedroom it is clear that Mary Elizabeth does not recognise her father. Johnny senses the awkwardness of the situation and offers the rather coy explanation that he is a "friend" of her mother. As he moves closer to the bed, Mary Elizabeth begins to recognise Johnny as her "old daddy" from photographs shown to her by her mother. Despite this recognition, however, it is clear that Mary Elizabeth regards her absent father as a stranger and she initially refuses him a kiss because "mummy said I mustn't kiss strangers", relenting only when he convinces her that he cannot be a stranger because he has known her since she was very young. Feeling reassured, Mary Elizabeth is pleased to receive the attention of this friendly male figure, whom she asks to sing her a song. The song, *Running Around in Circles*, given a childlike, nursery rhyme quality by its orchestration, allegorises Johnny's situation—he's been "running around in circles, getting nowhere ... very fast"—and in the few brief moments in which he sings to his daughter, Johnny comes to recognise what he has lost through his prioritization of his business interests over his family. What makes this scene such a distinctive moment is the fact that it is focused so intensely on the relationship between father and child. In the context of a musical, in which the narrative is primarily concerned with the romantic relationship between Johnny and Mary, and in which equilibrium is ultimately restored by reuniting them as a romantic couple, it is highly significant that this turning point in the narrative, this moment when the increasing separation of the romantic couple is halted and the process of bringing them back together begins, is focused not on their romance, but on the relationship between father and daughter. It is not Johnny's realization of what he has lost through his separation from Mary that begins to reunite the couple, but his recognition of the pleasures he has missed as a father, that initiates the process of reconciliation. This sense of loss is evident in Johnny's facial expression, which captures his feelings of joy and pain while he embraces Mary Elizabeth. Read in this way, the scene can be understood as an allegory of the pleasures of fatherhood, offering a rare instance of the articulation in film of this emergent discourse, perhaps most clearly in evidence in Spock's (1946) writing, concerning the changing perception of the role of fathers within the family during the period immediately following the end of the war.

While *Notorious* and *Saratoga Trunk* are linked by a discourse that attributes a rise in juvenile delinquency to the absence of paternal authority, *Margie* and *Blue Skies* are connected by a different discourse that causatively links paternal absence to the separation of the social world into gendered spheres of activity: in both films the fathers are absent from the family because of the priority they have given to their business activities and public life over family life and the private sphere. The different ways these two pairs of films (*Notorious* and *Saratoga Trunk* on the one hand *Margie* and *Blue Skies* on the other) deploy the figure of the absent father suggests a retrospective orientation in the case of the former pair—looking back to the recent past, during the war, when fathers were physically removed from family life—and a prospective orientation in the case of the latter, looking forward to the re-establishment of a civilian order in which a masculine public sphere will provide the reason for paternal estrangement from the family. *Margie* is the more conservative of this latter pair, framing the separation of spheres as a return to equilibrium, a re-establishment of the "way things ought to be". Here the father remains remote from his family (as his posting to Nicaragua emphasizes) and patriarchal order is reasserted by the inter-generational reproduction of the power dynamics of traditional, patriarchally-structured family life: the husband substitutes for the father as the source of paternal authority and becomes the father in his own turn. *Blue Skies*, however, offers a more progressive vision, in which the father comes to realise what he has lost by prioritizing his business activities over family life. Johnny's return to the family is not framed in terms of the restoration of paternal authority, but indicates more strongly the acceptance of an active nurturing role in relation to his daughter and a capacity to appreciate the pleasures of fatherhood, which were key elements of emerging postwar discourses relating to childcare and which signal a movement towards the more domesticated masculinities that would become the focus of discussion about American masculinity during the 1950s.

Momism

Another discourse about parenting rose to prominence in the postwar period and in some ways can be seen as a disturbing counterpart to the warm, sympathetic representation of the relationship between a father and daughter contained in the scene discussed immediately above. This discourse cast mothers—or at least a certain kind of mother—in a distinctly unfavourable light and centred on another allegorical figure: the "mom".

The figure of the mom was not entirely a construction of the wartime and postwar era. Citing the publication of Sidney Howard's play, *The Silver Cord* (first performed in 1927) as an example, Gorer observed that "many books and plays have been written in which she is the villain" (1948: 45). However, the figure of the mom gained a much firmer hold on the American popular imagination following the publication, in 1943, of Phillip Wylie's intensely misogynistic critique of American society; *Generation of Vipers*. The publication of Wylie's diatribe represented such a significant contribution to discourses about momism that it is frequently assumed by later writers, [for example Cohan (1997: 314 n.14) and Fischer (1993: 80), who use this figure to frame analyses of films in terms of a "postwar crisis of masculinity"], and even by contemporaries of Wylie, such as Strecker (1946), to mark the origin of these discourses. While this is not strictly accurate, Wylie's book was certainly of such significance that its publication represents at least the moment at which these concerns were brought to the fore in the general public consciousness.

Notwithstanding reservations about the origins of the figure of the mom, there are compelling reasons for using this figure as a focal point for interpreting postwar representations of gender and the family. Although Wylie's book may not have been the first expression of concern about momism—and so it would be misleading to assume a generative relationship between the war and this discourse—its treatment as such by later scholars and its evident importance to Wylie's contemporaries attest to the exceptional significance of this volume. This might not justify attaching so much importance to the figure of the mom if Wylie's book had been an isolated example. However, the period from the end of the war until at least the mid 1970s (see Sebald 1976 for a later example) saw an enormous volume of writing about momism. Although there remains, then, a doubt about whether momism troubled American society as much before as after the Second World War, this does not alter the fact that there demonstrably was significant concern about momism in the period following the end of the war. This in itself renders the figure of the mom deserving of critical attention in relation to popular postwar films, notwithstanding the earlier emergence of this figure.[3]

Postwar anxiety about momism resonated with contemporary concerns about the effects of military life: both were thought to represent a risk of infantilizing men. Wylie was certain that:

> war is a demonstration of infantilism in man. It is a reduction of all his efforts, schemes, ideals, aims, hopes, faiths, purposes, plots and possessions to the nursery level ...
>
> There is no other way to look at war than as the final proof of the infantilism of man—the revelation of ... his failure to achieve adulthood.
>
> (1943: 256)

Edward A. Strecker took this argument even further in his book, *Their Mother's Sons: The Psychiatrist Examines an American Problem*. As well as mothers who exhibited "momish" characteristics, Strecker identified the existence of other relationships characterized by the same dynamics as that between a mom and son. Styling these as "mom surrogates", Strecker argued that:

The army is so structured that it could become a mom surrogate.
Necessarily there must be regimentation and discipline. Soldiers
must be told what to do and what not to do, and there is not the
time or place for explanatory detail.

    ... In a good army, there is a close dependence-relationship
between soldiers and officers. The right kind of officer feels
responsible for his men and in some sense regards them
affectionately and protectingly as his children ... The stage
would seem to be set for "child-soldier" "mom-officer"
relationships, dangerously promoting immaturity.

(1946: 117-118)

In the period immediately after the war there was, then, a clear
concern about the maturity of men, which can be identified in
discussions of both momism and the effects of military life and which,
in the latter case deployed the mom as a metaphor for the infantilizing
effect of military life. The mom also became a key representational
figure in the movies of the postwar period.

    Readily recognizable representations of momism feature in two of
the most popular films released in the aftermath of the war: *Notorious*
and *The Green Years*. The character of Madame Sebastian (Leopoldine
Konstantin) in *Notorious* provides the most sustained study of momism
in any of the popular films examined for this book. Konstantin's
performance of this character perfectly captures some of the
distinctive characteristics of the mom; a combination of over-
solicitousness towards her own son, Alex—a desire to bind him to her
in a relationship of dependency—and extreme hostility toward
anyone perceived as presenting a threat to him or the continuance of
this relationship, particularly women who interest him romantically.
Madame Sebastian's momish proclivities are apparent from her first
appearance in the film, manifested in an aura of palpable menace
which Konstantin's remarkable performance creates.

    Madame Sebastian is introduced in the first scene in which Alicia
visits Alex at his home. Alicia arrives at the house and, as she waits for
Alex, Madame Sebastian appears at the top of an imposing staircase
at the rear of the shot and begins to descend, filmed in a long shot
from approximately Alicia's position. The distance from the top of the
stairs to the position where Alicia waits necessarily makes this a long

take and the duration of the take increases the feeling of tension in the scene. Shots showing Madame Sebastian's descent of the stairs and her passage across the hallway towards Alicia are interposed with shots of Alicia's nervous reaction to create a feeling of intense anxiety about the meeting of the two women. In the final seconds of the take, Madame Sebastian moves through a dark shadow before finally emerging into the light to greet Alicia. During the women's conversation, Konstantin's facial expressions—her unsmiling mouth; the cold, unflinching glare of her eyes—undermine her polite, solicitous words, investing the scene with an almost unbearable tension between the formal, superficial level of the women's relationship and the deeper reality of Madame Sebastian's feelings towards a woman she perceives as a threat to her own relationship with her son. Their conversation does not last long before this hidden level begins to rupture the conventions of polite conversation, when Madame Sebastian begins to question Alicia about the reasons why her father had not called her to give evidence at his trial. This eruption of hostility is only contained by the arrival of Alex, which deflects his mother from her interrogation of Alicia.

Two later scenes make Madame Sebastian's dislike of Alicia and her desire for control over Alex explicit. In the first, Alex and his mother sit together in a box at the races waiting for Alicia to return. When Madame Sebastian observes that "Miss Hubermann has been gone a long time", Alex asks whether his mother could try to "be a little more cordial to her". His suggestion that Madame Sebastian could at least attempt to smile at Alicia is met with her rebuke, "wouldn't it be too much if we both grinned at her like idiots". In the second scene, Alex and Madame Sebastian argue about his plan to marry Alicia. Madame Sebastian suggests that Alicia might have come to Rio intending to "capture the rich Alex Sebastian for a husband". When Alex dismisses this possibility, Madame Sebastian's curt response, "we will discuss it more fully tonight", reveals the extent of her expectation to control her son. Alex's response, rejecting this suggestion, reveals the momish nature of their relationship:

all these carping questions are just expression of your own jealousy, just as you've always been jealous of any woman I've ever shown any interest in.

Figure 3.3 "Mom" as a masculinized type of womanhood. Madame
Sebastian (Leopoldine Konstantin) in *Notorious* (1946).

Alex rebels against his mother's controlling, momish impulses by
marrying Alicia, but he turns to his mother once again when he
discovers that his wife is an American agent. This scene provides a
striking display of the type of domineering womanhood that was the
focus of anxieties about momism. As Alex tells his mother that there is
a problem in his relationship with Alicia, Madame Sebastian allows
herself a self-satisfied smile, assuming that her son's disenchantment
with his new wife results from the latter's infidelity with Devlin. She
dismisses Alex's thoughts of Alicia's "clinging kisses" as "foul
memories" and, even as she comes to understand the real nature of
the danger faced by her son, takes the opportunity to consolidate her
power over him by belittling him: "you're protected by the enormity
of your stupidity". Finally she takes control over her son's actions,
planning how the two of them will kill Alicia without arousing the
suspicions of their fellow conspirators. In *Generation of Vipers*, Wylie
presented an image of the mom as a masculinized type of
womanhood; "mom, however, is a great little guy. Pulling pants on

her by these words, let us look at mom" (1943: 189). Konstantin's performance in this scene employs a number of purposefully unfeminine mannerisms, which conform to the reversal of gendered norms suggested by Wylie. When told of Alex's suspicions, Madame Sebastian reaches for a cigarette box beside her bed, tosses it deliberately onto the bed and takes out and lights a cigarette. The slow pace and deliberateness of her actions magnify their significance and—taken together with the disregard for appearances, evident in Madame Sebastian's demeanour in throwing the box onto the bed and in the very masculine image of her sitting in bed with a cigarette dangling from her mouth—contribute to a sense of the peeling away of Madame Sebastian's facade of genteel motherliness and the revelation of her true, masculinized, momish character (see fig. 3.3). Near the end of this scene, the postures of mother and son and their relative positions within the frame reveal the relationship of dominance and subservience between them. Still smoking her cigarette, Madame Sebastian stands alongside Alex, who sits hunched on the end of her bed with his head in his hands, while she explains her plan to poison Alicia.

The same power relationship is evident in the later scene in which Alicia realizes that she is being poisoned. Dr. Anderson mistakenly picks up Alicia's poisoned coffee cup, causing Alex and his mother to react with alarm. There is then a cut from a middle distance shot of mother and son to a close up of the coffee cup, followed by another cut to a close up of Alicia's face as she comes to realize what has been happening. Alicia looks across the room at each of her poisoners in turn. As she does so there is an edit to a shot in which the camera rapidly zooms into a close-up of Madame Sebastian's face, defiantly returning Alicia's look with her own chilling, unflinching glare. The shot returns to a close-up of Alicia's face followed by a further cut to a shot which zooms into a close up of Alex's face, his eyes averted toward the newspaper he is reading (see shot sequence in fig. 3.4).

The triumphal defiance evident in Madame Sebastian's withering glower, returning Alicia's own look, juxtaposed with the studied avoidance of Alex's averted gaze signals the power dynamics in the relationship between mother and son. Madame Sebastian is in control. She is poisoning Alicia while Alex merely obeys her murderous instruction. These shots, together with that which follows, in which Alex and Madame Sebastian are cast into black silhouettes, distorted by Alicia's increasingly hallucinatory perception (see fig. 3.2), provide a disturbing vision of demonic momism and its potentially awful consequences.

Figure 3.4 Shot sequence from *Notorious* (1946)

The image of the mom provided by *The Green Years* is both less central to the film's plot and less pointedly sinister than that offered by *Notorious*, but it nevertheless captures very clearly some of the defining features of the phenomenon identified by Wylie. Arguing that "momworship has got completely out of hand" (1943: 185), Wylie suggests that "our land, subjectively mapped, would have more silver cords and apron strings crisscrossing it than railroads and telephone wires" (185). The image of "silver cords" and "apron strings", used to bind children to their moms, is a recurring one in the discourse about momism. Strecker (1946) devotes an entire chapter to "mom and her silver cord" in which he employs umbilical imagery to describe the relationship between a mom and her children:

> A mom does not untie the emotional apron string—the Silver Cord—which binds her children to her ... [moms] have one thing in common—the emotional satisfaction, almost repletion, she derives from keeping her children paddling about in a kind of psychological amniotic fluid rather than letting them swim away with the bold and decisive strokes of maturity from the emotional womb.
>
> (30-31)

Gorer identified this "picture of the clinging mother" and a "fear of such vampire-like possession" as "one of the components in the very strong ambivalence American men feel towards women" (1948: 45-46). The ambivalence toward women, typified by Wylie and Strecker, was probably a factor in the development of the figure of the femme fatale in film noir as well as the construction of domineering, controlling female roles—exemplified later in the 1940s and in the 1950s by characters such as Cody Jarrett's (James Cagney) mother in *White Heat* (Walsh, 1949 USA) and Jim Stark's (James Dean) mother in *Rebel Without a Cause* (Ray, 1955 USA). Similar concerns and a like mode of construction of mature womanhood are also apparent in the character of Grandma Leckie (Gladys Cooper) in *The Green Years*.

The Green Years tells the story of a young boy, Robert Shannon, who is sent from Ireland to live in Scotland with his maternal grandparents, following the death of his parents. Also living in the home are Robert's grandmother's father, Alexander Gow (Charles Coburn) and Grandma Leckie, his grandfather's mother. Early in the film the household appears to be dominated by Robert's grandfather, Papa Leckie (Hume Cronyn), a petty official who compensates for the inconsequence of his occupation by asserting his authority in the home. Papa Leckie resents the presence of his wife's father in the house and is less than happy about Robert's arrival on the scene. For the first few days Robert sleeps in his great grandfather's bed at night and is entrusted to the old man's care during the days. The return of Grandma Leckie to the home after a few days radically changes the dynamics of power within the house, and the arrangements for Robert's care.

Figure 3.5 "And now the material". Grandma Leckie's (Gladys Cooper) petticoat serves as a "silver cord" for the young Robert Shannon (Dean Stockwell) in *The Green Years* (1946).

Grandma Leckie is a domineering woman who is the ultimate source of authority in the family home. She immediately over-rules her son's decision concerning Robert's schooling, insisting that he attend a more expensive institution. Grandma Leckie then assumes control over Robert, over-riding Grandpa Gow's objections, and insisting that the boy sleep in her room and share her bed. Her most overtly momish action takes place when she decides that the only suit possessed by Robert is too shabby for him to wear to school. Grandma Leckie resolves to make him a new suit and, having measured the boy for this garment, she opens her wardrobe and looks through her dresses to find a suitable fabric. Finding nothing appropriate, she then removes the skirt she is wearing and begins to examine her many petticoats, removing one after another until she eventually finds what she considers a suitable material; a green, floral patterned cloth. Robert is horrified at the prospect of wearing a suit made from this material but Grandma Leckie overrules Robert's objections (see fig. 3.5).

It is difficult to imagine a more explicit example of the "apron strings" discussed by Wylie, Strecker and their contemporaries, or the "vampire-like possession" referred to by Gorer than this suit, cut from a quite inappropriate fabric for a young lad and literally enveloping the boy in his great grandmother's petticoat in a way that resonates with Strecker's use of umbilical and amniotic metaphors. Furthermore, this brightly coloured, floral-patterned fabric threatens to feminize Robert in much the same way that Gorer suggested that the influence of American mothers over their children produced men with a feminized conscience:

> The idiosyncratic feature of the American conscience is that it is predominantly feminine. Owing to the major role played by the mother ... far more aspects of the mother than of the father become incorporated ...
>
> This makes the role of the daughter, herself to become a mother, particularly easy and straightforward ... But for the son, the American male, the situation is far more complicated and confusing. He carries around, as it were encapsulated inside him, an ethical, admonitory, censorious mother.
>
> (1948: 39)

Robert eventually rejects Grandma Leckie's over-solicitous and ultimately suffocating care. The green suit fashioned from her petticoat marks Robert as an object of ridicule and a target for bullying when he starts to attend school, providing a visual reminder of his difference from the other boys, not only because of his Irishness and Catholicism, but also because of the extraordinary dominance of his grandmother. A montage sequence showing Robert's early days at school reveals the repeated bullying to which the boy is subject. Desperately unhappy at school, Robert turns to his great-grandfather for help. Grandpa Gow advises that the boy must fight, and beat, the most respected boy in the class in order to stop the bullying, and he instructs Robert in the art of fisticuffs. The fight that follows, in which the two boys fare equally, wins Robert new respect from the other boys and the friendship of his adversary. More importantly, the green floral-patterned suit is destroyed in the skirmish, severing Grandma Leckie's "silver cord" and Robert's former opponent and new best friend supplies him with a more suitable garment. Grandpa Gow completes the severance of Grandma Leckie's "silver cord" by burning the remains of the old suit. Encouraged by his great grandfather, Robert stands up to Grandma Leckie, refusing to attend a prayer meeting with her at her church, insisting on being able to worship in his own faith and returning to the care of his great grandfather. Although this image of domineering womanhood provides only a relatively brief interlude in the film, its inclusion is indicative of the extent to which momism was a source of anxiety in the wider culture and how this concern was reflected in a wider range of films than film scholars have generally considered in the past for their representations of domineering womanhood.[4]

The inclusion of characters and themes referable to discourses concerning momism is less consistent in the popular films than the presence of femmes fatale—that other characteristic expression of postwar anxiety about powerful women—in film noir. Only two of the popular films feature unambiguous representations of mom-like women among their major characters. These are not the only instances, however, and further examples might include characters such as Ma Baxter in *The Yearling*—on the basis of the over-protectiveness that lies behind her stern demeanour towards her son and her efforts to exercise authority over him—and Mrs. Bellop in *Saratoga Trunk*, because of the conformity of her corpulent figure and ability to live a life of luxury on the back of other people's efforts to some of Wylie's characterizations of the mom, and Clarissa Van Steed, in *Saratoga Trunk*, who clearly dominates her son. However, none of these characters is as central to the films in which they feature nor as unequivocally momish as either Grandma Leckie or Madame Sebastian and none attracts anything approaching the degree of disapproval that attaches to these more obviously momish characters. It may be significant that the least ambiguous and most sustained portrayal of the mom occurs in *Notorious*, the only one of the popular films released in 1946 to have been subsequently classified as a film noir. Whether or not this way of classifying the film is accepted, the fact that it has been so classified by other critics, taken together with the presence in the film of this key female character, constructed as a rather frightening, unfeminine figure, suggests that films noirs might have constituted a privileged site within early postwar American culture; a site in which anxious and uncomfortable aspects of postwar discourse, such as those concerning momism and domineering women more generally, could be articulated. As this chapter illustrates, however, this did not completely preclude the presence of similarly constructed characters in a wider range of Hollywood's genres.

The disruptions to family life brought about by America's involvement in the Second World War were a cause of considerable anxieties that came to a head after the end of the war, when American society began the difficult process of adjusting to the lasting changes to social structures and institutions that had been effected by the exigencies of wartime living. While some commentators, such as Spock, seem to have seen this period of readjustment as an opportunity for more progressive visions of family relations to influence the way families were structured and roles shared between parents, others, such as Overton and Lundberg and Farnham, lamented the loss of traditional family roles and values. The range of opinions covered by these varying attitudes to postwar family life also found expression in some of the most popular films released just after the war. The absent father and the mom provided filmmakers with representational figures capable of articulating these attitudes. Both figures were capable of being used in support of a conservative discourse promoting a return to traditional gender and family relations, as seen in the use of the absent father in films such as *Notorious*, *Saratoga Trunk*, *Margie* and in the use of the mom in *Notorious* and *The Green Years*. But these figures could also be used to present a more progressive vision of family and gender relations, as the scene from *Blue Skies* discussed in this chapter and the characters of Ma Baxter in *The Yearling* and Mrs. Bellop in *Saratoga Trunk*—who both arguably exhibit momish characteristics, but are hardly unsympathetic characters for that—illustrate. In the contradictions between these different uses of these figures an impression begins to develop of the complicated and often contradictory attitudes towards gender and the family that emerged in America as the nation moved from war to peace.

Chapter 4

Performing postwar masculinities

The place of the ex-serviceman in postwar society was one of the major issues of the period immediately following the end of the war. As a result of America's involvement in the war, around 31 million men were processed through selective service and around ten million of these men were actually drafted into the military (de Bedts 1973: 319). The prospect of the re-assimilation of such a large number of veterans into civilian society at the war's end was a source of considerable anxiety. Of particular concern was the impact that the return of such a large number of men of working age might have on an economy that had been extremely buoyant in their absence. Other concerns centred on the effects that the combination of training in the efficient use of violence and the brutalizing experiences of military service may have had on the psychological disposition of returning veterans, and consequently on their behaviour on returning to civilian life (see, for example Waller, 1944: 13 and 124; "Crime Wave Coming", *Time* Magazine 3 April 1944: 6; Kupper, 1945: 43; "Does War Brutalize Men?" *Ladies Home Journal*, November 1943: 120-1; Cherne 1944: 69). A further concern was that the all-male milieu inhabited by men in the armed forces might have led to an increase in homosexual conduct among returning veterans.

Related to these anxieties and equal in importance to any of these postwar concerns about returning veterans was a more fundamental question about masculine identity—about what it meant to be a man—that accompanied the movement of men from the relative certainty afforded by the military environment to the less regimented arena of postwar civilian life. Military service provided men with a clear sense of identity, but the corollary of the certainties provided by military life was increased uncertainty about the meaning of masculinity as these ex-servicemen began to move into a postwar civilian world in which the sureties of the military milieu no longer held sway. A strong sense of this uncertainty is captured by an advertisement for the New England Mutual Life Assurance Co., published in *Life* magazine in on 10 July 1944. The caption, "Where do I go from here?" juxtaposed with an image of a young man replacing a military tunic on a coat hanger operates on several levels. Superficially the image registers mundane concerns about the employment and educational opportunities that would be available to veterans on their return to civilian life. At a deeper level, however, there is something about this image that suggests more fundamental uncertainties. The juxtaposition of the image of the male figure hanging up his military uniform with the question posed by the caption endows the act of discarding one type of clothing in favour of another, with a quality more like the shedding of an identity, and the certainties that accompanied it, without any clear sense of the character of the new identity that will replace it. The image in this advertisement reveals, then, a strong sense of masculinity being understood as an inessential identity, constituted through performance and dependent on items such as the military tunic to construct that performance.

The conception of masculinity as a performance of gender provides the focus of this chapter. This understanding of masculinity not as an inflexible, essential identity consequent on biological maleness, but as a construct, a complicated assemblage of exterior signifiers, such as clothing, and acquired behaviours that position the male body not as the source of masculine identity but as the site of its performance has acquired considerable currency in cultural theory in recent years, under the influence of the work of Judith Butler (1990), and this conception of gender as a performance radically challenges more traditional, essentialist conceptions of masculine identity. Although this way of conceptualizing gender is a relatively recent theoretical development, some of the popular films and other material examined for this study reveal that this understanding of masculinity became an element of certain discourses about men in the early postwar period. It is important to be clear that I am not suggesting that journalists, filmmakers and other contemporary commentators on American society after the Second World War pre-empted Butler's insights and began to espouse whole-heartedly a conception of gender as a performative identity. The situation was more complicated than that and where limited recognition was given to the performativity of identities, this was restricted to a context within which the acknowledgement of performativity supported a rhetoric aimed at easing anxieties about whether war veterans would be able to make a successful re-adjustment to civilian life. What we can observe in these discourses of the early postwar period is an opportunistic use of the idea that men's identities may be performatively constituted rather than essential and inflexible. What is remarkable, however, is the fact that such a radically unsettling concept as the performativity of masculinity should be mobilized in this way and particularly in service of a rhetoric directed at offering reassurance to an anxious American public.

So far as the popular films are concerned, discussing performative masculinities solely in relation to discourses about postwar readjustment presents a problem. Film is an inherently performative medium and so the ability to recognize explicitly performative masculinities in movies is not at all surprising. What is more surprising is the use of explicit indices of the performativity of masculinities in some of the quality narrative films released after the war; films of a type that have more usually effaced the performative aspects of characters than genres such as, say, the musical, in which generic conventions have more readily permitted the foregrounding of performance in the construction of character. That one of these quality narrative films, *Best Years of Our Lives*, should be explicitly concerned with veterans' readjustment and the other, *Two Years Before the Mast*, implicitly so, is even more surprising (and more instructive). In addition to these quality narrative films, a larger number of the popular musicals, romances and comedies present images of performative masculinity within a more predictable generic frame. This generic split is followed in the structure of this chapter, with the quality narrative films receiving consideration separately from these other genres. Despite splitting the chapter in this way, my argument is that both sets of films speak to the same concerns of the postwar moment. So far as the quality narrative films are concerned the discourse is explicit, but there is also a distinct resonance between the images of performative masculinities in the other genres and the deployment of the conception of masculinity as a performative identity in contemporary discourses concerning veterans' readjustment.

Soldier to civilian: masculinity and performativity

America's involvement in World War 2 brought the performativity of masculinities to the fore in a rather unexpected way. Although there was a professional army consisting of men who had chosen to enter military service, the majority of men who served in the war were conscripted under the Selective Service Act. When the number of men leaving civilian life to enter the military as professional soldiers had been relatively small, and the movement of men between military and civilian life limited, it had been easy for the masculinities of both civilian and military men to be taken for granted as natural, essential identities. As a result of conscription, the size of the military during the war grew to over ten million men (de Bedts, 1973: 319). This increase in size and the concomitant increase in the movement of men between civilian and military life precipitated the opportunistic deployment of a radically different way of conceiving masculine identity.

Writers such as Filene (1998: 165) have noted the importance of men's occupational or professional roles in defining their identities. The nature of the military milieu—its all-encompassing institutional setting, its removal of men from the ordinary life of the civilian, and its provision for every physical, mental and social need appropriate to the life of a soldier—exaggerates this tendency. In relation to the masculinity of the soldier, the basic military training undertaken by new recruits to the armed forces fulfilled a dual purpose—first the functional requirement of equipping men with the physical fitness and skills in using various weapons and other military technologies necessary for life as a soldier, and second the, equally important, ideological purpose of instilling in men the values and attitudes of the soldier: of effecting a transformation of civilian men into soldiers.[1] The masculinity of the soldier can, therefore, be seen as a highly self-conscious performance of gender.

Waller recognised that the soldier's masculinity was a performative identity but maintained a distinction between this and the "real" identity of the civilian. He argued that war itself is a masquerade in which men are required to adopt different roles and comply with new codes of morality and behaviour (1944: 130), but he retained a sense of civilian society as an underlying reality, fundamentally more authentic than the masquerade of war. Waller saw identity as a social production:

> A human being is the creature and the creation of the society in which he lives ... Change the society and you change the man. The civilian-turned-soldier derives his distinguishing characteristics from the social environment of the army.
>
> (19)

This is an ambiguous formulation, however, and while it leaves open the possibility to see both soldierly and civilian masculinities as performative, Waller's emphasis on the performativity of the former contrasted with his silence about the latter does imply that the identity of the civilian is somehow more authentic. An additional ambiguity in Waller's formulation lies in the fact that, while this account of the performativity of soldierly identity would seem to imply a reasonably easy adjustment to civilian life after discharge from the army—the civilian social environment providing the setting for the reversal of the transformation referred to in the above quotation—Waller apparently regarded the transformation of civilian men into soldiers as, if not exactly a one-way process, then certainly as one which was considerably easier in one direction than the other. Thus while Waller regarded the process of turning civilians into soldiers as little more than a matter of immersion in a military setting and exposure to the culture of the armed forces—"the army has its own culture, and as a soldier becomes immersed in it, it becomes part of him, and he grows away from his civilian personality" (28)—reversing this process was more difficult:

we know how to turn the civilian into a soldier. History has taught us that all too well; tradition has given us marvellously adequate techniques. But we do not know how to turn the soldier into a civilian again. This is the art we must perfect if we are ever to solve the problem of the veteran in our society.

(15)

This apparent intractability of soldierly masculinity is not entirely consistent with the idea that this identity was a performative element in what Waller characterized as the masquerade of war. The rhetoric employed by Waller in his consideration of the problems of veterans' readjustment to civilian life oscillates between contradictory positions, conceptualizing the soldier as, on the one hand, a highly performative masculinity and on the other hand as an identity which, once acquired, was highly resistant to further change, even where this amounted to the restoration of an earlier (and in Waller's conception, more authentic) masculine type.

While Waller's account of the transformations from civilian to soldier and back again presents a rather contradictory image of the performativity of masculinities, the recognition of identity as a performance in certain circumstances is sufficiently marked in Waller's writing to be worthy of comment and does give a clear sense of the existence of a willingness, in the early postwar period, to accept the idea of masculinity as a performance when it suited the immediate rhetorical context.

Waller was not alone in tentatively recognizing soldierly masculinity as a performance of gender. In an article published in *Collier's* magazine, Leo Cherne gave an account of the soldier's identity that also acknowledged the performativity of that identity. Cherne referred to a "veneer of civilization" which military service would cause to be "rubbed off some of the boys and rubbed thin on many others" (1944: 69). Insofar as both writers assert the existence of an essential core identity beneath the performances of different masculinities, Cherne's formulation is consistent with Waller's. The two differ, however, over the precise character of this essential masculine identity. While Waller equates it with the civilian man, Cherne regards civilian identity itself as being a performative veneer laid over an altogether more brutal, essential masculinity that would be released by exposure to the military milieu. Cherne's account is further complicated, however, by his suggestion that "the crust of dissatisfactions that formed while he was in uniform will not peel off when he puts on his Sunday best" (69). Cherne's formulation works against any simple conception of civilian and soldierly masculinities as a dichotomy between essential core identities that are overlaid with the performance of civilized (civilian) masculinity. Instead it suggests an identity consisting of a layering of successive performances leading to the production of particular synchronic performances of masculinity conditioned by the immediate social context, but which always retain traces of earlier performative modes, and are susceptible to being overlaid by further performances.

Kupper also emphasized the importance of exposure to the culture of military life in forming the identity of the soldier. Unlike Waller or Cherne, however, Kupper also recognized the existence of ideological institutions within the civilian world that functioned in a similar way to the military culture in socializing the individual to particular modes of identity:

> In the returning veteran we have an ego which has been remolded and restrained by military experiences and consequently weakened for civilian life ... that part of every individual which *family, society, church and authority of every kind* have helped form is in need of reconstruction.
>
> (1945: 165-166, my emphasis)

Kupper recognized, then, the possibility of restoring ex-servicemen to their civilian identities and acknowledged the role to be played in this process by the ideological structures of civilian culture, calling for "economic, educational and psychological" resources to be mobilized to assist "the rebuilding of the ego of every veteran" (166).

There is little consistency between these three writers over precisely which dimensions of men's identities they considered essential and which performative. The important point about these writings, however, is that all three writers were prepared to accept that masculinities are in some respect performative, and also to acknowledge the central role of the immediate cultural and social setting in producing particular performances of masculinity. This way of conceptualizing masculinity recognizes a fluidity of identity which the essentialist view does not, and thus allows for the changes in the character of masculinity that would be a vital element of the military man's readjustment to civilian life after the war.

Any performance of identity must have distinctive ways of constructing and signifying itself. These might include characteristic styles of dress, gestures, speech and mannerisms that provide a way of both constituting the performance and of signifying it to the rest of the world. In his formulation of the concept of identity as an act of self-presentation, Erving Goffman (1969) describes such devices as "sign equipment". In some of the publications of the late-war and postwar period, it is possible to detect an emphasis on the use of distinctive styles of dress as sign equipment that signified particular performances of masculinity. An article by Coleman R. Griffith, published in the *Journal of Home Economics* in 1944 recognized the importance of clothing and weapons as constituent elements of a soldierly masculinity, but predicted that the readjustment of veterans to civilian life could be as simple as merely discarding this military "sign equipment":

> Multiplied thousands of veterans will throw away their lonely nights, their fire-swept days, their wounds, hurts, and aching hearts, and their brutal thoughts as speedily as they throw away the weapons and clothes of war.
>
> (1944: 385)

Similar emphasis on the importance of military uniform in defining a particular kind of masculine identity can be seen in an article, "When Twelve Million Come Home", concerning the readjustment of First World War veterans to civilian life, published in *The New Republic* in 1944: "once they got out of their uniforms, they seemed only too glad to merge again with the civilian population and take up once more where they left off" (707-8). This emphasis on the importance of military uniform in constructing soldierly masculinity also recalls the image of the ex-soldier replacing his military tunic on a coat hanger referred to earlier in this chapter. Here again the status of the military uniform as "sign equipment" is foregrounded and the uncertainty expressed in the caption, "where do I go from here", captures a clear sense of a loss of identity resulting from the move from military to civilian life. All of these accounts convey an impression of masculinity as a performance of identity and, despite the contradictions between the different accounts there is a real sense of the debate about veterans' readjustment being informed by a conception of masculinity as a performance of identity.

The performativity of masculinities, either explicitly in relation to veterans' readjustment to civilian life or in relation to a clearly analogous situation, is also foregrounded in two of the popular films of 1946, *Best Years of Our Lives* and *Two Years Before the Mast*. In *Best Years of Our Lives* the military uniform is an element that delineates the boundaries between the armed forces and civilian life. When Al Stephenson arrives home, he is greeted by his wife, Millie, who embraces him in the hallway of their apartment, then removes his cap while saying, "let me look at you". The juxtaposition of the act of removing part of Al's military uniform with these words gives a strong sense that the Al who Millie knows, the "real" Al, exists somewhere beneath the performance of "Sergeant Al Stephenson" that is visually signified by the uniform. Millie can only see the "real" Al once she has stripped away some of the sign equipment associated with the performance of Al's soldierly masculinity. Even more significant in this respect is Millie's later removal of Al's "dog tags", the part of the uniform that most particularly specifies Al's soldierly identity—name, rank and number—while she is dressing him in his pyjamas later that night.

A clear sense of the shift between different performances of masculinity associated with the move from military to civilian life is provided by the later scene which shows Al waking up after his first night at home. On awakening, Al looks across from the bed to his old uniform, which is lying on a chair in the room. Al sits up in bed for a while, seemingly confused by his presence in his own (civilian) bedroom. Still worse for wear after his excessive drinking the night before, Al appears disoriented by his presence in this civilian setting, as if he cannot reconcile the contradiction created by the presence of his soldierly self within the domestic setting of his earlier, civilian life. Rising from the bed, Al picks up his army boots and throws them out of the window, signalling the start of a process of disinvestment in the soldierly masculinity that his uniform represents. Next, Al picks up a photograph of himself taken before the war and stands in front of the dressing table mirror comparing this image of himself with his reflection in the mirror, attempting to recognize in the picture of the immaculately groomed pre-war civilian who appears in the photograph, the bleary-eyed ex-serviceman whose reflection appears in the mirror, pulling at his face and hair in an attempt to recreate the image of his civilian self in the photograph (fig 4.1). Struck by the differences between the two images that gaze back at him, Al replaces the photograph and moves into the bathroom to take a shower and to shave, in an attempt to restore his appearance to something more closely approximating that in the photograph. After his shower, Al stands in front of his wardrobe examining his civilian clothes; the sign equipment which will play a central role in the reconstruction of his civilian self.

Figure 4.1 Sergeant Al Stephenson (Fredric March) struggles to recognize his civilian self in *Best Years of Our Lives* (1946)

Later, over breakfast, Al remarks to Millie that his trousers no longer fit him because he has lost so much weight in the army. In the context of a discourse that maintains a strong link between clothing and different modes of masculine identity, this comment signifies more than the simple fact that Al's waistline has reduced. It also hints at the veteran's difficulties in readjusting to civilian life. In a sense, it is not only Al's clothing that no longer fits, but his whole civilian identity that no longer "fits" him properly. However, the film promotes a strong feeling that successful re-adjustment to civilian life will simply depend on the ex-serviceman being given sufficient time to adjust. Millie's response to Al's suggestion that he might have to have his clothes adjusted registers this perfectly: "couple of weeks of heavy eating and those pants will fit perfectly".

Best Years of Our Lives contrasts Al and Fred's experiences of readjustment to civilian life. Millie anticipates the return of Al's civilian identity, given sufficient time, and initiates the process of effacing Al's soldierly masculinity by her actions in removing his cap and "dog tags" in the scenes described above. Fred's wife, Marie, on the other hand actively impedes Fred's rehabilitation by insisting on his retention of the sign equipment associated with his soldierly masculinity long after his return home. Fred and Marie met during his military training and she has never known Fred as anything other than an Air Force Captain. For Marie this performative identity defines Fred's true masculinity. A comment she makes after she has convinced Fred to once again wear the uniform he had stored in his closet confirms this: "oh, now you look wonderful. You look like yourself". Fred's retention of elements of military dress throughout the film becomes an index of the difficulties he experiences in readjusting to civilian life. In the scene discussed in chapter 2, in which Fred and Al meet to discuss the former's relationship with Peggy, the only element of the scene that disrupts its symmetry is the difference between the men's clothing. While Al wears a light-coloured business suit, Fred wears a leather jacket (see fig. 2.1). This difference in clothing is vital to the creation of the sense of equality between Fred and Al that I have suggested the scene promotes: the leather jacket is Fred's old Air Force flying jacket and so is associated with the military milieu in which Fred's status more closely approximated that which Al enjoys in civilian life. In this way, by creating a sense of equivalence between the two men, but making this equivalence contingent on Fred's retention of his soldierly masculinity, the film illustrates Fred's difficulties in shedding his military identity and adjusting to civilian life, since it makes this shift dependent upon his acceptance of a sharp reduction in status. The difficulty of accepting this loss of status is signalled by Marie's declining attraction to Fred as he becomes increasingly reintegrated into civilian life, but also in Fred's habit of continuing to wear items associated with his military past long after he has been forced to accept the reality of his civilian present.

The idea of masculinity as a performance of gender enacted through the deployment of different aggregations of sign equipment is strongly marked in *Best Years of Our Lives*, and the film's use of this conception of performative masculinity is consonant with contemporary discourses concerning veterans' re-adjustment to civilian life. In a similar manner, *Two Years Before the Mast* uses changes in styles of dress (different sign equipment) to foreground the contrasts between alternative performances of masculinity.

In an early scene, in which Charles becomes involved in a fight with Amazeen (William Bendix), first mate of the *Pilgrim*, it is Charles's clothing that marks him as different from Amazeen and the other patrons of the dockside bar in which the action occurs. Amazeen enters the bar looking for a crew for the *Pilgrim*. Spotting Charles and his friends, Amazeen passes comment on their dandified appearance to his companion: "look what we've found, lace and everything. Not for us". Overheard by Charles, this comment leads to an argument between the two men in which the contrast between the supposed effeminacy of Charles and the brute masculinity of Amazeen is foregrounded and is articulated through their different modes of dress. The dandy's outfit, which Charles wears, emphasizes the differences between the men and provides a pretext for Amazeen to characterize Charles and his friends as "daisies". After the ensuing fight, Charles awakes aboard the Pilgrim, having been shanghaied by Amazeen. The Captain refuses Charles's demand that the ship should return to port and Charles is given clothing more suitable for his new life as a sailor. This clothing, particularly the tight-fitting checked shirt worn with the sleeves rolled high over the biceps to reveal the muscularity of Alan Ladd's arms and unbuttoned in order to display his expansive chest, presents a stark visual contrast with the rather effeminate outfit which it replaces, foregrounding Ladd's conventionally masculine attributes, previously concealed under the "lace doilies" of his dandy's suit. This change of clothing coincides with the start of the process of transforming Charles's character from an idle, spendthrift dandy into a sailor. This transformation is symbolically completed when the ship sails around Cape Horn, a well-known rite of passage for novice sailors, the significance of which, in relation to the transformation of Charles's masculinity, is registered in the cabin boy's comment, "why a man's not a sailor until he's been around the Horn".

In both *Best Years of Our Lives* and *Two Years Before the Mast*, changes in clothing are symbolically linked to shifts in masculine identity. In both films the circumstances surrounding these shifts involve movement between a bounded, disciplined, all-male setting (the armed forces, the merchant navy) and ordinary civilian society. While only *Best Years of Our Lives* explicitly constructs this bounded setting as the military services, the milieu aboard the ship in *Two Years Before the Mast* is clearly analogous. There is a resonance, then, between the situations represented in these two films and the experiences of numerous American men at the end of the Second World War. The films deploy representations of performative masculinities as part of a re-adjustment narrative that is structured in a similar way to the rhetorical strategies employed in a wider range of discourses concerned with the problems of veterans' postwar readjustment. All of these different cultural forms use the idea of masculinity as a performance as a way of showing that men can change and therefore will be able to readjust to civilian life. While only these two films employ images of performative masculinities in the context of narratives that are overtly concerned with changes in masculinity resulting from the move from military or naval service to civilian life, a larger number of the remaining popular films also present masculinities as performative identities.

Staging masculinities: performativity and genre

The Jolson Story provides the most striking depiction of performative masculinity. It is also one of the most complicated films to discuss in relation to the performance of masculinity, since the film presents an elaborate web of performances of identity operating at different diegetic and extra-diegetic levels. Any consideration of performativity in *The Jolson Story* must engage with this issue not only in relation to the diegetic construction of character, but also in connection with the extraordinary performance of Larry Parks, playing the lead role, and the unusually overt performativity of the "real" Al Jolson. Taking all of these different levels of performance into account, the film provides one of the clearest cinematic representations of identity conceived as a multi-layered conglomeration of performances.

The construction of Jolson's character in the film relies heavily on the use of a distinctive repertoire of sign equipment: costume, make-up and gesture. Some of Jolson's characteristic gestures are evident in the early stage performances of the young Asa Yoelson (before he changes his name), but these performative devices become a more central part of Jolson's stage act as his career progresses and he refines the trademark Jolson performance. This performance is perfected when these gestures and vocal mannerisms are combined with the most readily recognizable elements of Jolson's mature stage persona; the use of blackface makeup and white gloves.[2] All of these elements are crucial to the construction of the well-known and highly performative persona of "Al Jolson". Even the adoption of this name is a vital part of the performance, providing Jolson with a more American image and effacing the Jewishness of his background.

The extraordinary performativity of this stage persona marks "Al Jolson" as an identity that is quite distinct from that of Asa Yoelson. This sense of a separation of "Al Jolson" from Asa Yoelson is intensified by the fact that the sign equipment used in Asa's staging of a performance of "Al Jolson" also allows other characters in the film to enact performances of "Al". This is demonstrated in a scene in the middle of the film in which Julie (Evelyn Keyes) performs a convincing impersonation of Al at a party after one of his shows, mimicking perfectly his vocal inflections and bodily movements to create an unmistakable performance of "Al Jolson". The same performative devices are also central to Larry Parks's onscreen re-creation of Jolson's character. Parks's performance goes beyond mimicry to achieve a verisimilitude that, as Babbington and Evans observe, approaches perfection (1985: 125). The degree of perfection achieved by Parks draws attention to the performative dimensions of the "real" Jolson's character: Parks's performance never seems like mere impersonation of a well-known individual, but is more akin to a highly proficient performance of an established theatrical role. In this respect the performativity of the character Al Jolson resembles that of characters in theatrical traditions such as the Commedia dell' Arte, in which the actors performed highly stylized roles which they retained for the whole of their professional lives and which, to some degree, became inseparable from their "real" personalities.

This sense that "Al Jolson" existed only as a performative identity is reinforced by a remark made by Evelyn Keyes to Jolson's biographer: "it's true, he was always performing ... if you were sitting alone with him in a room he was giving you a performance" (quoted in Freedland 1995: 250). There is some evidence that the unusual explicitness of the performativity of Jolson's persona was publicly acknowledged around the time of the release of *The Jolson Story*. Michael Freedland's biography of Jolson contains a photograph of Larry Parks and Al Jolson together, bearing the caption, "the two Jolsons: Al 'Larry Parks' Jolson and Al 'Asa Yoelson' Jolson". Although the juxtaposition of the photograph and this particular caption is a later imposition, Freedland does note that contemporary columnists did use the phrase, "the two Jolsons" to describe the pair (239).

The obviousness of the means by which Jolson's character is constructed, and his unavoidable association with the theatrical milieu might suggest that this character should be regarded as a special case; one that originates in, and never transcends a milieu explicitly built on performance, and separated from everyday life. Throughout the film, however, Jolson's character transgresses the boundaries of the privileged performative space offered by the theatre's stage and, in so doing, foregrounds the performances involved in both his own offstage self and the identities of other characters in the film. Early in the film, the young Asa Yoelson, sits anonymously in the audience, dressed and behaving like any other member of the audience until cued to begin singing, which he does, again, from within the space of the audience. This breaching of the conventional boundary between the performative space of the stage and the ostensibly non-performative space of the audience continues throughout the film. Later, after Al has become famous, he insists on having a runway constructed from the stage to the rear of the auditorium. This allows him to walk through the audience's space while he performs his act and, on occasion, he engages in particularly intimate performances, sitting down on the runway and singing apparently to a single member of the audience, as when he sings one song to Julie, "just for you, just for you". Jolson also transforms the audience into performers for his own spectatorship by insisting that the house lights be turned up so that he can see their faces while he performs his act. This radical reversal of the conventional relations of looking involved in a theatrical performance once again disrupts normative conceptions of performance in the theatre, transforming the audience into performers in their role as audience. While the artist on stage continues to enact the traditional role of performer for the audiences' spectatorship, the latter also become performers for the artist's spectatorship.

As well as breaching the conventional spatial divide between performers and spectators—between performance and "reality"—Al also transgresses temporal boundaries. When Al is given his first solo slot in a Broadway show, the stage manager attempts to cut his act because the show is running over time. Al only gets to perform by forcing his way on stage and exceeding the end-time for the performance. This motif of Al's performances running beyond their allotted time continues throughout the film. Al finds it difficult to ever really end a show and his performances extend far past their supposed finishing times. As he remarks at the start of one show, "tonight folks I'm only going to sing 2,000 songs, one to a customer". Even when his stage performances are finally finished, Al hosts private after-show parties at which he continues to perform his songs to a private audience of invited show-business friends into the early hours of the morning.

This blurring of the conventional spatio-temporal boundaries of performance exposes the indivisibility of Al's performative self from his "real" self. This sense is reinforced by a gesture, which Al makes on several occasions in the film, most notably near the start of the film when Asa/Al is first discovered, but also later on when he sings at his parents anniversary. Al is singing on each of these occasions and, at the end of the song, appears to awaken from a trance-like state. This gesture creates a feeling that Al has been unaware that he has been performing; that the performance is a spontaneous expression of his true self, a self that exists only in performance. The feeling that Al's true self and the performance of his public persona cannot be separated becomes particularly marked toward the end of the film. By this point in the film, Al has withdrawn from public performance for several years because his irresistible compulsion to perform threatened to destroy his relationship with Julie. Fearful that this compulsion might prove too strong, he has refrained from any kind of musical activity, even singing around the house, and turned his back on the theatre, refusing to even look at outlines for future productions and becoming bad-tempered when pressed to do so. Al's parents' anniversary provides the occasion on which Al relaxes both of these disciplines, finally agreeing to look at the manuscript for Tom Barron's new show and, later, singing a duet with his father. When the party moves on to a night-club, Al is quickly recognized and he is cajoled into performing, reluctantly at first, but with increasing enthusiasm until, at the film's end, he is once again in the full swing of his act; "Al Jolson" once again.

If the ending of the film is ambiguous in its presentation of Al's ability to adjust to family life, this results from Al's rigid adherence to a performative mode that directs him toward the public sphere. Al is unable to shift from this public oriented performance to one that would enable his satisfactory integration into domestic life. While this is not consistent with the use of the conception of masculinity as a performance in *Best Years of Our Lives* and *Two Years Before the Mast*, it is possible that *The Jolson Story* addresses the emergent discourse concerning male domestication that would gain considerable momentum in the decade following the end of the war, rather than discourses relating to the resettlement of veterans after the war.

Stars and performance

Some of the complexity surrounding the presentation of masculinity as a performative identity in *The Jolson Story* results from the operations of the Hollywood star system. As a star, the "real" Jolson's identity involved a particularly explicit performance of persona. The fact that another actor performs this star persona in the film reinforces the sense of its performativity. Having someone other than the "real" Al Jolson play Jolson foregrounds the use made of sign equipment—gestures, mannerisms, clothing, voice etc.—in constructing this performance of persona. The sign equipment remains the same whether the persona is performed by another actor or by Jolson/Yoelson himself. This produces a rather unusual reversal of the more conventional operation of the star system, which usually operates to ground the disparate range of characters played by a star in a well-known, coherent and consistent persona embodied by the star himself, thereby allowing a star to play a wide range of characters without disturbing the viewers' belief in a singular, coherent masculinity represented by the embodied star character. The denaturalization of Jolson's star persona in *The Jolson Story* has the opposite effect, revealing that Jolson's star character lacks any empirical coherence apart from its performance. The star character is revealed to be a pure sign, separable from the body of the performer.

The various roles played by Fred Astaire in *Ziegfeld Follies* represent a more conventional use of a star character to ground a diverse range of performances in a coherent single identity. Astaire appears as himself early in the film, wearing the trademark top hat and tails which, as Cohan observes (1993a: 62), became instantly identifiable with the star character, "Fred Astaire". This early appearance establishes Astaire's familiar star persona as an objective exterior reality against which the subsequent performances within the movie are differentiated; set apart as explicit performances. Conversely, the explicitness of these performances is equally important in establishing the "naturalness" of the—no less performative, but less explicitly so—star persona, Fred Astaire.

Ziegfeld Follies has an unusual structure, consisting of a series of discrete segments, each featuring a song, dance or comedy routine performed by one or more stars. While the film lacks a conventional narrative structure, this collection of segments is provided with a minimal narrative coherence by the opening segment, in which the late Florenz Ziegfeld Jr. (William Powell), looking down from heaven, remembers his past theatrical successes and fantasizes about producing one last show. The remainder of the film plays out this fantasy show.

In his first performance in the film, Astaire appears as a "Raffles" character, an upper class thief who tricks his way into a society ball in order to steal from the guests. This sequence is most interesting for the way it reveals the susceptibility of the sign equipment used to stage a performance of identity to recontextualization and, through this, to shifts in meaning. In the role of "Raffles", Astaire wears a top hat and tails similar to those he wore when appearing as himself in the earlier sequence. Here, however, these do not simply signify Fred Astaire (although residual traces remain). The addition of a long cigarette holder and monocle heighten the class connotations of Astaire's costume and make the costume sufficiently different from that associated with Astaire's star character to endow the top hat and tails with meanings quite distinct from the connotations of "Fred Astaireness" carried by these items of clothing. Astaire's star persona ensures, however, that this performance is never simply the playing of a role, but is always inflected with connotations of his star character.

The later *Limehouse Blues* segment involves a more radical use of costume, gesture and make-up to create another character for Astaire. Here Astaire plays the part of a mysterious Chinese man who follows a beautiful Chinese woman (Lucille Bremer) through a mythologized version of London's East End, inhabited by shady underworld characters, immigrants and pearly kings and queens. In this segment of the film Astaire and Bremer wear far Eastern costumes and, when not dancing, Astaire adopts a shuffling gait that reinforces the sense of his character as Chinese[3] and establishes a distance between this role and his star persona in order to create a clear sense that he is playing a part in a production. The most striking aspect of this character's visual construction is the use of make-up to change the shape of Astaire's eyes in order to give them a more oriental appearance. This character represents the most radical departure from Astaire's own star persona in *Ziegfeld Follies* but, despite the remarkable use of make-up and gait, his star character is not completely effaced by the performance: as soon as he begins to dance the awkwardness of his shuffle is lost and replaced with the fluid bodily movements characteristic of Astaire's unmistakeable performance style.

Towards the end of the film Astaire appears as himself once again, in a sequence that also features Gene Kelly. Although Astaire and Kelly are performing as themselves, a number of costume and make-up changes are used to show the ageing of the performers. The obviousness of the devices used to depict the ageing process functions in the same way as those used in constructing the Chinese character discussed above, to naturalize Astaire's star persona, denying its performative dimension by providing a set of performances of other identities in which the elements used in constructing the performance are foregrounded, in contrast to the concealment of the performative devices through which Astaire's star character is created.

While *Best Years of Our Lives* and *Two Years Before the Mast* provide examples of performative masculinities within realist, narrative generic modes, and *The Jolson Story* and *Ziegfeld Follies* demonstrate the presence of a similar emphasis on the performativity of masculinities within the spectacular, less narrative-driven generic mode of the musical. *Road to Utopia*, *Easy to Wed*, and *The Kid From Brooklyn* all feature performative masculinities in musical/comedies, a generic hybrid which combines narrative with spectacular moments derived from its generic heritage in the musical.

In *Road To Utopia*, the two central male characters, Duke (Bing Crosby) and Chester (Bob Hope) are, from the outset, strongly associated with performance and masquerade: they are partners in a vaudeville act, part of which (essentially a "con-trick") involves Duke impersonating an Indian mystic. Although the act—in which Duke wears an exotic gown, a turban and a fake beard—is obviously false to the viewer of the film, it is clearly intended to have diegetic plausibility. It is certainly treated as genuine by the diegetic vaudeville audience watching the performance, and members of that audience freely part with their money when requested to by Chester, believing that Duke genuinely does posses mystical powers. This disjuncture between the capacity of the film's minor characters (the diegetic audience), and that of the film's viewers, to recognize the obvious deceptions performed by the two protagonists is a major source of the film's comedy. In short, its humour results from the film's audience being "in on the joke", and throughout the film a number of devices are used in order to engage the complicity of the viewer in this way. These devices transgress the boundaries of performative space in a similar fashion to the transgressions which occur in *The Jolson Story*, extending the film's performances of identity beyond the stage of the diegetic vaudeville theatre into all areas of the diegesis and beyond, even implicating the film's audience in a staged performance as "audience" by circumscribing the moments when the audience is "let in on the joke" and thereby attempting to prescribe the audience's response (laughter) at those moments. The film's jokes allow the performativity of its characters to become explicit, providing moments at which performativity erupts through the appearance of diegetic realism. One of the film's main uses of explicitly performative masculinities is, however, more tightly woven into the narrative. When Duke and Chester lose all their money aboard a ship bound for Alaska they are unable to pay their fares and are forced to work their passage. While cleaning a cabin they discover a map to an Alaskan gold mine, stolen by the cabin's occupants—two murderous outlaws named Sperry and McGurk—from the late father of Sal Van Hoyden (Dorothy Lamour). When they are discovered poring over the map by the outlaws, Duke and Chester manage to overcome Sperry and

McGurk and adopt their identities, donning false beards and the renegades' clothes in order to get off the ship. Once ashore they find that their adopted personas inspire fear and awe among the town's inhabitants, as well as attracting numerous young women. Enjoying these benefits of their adopted identities, they maintain the masquerade for much of the remainder of the movie. Like the earlier performance as an eastern mystic in their vaudeville act, Duke and Chester's impersonation of Sperry and McGurk relies on an obviously unrealistic use of sign equipment, especially the false beards and moustaches sported by the characters (fig. 4.2). However, while the absurdity of this masquerade may be a source of humour for the film's audience, it is accepted unquestioningly by the film's other characters, and these performances of different identities are seamlessly incorporated into the film's narrative, with Duke and Chester able to switch from their "real" diegetic identities to their impersonation of Sperry and McGurk as circumstances require. The film presents, then, images of performative masculinities that are not restricted to a privileged performative arena, such as the vaudeville stage, but which work their way into all areas of the diegetic world.

The explicit un-realism of these performances makes the complicity of the film's viewers a precondition of its humour, and a number of other explicit devices operate to secure and maintain this complicity. The first of these is the use of a narrator (Robert Benchley) who appears onscreen from time to time in order to explain the cinematic techniques employed in the film. Additionally, the narrative is halted periodically in order to allow Hope to address the audience directly, passing comment on diegetic events. These frequent interjections, supplemented by further anti-realist visual gags within the movie, such as a talking fish, a talking bear, an actor—supposedly from a different movie—who walks across the set while "taking a short cut" to another sound stage, and a ring of stars that appears around a mountain in one scene to form the Paramount Pictures logo (accompanied by Hope's comment, "may be a mountain to you but it's bread and butter to me") all serve to foreground the unreality of the film's narrative and its status as a production of the movie industry.

Unlike the other films discussed earlier in this chapter, *Road to Utopia* presents the performances of its stars as deliberate deceptions. Admittedly the "real" diegetic identities of the protagonists are not portrayed in this way, but given the fact that the film was the fourth in a series in which Crosby and Hope played the same parts, the characters of Duke and Chester were well established and were so close to the actors' star characters as to be almost indivisible from them: although given different names in the films, Crosby and Hope are essentially playing themselves. This proximity of the films' characters to the stars' public personas endows the characters of Duke and Chester with an authenticity against which their masquerades as Professor Zambini (the Eastern mystic) and Sperry and McGurk are marked as especially artificial. Similar patterns of blatantly false performances of identity set in contrast to a more authentic character that is equivalent (or nearly so) to a star's public persona typify the construction of central characters in *Easy to Wed* and *The Kid from Brooklyn*.

Figure 4.2 Bing Crosby and Bob Hope as Duke Johnson and Chester Hooton as Sperry and McGurk. Layered performances of identity in *Road to Utopia* (1946)

Like *Road to Utopia*, *Easy to Wed* foregrounds its use of sign equipment in constructing the character of Bill Chandler (Van

Johnson). In so doing, the film flouts realist conventions and provides some rather incoherent narrative moments. These moments of narrative incoherence and the obviousness of the means through which Bill's character is constructed all contribute to the foregrounding of the performativity of his identity. Bill Chandler presents a particularly chameleon-like identity. An ex-vaudeville performer turned newspaperman, his function at the newspaper seems to have been to involve well-known women in contrived sex scandals which the paper can report. Achieving these ends necessitates his performance of a series of elaborately staged masquerades.

At the start of the film Bill is brought back to work for a paper from which he had previously been fired in order to help it defeat a large lawsuit brought against the newspaper by Connie Allenbury (Esther Williams), a millionaire's daughter, arising from the paper's erroneous reporting of her romantic involvement with a married man. Bill's job is to charm Connie into having an affair with him so that the liaison can be "discovered" by one of the newspaper's photographers and Connie can be coerced into dropping her lawsuit in order to avoid the scandal that would follow from the newspaper's publicizing of her involvement with a married man. This scheme involves masquerade at every level. Bill is not married when the plan is conceived (although he is soon tricked into a marriage which, while legally valid, is every bit as fake, in terms of the film's ideology of romantic love, as every other aspect of Bill's character), and realization of the plan requires Bill to adopt an identity that is false in every other respect.

At certain moments in the film the performativity of Bill's identity is foregrounded. Some of these instances, such as his wearing of a duck hunter's outfit and carrying the lures and guns of a hunter, are given a narrative motivation while others, such as the Mexican outfit Bill inexplicably wears in one scene while horse riding, have a motivation that is considerably underdetermined by the narrative. This latter instance—not entirely unmotivated (the horse ride does take place in Mexico) but lacking sufficient motivation to be plausibly realist—is highly effective in drawing attention to the use of particular sign equipment to construct Bill's character. A charity gala hosted by Connie's father provides another clear instance of this by allowing for an extended sequence in which the movement of the narrative is temporarily suspended in favour of the pure spectacle of a performance of music, song and dance in which Bill plays a major role, singing a song with Connie and Ethel Smith (playing herself), and dancing an extended routine with Connie.

Beneath the performative identity constructed by the scantly motivated adoption of different costumes, Bill's character is grounded by the star persona of Van Johnson. Given Johnson's status as a leading Hollywood heartthrob at the time of the film's release—an almost contemporary article in *Life* magazine noted that he was, "according to the best available statistics, the most adored male in the U. S. today" (Butterfield 1945: 115)—there is a clear fit between star persona and the character Johnson plays in the movie: both apparently irresistible to women. Despite the overtly performative diversions provided by the elaborate costumes worn by Bill from time to time, *Easy to Wed* ultimately assures the viewer that this performativity is founded on the more solid and coherent masculinity of Johnson's star character. The contrast between the understated clothing worn by Bill in his "real" character and the elaborate costumes worn at moments of heightened performativity provides a clear sense of this, and this feeling is further reinforced by the equivalence which the film creates between the character, Bill, and the star persona of Van Johnson.

Similarly, in *The Kid from Brooklyn*, Danny Kaye's star persona provides the basis for his character, Burleigh Sullivan. Burleigh, a clumsy incompetent man employed as a milkman, is mistakenly assumed to have a natural talent for boxing after he accidentally knocks out a champion boxer. Under the influence of a promoter he is put into training for a championship bout, exchanging the sign equipment that indicates his occupation as a milkman for that which signifies the pugilist. Much of the film's humour results from the incongruity between Kaye's typecast performance as the shy milkman and his attempts to create a convincing performance as a bloodthirsty boxer. Although successful in performing this latter role, in that he does unexpectedly well in the boxing ring, his success is achieved as a result of a series of accidents rather than his skill in enacting a different performance of masculinity. Like *Road to Utopia* and *Easy to Wed*, *The Kid From Brooklyn* provides an image of masculinity that, although performative in some respects, is built on the foundation of a coherent and non-performative masculine self. In all three of these films, the well known personas of the films' stars function to authenticate a particular version of their character's masculinities and so to assert an essential masculinity which contrasts with the explicitly performative identities adopted at various times by those characters.

All of the films discussed in this chapter negotiate a contradiction between two incompatible conceptions of masculinity; either a coherent, essential condition of selfhood or a fluid identity constituted entirely through performance. The contradiction between these two alternatives was particularly pertinent at the time these films were released because of the existence of two equally contradictory social pressures: firstly the need to maintain a sense that there was an essential difference between the sexes, which was the basis of the patriarchal ordering of society, and secondly the pressing need, after the war, to be able to recognize men's abilities to adjust to the different conditions of war and peace. Because this contradiction is irreconcilable, it is hardly surprising that the attitudes toward the idea of masculinity as a performance revealed in these films are also contradictory. At one extreme, the extraordinary degree of performativity involved in the construction of the central character (and his real-life counterpart) in *The Jolson Story* presents a vision of masculinity so inextricably bound up in its own performance that there remains almost no sense of a coherent self underneath its enactment. At the other end of the spectrum lie films such as *Road to Utopia*, *Easy to Wed* and *The Kid from Brooklyn* which, while they play with images of performative masculinities, do so only from a position of relative security, with the well-known public personas of their stars operating to ground the most performative moments in these films in the apparently concrete masculinities of their male stars. While these films reveal contradictory attitudes in relation to the constitution of masculine identity, there is a certain sense in which the ability of these films to put these contradictions on display stems from the degree of representational latitude afforded to them on the basis of their genres. Musicals and comedies may be less tied to the conventions of realism which characterize the quality, narrative films and, therefore, enjoy greater liberty to play with representations of gendered identity, without seeming to threaten the stability of gendered identities in the real world, simply because another convention of these genres decrees that they are understood as escapist entertainment and are not to be taken seriously. In this respect the fact that quality, realist, narrative films such as *Best Years of Our Lives* and *Two Years Before the Mast* also depict highly performative masculinities is particularly revealing of the importance this way of conceptualizing men's identities assumed in film and other media discourses in a period in which large numbers of men were actually shifting between different masculine modes, as they left the armed forces and returned to civilian life. While genre may operate to disavow the performativity of masculinities in the musicals and comedies by denying the seriousness of the films, the same cannot be said of these prestige productions. Indeed the opposite would seem to be the case given the interest these films have in dealing with real social issues, and this reinforces the feeling of seriousness surrounding their portrayals of performative masculinities. This generic disavowal may also partially explain the predominance of musicals and comedies among the most popular films released in the early postwar period: while people sought reassurance about men's capacity to change, and so were attracted by the presentation of fluid identities permitted by the conventions of these genres, they may not have been entirely comfortable about accepting that masculinity is a gendered identity that possesses no essential basis.

Chapter 5

Military service and male companionship

Studies of representations of masculinity that have focused on anxieties about masculinity, or the so-called "crisis of masculinity" have tended to neglect the matter of masculine pleasures. Where film studies has considered male pleasures at all, the concept of pleasure has regularly been approached from a psychoanalytic perspective that has focused attention on the pleasures to be derived from the male's erotic objectification of the female body. All-male activities and the pleasures of relationships between men have received little attention other than in the context of debates concerning the homoerotic potential of these all-male relationships and anxieties that this provokes. But an examination of some of the higher earning films released shortly after the war reveals that popular movies were very often concerned with exploring men's relationships with other men. My argument in this chapter is that, far from revealing thinly concealed homoerotic impulses, analysis of these popular films reveals that they frequently provided a space in which the dynamics of close friendships between men could be explored without necessarily hinting at homoerotic undercurrents or the anxieties that concealed homoerotic impulses could provoke: Hollywood's films provided a space in which the pleasures of male companionship could be celebrated. Three distinct types of male relationships present themselves in the movies—the all-male group, the "buddy" relationship, and relationships between older and younger men that reveal a dynamic of patriarchal continuity. Each of these is considered separately in this chapter.

The all-male group

Life within an almost exclusively male environment was a key feature of military experience. Accordingly the all-male group became one the major institutions of the social order within which numerous men lived throughout the Second World War. This basic social unit occupied a position in military life analogous to that occupied by the family within the civilian social order and was treated as a type of military "family" in contemporary debates concerning the postwar readjustment of veterans to civilian life. In these readjustment discourses, the all-male group was frequently cast in a negative light, as a potential impediment to veterans' rehabilitation. Waller argued that the all-male setting of the military and the inevitable estrangement of men from the "feminizing" influence of family life were important elements of the culture of the armed forces which Waller viewed as a crucial factor in the transformation of civilian men into soldiers:

> One important phase of the soldier's isolation is his severance from family life. There are women in the army now, but they are not there as women, and the soldier is almost entirely devoid of the feminine influence
>
> (1944: 30)

Once transformed into military personnel by this over-masculinized milieu, it was suggested that men were likely find it difficult to readjust to the dynamics of normative hetero-social relationships on their return to civilian life. Waller's writing promotes a strong feeling that the all-male group might prove too successful as a substitute for the family and that prolonged immersion within the all-male group could lead to an inability to readjust to family life. Waller illustrates this argument with a quotation from a letter written by a soldier to his wife upon returning to his regiment after a period at home on leave:

> All the time I was with you, I had the most curious feeling that I was waiting to go back—to go "home" to Camp X ... Now I realize why. I'm really home now, hard as it is to say this. But that's what happens, it seems, when you join the army. You don't feel that you belong anywhere else—you can't, when you're in a uniform.
>
> (31)

A belief that the level of commitment to the all-male group demonstrated by this soldier would be commonplace in the postwar period informed Waller's account of veterans' rehabilitation and led him to conclude that many ex-servicemen would display a marked preference for the company of other men over that of their families after the war, as they sought to recover the sense of male comradeship they experienced in the armed forces, which for many men would have been "the high point of their lives" (42).

Sounding a similar note, but inflecting it with concern about the possible development of homosexual relationships within this all-male setting, Kupper noted that the exclusion of feminine influence from the all-male group might lead to the development of sexual anxieties in veterans returning to civilian life; "some returning veterans find themselves actually afraid of women and conscious of the wish to return to whatever sexual equilibrium the company of men could provide" (1945: 95). Kupper further argued that it would be quite understandable if these veterans were inclined to retreat from family life and to attempt to recapture the homosocial camaraderie of the all-male group: "small wonder, actually, if his immediate impulse is to leave his wife, go out with men friends, drink heavily" (159).

While undoubtedly coincidental, the resonance between Waller's evaluation of men's military experiences as "the high point of their lives" (42) and the title of *Best Years of Our Lives* is hard to ignore and, as in Waller's account of veterans' readjustment, the all-male group is an important element of the film. A key dimension of the film's narrative is the contradiction presented by the three central male characters' allegiances to both the all-male group and the family as they attempt to make the adjustment from military to civilian life. The binary-oppositional pair formed by the all-male group and the family serves as a metaphor for the shift from military to civilian life in the film, and the characters' ultimate rehabilitation to the latter is articulated through a shift of allegiances from the male group to the family.

The early scenes in the film are concerned with constituting the all-male group formed by Al, Fred and Homer and with establishing this group as a synecdoche for the military services generally. On numerous occasions early in the film, the characters are identified by reference to the branch of the armed forces in which they served. Al's reference to himself during their flight home, "you trying to kid the army?" is typical, as is Uncle Butch's later instruction to his barman to "draw a beer for the navy", when Homer comes to his bar for a drink. The sense that the three male characters each represent their branch of the services is intensified by their habit, in the early parts of the film, of referring to each other by their former military rank in preference to their names.

This all-male group is formed when Fred, Al and Homer meet at the start of the film, during their flight home to Boone City. The flight itself establishes the film's ideological direction—a movement away from the world of the military towards civilian life: from the all-male group to the family. But the shift from one to the other is not a simple matter of physically returning home, and after their arrival in their home town the three men continue to be drawn to one another in preference to their families. Indeed, the return to the family is initially problematic for each of the men. There is a tangible sense of awkwardness about Al's return home. Before Al even reaches his apartment he is challenged by the porter in the building, who doesn't appear to know that Millie has a husband. It seems as if, in his absence, Al's very existence has almost been forgotten. This feeling of awkwardness is reinforced when Al rejoins his family. Al's difficulties in returning to family life are most clearly marked in his relationship with his son, Rob (Michael Hall). The boy has grown considerably while Al has been away and has developed a personality and set of attitudes that are at odds with the military values that Al still holds when he returns. This is particularly evident in Rob's reaction to the presents—a Japanese soldier's cap, a Japanese flag and a samurai sword—Al has brought back from the war for him. While these war trophies would undoubtedly have held considerable prestige within the value system of the all-male group they possess so little interest for Rob that he even forgets to take them with him when he retires to his bedroom and he needs to be prompted by Millie to express any gratitude for the gifts. Homer's return to his family is also signalled as problematic. Here the difficulties of readjustment to family life are articulated through the contrast between Homer's considerable dexterity with his hooks in the company of Al and Fred—which he demonstrates by, for example, lighting matches, holding a beer glass and, later, by playing the piano—and his clumsiness in the presence of his family, where he drops a glass of lemonade and is denied the opportunity to display his ability to light a match by Wilma's father's swift action in lighting his own cigar. Fred's difficulties in returning to his family are the most problematic, however. Arriving at his father's home, Fred finds that his wife, Marie, has moved to her own apartment. Unable to find Marie at her new home or locate the night-club at which she works, Fred spends his first evening in his home town drifting from bar to bar, eventually finding his way to *Butch's Place*, a bar owned by Homer's uncle. Fred's first night in his home town passes, therefore, without his even discovering where "home" really is.

All three men find their way to *Butch's Place* that evening, allowing the film to reconstitute the all-male group. Al's arrival at the bar illustrates particularly well the continuing importance of the emotional bonds between the three men and their residual attachment to the all-male group. When Al enters the room the men embrace and greet each other warmly. The warmth of this reunion of men who are, in reality, relative strangers contrasts with the awkwardness associated with each man's return to his family home. This contrast is intensified by the rather pointed exclusion of Peggy and Millie from the men's displays of affection: the women stand apart from the men and are visually separated from the male group by framing which positions the women and the all-male group in separate shots.

The fact that this reunion takes place in a bar is also significant and connects the film to postwar discourses concerning the gendering of space. Two articles published in *Life* magazine after the war create a strong sense of the public bar as a masculine space (albeit one that is under constant threat from feminine influence). *Life Goes to Bleecks*, (26 November 1945: 138-141) describes the public bar as "man's last citadel" (141) and recounts the protests that had accompanied the decision to admit women to the bar. *Man's Stance Declines* (21 January 1946: 14) adopts a similar rhetoric, calling the public bar man's "last citadel of escape and evasion", and attributing a recently observed tendency of men to adopt a slouching posture to the fact that the bars against which they leaned for many hours had recently been lowered by several inches in order to allow the newly admitted women to order across them. Despite the fact that they recognize that women were present in public bars, both articles retain a strong sense of the bar as a masculine space. This masculine gendering of the public bar is reinforced in *Best Years of Our Lives* by the naming of the bar; it is *Butch's Place* after all, a name that emphasizes masculinity and suggests the total exclusion of femininity.

While the all-male group provides the principal emotional nexus for the men in the early part of the film, the film's ideological direction propels the men toward a renewed commitment to the family. The progressive increase in the men's commitment to the family inevitably entails a concomitant decline in the importance of the relationships between the men. The romance that develops between Fred and Al's daughter, Peggy, places considerable strain on relationships within the all-male group. This relationship precipitates a decisive break in the emotional bond between Fred and Al. In a scene already discussed in chapter 2, in which Al confronts Fred about the relationship, Al's clearly stated intention to prevent the relationship developing further is phrased in terms that demonstrate the shift of Al's commitment from the all-male group to the familial ideal:

> I give you fair warning, I'm gonna do everything I can to keep her away from you; to help her forget about you and get her married to some decent guy who can make her happy.

The film's ideological commitment to the family as the basic social unit of civilian life ultimately necessitates the loss of the sort of close emotional bond between men that was possible within an all-male group, and it is clear that the male group that is temporarily reconstituted for Homer's wedding at the film's end is very different to that which existed in the early part of the film. Despite the passage of time, relations between Fred and Al are evidently still strained and the men have lost the easy intimacy that they enjoyed earlier in the film. Ultimately, then, the film's ideological agenda promotes a process of male disinvestment in the all-male group and a renewed commitment to the family ideal. Despite this overarching ideological direction, however, the film's representation of the friendships that developed between men within the all-male setting is noteworthy for the glimpse it allows of the kind of intimate male friendships that became possible during the war between men who were, in reality, virtually strangers.

The dichotomy between the all-male group and the family, which is such a key feature of *Best Years of Our Lives,* is also central to the binary structure of *The Yearling.* A monologue spoken by Pa Baxter (Gregory Peck) at the start of the film establishes a clear sense of the shift of his emotional nexus away from the all-male group and toward the family, catalysed by his move from military to civilian life. In the monologue, Pa tells how he fought for the confederacy during the American civil war and, after the war's end, sought to find a more peaceful setting "away from towns and wars". He found this on "Baxter's Island", a small Florida isle, where he settled down with his wife in order to work the land and start a family. Although there are many differences in style, genre and narrative content between *The Yearling* and *Best Years of Our Lives*, as this early monologue illustrates, the direction of the ideological movement is the same in both films: a shift of men's loyalties from the all-male group to the family.

The binary opposition between the all-male group and the family is incorporated as a narrative element in *The Yearling* through contrasting constructions of the Baxter and Forrester families. Although superficially both would appear to belong on the "family" side of this binary, the Forrester family—consisting of two elderly parents and their seven sons—is constructed in such a way that it is also able to signify both the family and the all-male group at different times in the film. As an all-male group, the Forresters are held in opposition to the Baxter family, which performs a normalizing function within the binary opposition, representing a preferred family type that clearly excludes the sort of family represented by the Forresters.

The film clearly signals its preference for the kind of family represented by the Baxters over the Forresters before the latter have even appeared onscreen; Ma Baxter describes them early in the film as a "reckless, no account, black-hearted lot". The first appearance of the Forresters on screen confirms the impression that they are a problematic group. As Pa and Jody approach the Forresters' home they hear the sounds of a heated argument emanating from inside the house. The dispute soon spills out into the front yard and the Forresters appear on screen: a rough-and-ready group of men prone to violent disagreements. The Forresters' theft of the Baxters' pigs later in the film and the frequent references that Pa Baxter makes throughout the film to the possibility that Lem Forrester might try to shoot him reinforce the association between the Forresters and an atmosphere of over-masculinized lawlessness and violence situated within the all-male group. This impression is most clearly evidenced by Lem's behaviour while Pa and Jody are visiting the Forresters. Lem's attitude is aggressive throughout the visit and he appears to be constantly on the brink of violence: Lem's truculent interrogation of Pa's story about a hunting trip culminates in Lem taking a shotgun from the wall and discharging both its barrels over Pa's shoulder.

Although the degree of violence threatened by Lem is quite disproportionate to the ends he wishes to achieve, there is at least a slim narrative motivation for it in his desire to trade Pa's hunting dog for the gun. Later in the film, however, a fistfight between Lem and another man provides a demonstration of the Forresters' capacity for entirely unmotivated violence. Although Lem's involvement in the fight is a result of rivalry over a woman, two more of the Forrester brothers become involved purely for the pleasure of fighting:

First brother:	I ain't seen a fight as good as this for months.
Second brother:	Reckon I oughta get into it too. Coming?
First brother:	Might as well.

Despite the association that the film creates between the Forrester family, criminality and violence, the Forresters are not entirely unsympathetic characters. On the whole, with the exception of Lem, the Forrester men are warm and hospitable towards Pa and Jody throughout the film. In one scene, during their visit to the Forresters' farm, it is clear that there is an easy integration of the two Baxters into the all-male group constituted by the Forrester men. In this scene, all of the men and boys gather around Pa Baxter as he entertains the group by recounting the story of his pursuit of a bear, known as "Old Slewfoot", renowned for its cunning and keen survival instinct. As Pa tells of his battle of wits against this worthy adversary, the Forresters listen, enthralled, interjecting excitedly from time to time with their own comments as they enjoy the tale and the opportunity it provides for them to imagine themselves in the hunter's role. This activity of story telling, and the warm familiarity it fosters between the Baxter and Forrester men, cements a distinctly masculine bond between the men. In contrast to the obvious pleasure which Pa's story gives to the all-male group, Ma Baxter's attempt, in a later scene, to participate in this masculine activity by telling a story of her own falls flat: her anecdote, lacking the familiar masculine narrative structure of Pa's hunting stories, simply leaves Pa and Jody bewildered.

Although the Forresters are peripheral to the film's main focus on the tribulations of the Baxters, they nevertheless provide a crucial structuring opposite to the family unit represented by the latter. The Forresters occupy an ambiguous position in the film, associated with violence and criminality on the one hand, but also offering an opportunity to examine some of the pleasures of male friendships on the other. In this respect the Forresters are constructed in a manner that is consistent with the tone of contemporary discourses concerning male groups. While these discourses do not deny the pleasures of men's relationships with one another they do tend to portray these friendships as less appropriate, and therefore as problematic to some degree, within a postwar civilian order dominated by the family as the key institution around which social life was organized.

In *Two Years Before the Mast* a different slant is placed on the relationship between the all-male group and the family. Although the film focuses almost entirely on the all-male group constituted by the crew of the *Pilgrim*, scenes near the beginning and end of the film provide an insight into Charles's relationship with his family, and the beneficial transformation this relationship undergoes as a result of his immersion in an all-male group. Early in the film, the relationship between Charles and his father, Gordon, is shown to be particularly problematic. The two men could hardly be more dissimilar—Gordon, a thrifty, self-made merchant; Charles, a dissolute hedonist with a deep contempt for his father's thrift and industry and a predilection for drinking and gambling. Charles is content to live off the proceeds of his father's success, and when Gordon withholds money he simply circumvents Gordon's financial control by seeking the money from his mother, who seems very willing to undermine Gordon's authority by acceding to Charles's request. In this film too, then, the family is initially constructed as problematic. I have already discussed, in chapter 2, the transformational effect of Charles's immersion within an all-male group, as a member of the *Pilgrim's* crew, in terms of his changing attitude toward social class. This wholly masculine milieu also provides the context for a shift in his attitudes towards his family, and his father in particular. When the crew is arrested for mutiny on their return to Boston, Gordon visits Charles in his cell, offering to obtain the best lawyers to secure his release. Charles's rejection of the offer—"I'm sorry father, but I'm going to stay here and face the charges with my shipmates"—signals not only his rejection of class privilege and embrace of democratic principles, but also the strength of his commitment to the all-male group. While it may seem that this refusal of his father's help represents a continuation of the antagonism between Charles and Gordon, the refusal is accompanied by a look which passes between the two men and which signals a new level of understanding and respect between them. Gordon's hope that Charles's experiences aboard the Pilgrim "may do him some good" is shown to have been vindicated and the formerly problematic family relationship is reconfigured through a uniquely masculine bond between father and son.

Military service and self "improvement"

A different set of discourses relating to all-male groups provides another possibility for reading this aspect of *Two Years Before the Mast*. During the years immediately following the end of the war the question of whether national service should remain compulsory became the subject of much debate. In 1945, the *Annals of the American Academy of Political and Social Science* devoted an entire edition to the debate about whether there should be compulsory military service for all American men. In the introductory essay, "National Security in the Postwar World", Paul Anderson noted the existence of a widespread debate in America at the time about whether every American man should be required to undertake a year of military training (1945: 6). The remaining articles contained in this volume set out the terms of the debate between those writers who emphasized the benefits to the male character of exposure to the discipline of military service and those, such as Willard Waller, who feared that the requirement for young men to take a year out of civilian life "would strike a blow at the American family" (1945b: 99).

In a book advocating the continuation of conscription, Edward Fitzpatrick emphasized the educational advantages which military service could offer and the importance of these for ensuring the individual's participation in a democratic society. Answering the objections raised by those who feared that compulsory military service might damage men's ability to integrate into civilian society, Fitzpatrick argued that:

> a new seriousness, perhaps a high seriousness, will come to many of these men; and we shall have in our communities, after training, other influences for a better community and a better world
>
> (1945:279)

The rhetoric on this side of the debate about universal conscription promoted a strong belief that the discipline and rigours of the military regime would bring about the "improvement" of the masculine self. Inevitably the setting within which this "improvement" could be achieved was an all-male group. This is entirely consonant with the reading of *Two Years Before the Mast* as a contribution to this discourse. A key element of the "self-improvement" that conscription was understood to promote was the ability of men to develop supportive, caring relationships with other men. In the film, the transformation of Charles's character from a self-centred individualist, who thinks nothing of allowing the whole crew to suffer punishment in order to avoid a more severe punishment himself, into a socially responsible, mature man who cares for the needs of other men, reveals the benefits which the values associated with the all-male group could bring to society in general, providing a setting in which men could engage in expressions of care and concern for one another without provoking the suggestions of effeminacy or homosexuality that might accompany caring and supportive gestures between men in other contexts.

A brief glimpse of the sort of supportive friendships between men that became possible within the setting of an all-male group is provided by a short sequence near the end of *Blue Skies*. The sequence, which depicts Johnny's activities entertaining the troops during the

Second World War, takes the form of a montage of different shots showing Johnny singing to various groups of soldiers in different locations. Each part of this sequence, each individual location, is linked by the soundtrack, which consists of Crosby singing his hit song, *White Christmas*. One shot, late in the montage sequence, shows several soldiers, some stripped to the waist, with their arms around each other's shoulders. While one possible reading of this image could suggest that it revealed a latent homoeroticism within the all-male group, I would argue that there are elements of this scene that function to negate such an interpretation. Although several of the men are bare-chested and the men's bodies do touch each other, the direction of all the men's gazes towards Crosby, singing on a stage in front of them, disavows any sexual element in the physical contact between the men's bodies and instead produces an impression of a masculine closeness—they "lean on" each other for support—that lacks an erotic component (fig. 5.1).

Figure 5.1 An image of supportive male friendships in *Blue Skies* (1946)

Although all of the films discussed in this section employ representations of all-male groups, the use they make of these groups is not identical. *Best Years of Our Lives* and *The Yearling* both use the all-male group as an element in an opposition between the male-group and the family, which provides a metaphor for the shift from one system of values to another that was a characteristic feature of the movement of men from military to civilian life. In the context of a society emerging from a state of war, it is hardly surprising that the terms used to elaborate this opposition are hierarchically arranged, with the family clearly preferred over the male group. Notwithstanding this preference, the all-male group is hardly cast in a negative light in these films; it is more a case of the male group being portrayed as a desirable institution within the context of a society at war but less so in postwar civilian life. The remaining films, *Two Years Before the Mast* and *Blue Skies* adopt different approaches to the all-male group. *Two Years Before the Mast* illustrates the beneficial impact of immersion in an all-male milieu on the male individual and, as a result of the subsequent actions of these individuals, on society as a whole. *Blue Skies*, on the other hand simply provides a brief image of the emotional intimacy that was possible between men within the all-male group but which often tended to provoke anxieties about men's sexuality when expressed outside that context.

Buddies

One particularly close relationship that developed between men within the military setting, but which also tended to provoke concerns about homosexuality in the civilian postwar milieu, was the "buddy" relationship. This relationship was such an ubiquitous element of military life that, as Kupper noted (1945: 68), it came to be celebrated in a number of popular songs of the wartime period. Despite the position the buddy relationship gained within popular culture at the time, attitudes toward this extremely close friendship between men were often contradictory. The reciprocal care of buddies for each other's welfare was undoubtedly beneficial to the organization of military campaigns, but the very closeness of these relationships was a source of concern that this fraternal intimacy might acquire a homoerotic dimension within the military's bounded, all-male setting.

The military authorities officially endeavoured to exclude any person with a history of homosexual behaviour from the armed forces (see Kinsey et al 1948: 621 and Gorer 1948: 96), but the buddy relationship did gain a measure of acceptance by the military authorities. In all likelihood, a pragmatic approach to the realities of life within a group of men removed from much contact with women probably dictated that a "blind eye" be turned to discrete instances of homosexual conduct between buddies. As George R. Stewart speculated about the sexual behaviour of America's earliest settlers in his paperback, *American Ways of Life*, a few years later:

> As to what solution of the sex problem was attained by these hundred-odd lusty men, we are ... in ignorance. Probably there was some commerce with the Indian women, but relationships with the tribes were so commonly hostile that there was little opportunity for many of the colonists to acquire concubines. Doubtless the Jamestown colonists behaved about as we should expect of a battalion of United States marines garrisoned on a South Sea island with little chance to fraternize with the natives.
>
> (1954: 157-158)

Given the wealth of data contained in their study, it is surprising that Kinsey et al present no information as to any differences there may have been between the proportion of men participating in homosexual acts in the armed forces and in civilian life. Perhaps this attests to the sensitivity of the military authorities to the issue of homosexuality in the armed forces. Although Kupper does not refer directly to the question of homosexual relations between buddies, the anxiety this relationship provoked is easily recognizable in his observation that the bond between buddies might be so strong that veterans' wives might "wonder whom her husband prefers to be with" (1945: 67-68). Because of these anxieties, it became a matter of urgent necessity that the possibility that relationships between buddies might be sexual should be vigorously denied. And the closer the relationship between two men was, the greater was the need to maintain this denial. According to Gorer, a number of distinctive patterns of behaviour developed as strategies for denying any homosexual component within the buddy relationship:

[The] "buddy" relationship can be of any degree of warmth or intensity; but the greater the warmth and intensity, the more essential it is that the pair shall engage in "double-dating"; at its most intense they may even make a play for the same girl, preserving their relationship by sharing her favours ... the warmer the relationship is between friends, the more ardently shall they pursue women together, because of the panic fear of homosexuality.

(1948: 95)

The characteristic behaviours referred to by Gorer are evident in the relationship between Johnny and Jed in *Blue Skies*. Johnny and Jed are former vaudeville partners. They have enjoyed an extremely close friendship in the past, even if this has faded in the film's diegetic present. One evening Jed brings Mary (Joan Caulfield) to Johnny's nightclub. Jed wants to marry Mary but she is obviously less romantically interested in Jed. However, she does make her romantic interest in Johnny very clear and much of the remainder of the film is concerned with the competition between the two men for Mary's affection. Although Johnny participates in this contest, he seems reluctant to pursue it to its logical conclusion by asking Mary to marry him, even though her preference for him over Jed is clear. At first this might be explained by the fact that Johnny had assumed that Mary's display of interest in him was part of a "burn" on Jed. He remains reticent, however, even when he realizes that Mary is genuinely fond of him until finally, her patience exhausted, Mary is forced to ask "do I have to propose to you too?"

Johnny and Mary do marry, but their relationship is marred by the distance which Johnny maintains between them, and in particular by his repeated failure to consult Mary over the many sales and purchases of nightclubs he makes during the course of the film. This aspect of Johnny's character gives an ambiguous tone to their relationship. The ambiguity is clearest in the contrast between Johnny and Jed's attitudes towards Mary. While the latter's feelings towards Mary are evidently motivated by heterosexual desire, Johnny's feelings toward Mary are more difficult to discern. Certainly he shows some interest in her, but his reluctance to propose marriage until prompted by Mary and his resistance to her closer involvement in his business affairs suggests a considerable ambivalence towards the relationship. It does seem possible that Johnny's interest in the relationship might stem more from a need to engage in competitive behaviour with Jed than from any real interest in the marriage itself and, in this respect, the construction of the relationships between the three characters involved in this love triangle is consonant with Gorer's account of characteristic "buddy" behaviour.

Bearing in mind that it is the *anxiety* that the relationship might be perceived as homosexual that is at stake in concern about the nature of the buddy relationship, it is possible to identify another characteristic behaviour of buddies in Johnny and Jed's manner towards each other. Despite the fact that the two men are close friends, throughout the film they never display any warmth toward one another and they engage in a continuous banter, which takes the form of a mutual exchange of disparaging remarks. Far from creating an impression that the two men actually dislike each other, this conduct serves instead to reinforce the sense that there is an extremely close friendship between them, since only a relationship founded on a deep affection could bear the constant expressions of mutual disdain. Although this is not one of the disavowal strategies mentioned by Gorer, this banter does function in a similar way to the other behaviours that he discusses, to promote a superficial impression that the relationship is far less intimate than it really is.

It is not only Crosby and Astaire who engage in this characteristic behaviour, either in the roles they play in *Blue Skies* or in other films in which they are paired. Indeed it is a common feature of male partnerships in many musicals and comedies. In *Ziegfeld Follies*, for example, the insults traded by Fred Astaire and Gene Kelly in *The Babbitt and the Bromide* sequence only thinly mask the overriding impression of deep affection in the men's relationship which this segment of the film otherwise produces. Similarly, in *Easy to Wed* the apparent dislike of Bill and Warren (Keenan Wynn) for one another is so excessively overstated that it is easy to see that their true feelings must be extremely warm and that their behaviour towards one another is intended to obscure the truth about their feelings.

Road to Utopia provides a particularly clear example of this tendency to disavow affection within a buddy relationship through the use of expressions of mutual disdain and mistrust. In an early scene, the dialogue between Duke and Chester seems to express real emotional warmth between the men.

Figure 5.2 "What's mine is yours..." Simultaneous expression of affection and mistrust between buddies in *Road to Utopia* (1946)

However, the men's actions while they speak these words invests them with a second meaning which counters the first and transforms these expressions of affection into an articulation of mutual distrust:

Duke:	I can't let you go like this, without letting you know that, whatever happens, you can always count on me.
Chester:	Oh that's fine Duke, just fine.

Duke:	I want you to feel that whatever I have is yours, and somehow I feel that whatever you have is mine. [*He picks Chester's pocket and takes his wallet*]
Chester:	Duke, that little speech touched me. We're pals. If we want something we don't have to ask for it. We know it's there and we take it. [*He picks Duke's pocket and retrieves his wallet*]
Duke:	Well, this is it son. Let me have a last look at you.
Chester:	Duke, I...
Duke:	No, don't speak. Don't say it. Go quickly and don't look back. [*As Chester turns and walks away, Duke once again picks his pocket and takes the wallet*].

(see shot sequence in fig. 5.2)

One of the film's songs, *Put it There Pal*, makes a similar use of double meanings—this time by using the second line of a series of couplets in the song to alter the meaning of that which precedes it—to transform what appear to be compliments into insults. The song begins innocuously enough, with the line "I don't care where I'm going, just as long as I'm with you", giving a sense of genuine affection between the men. However, this quickly changes into an exchange of insults: "I like the way you wear those gaudy shirts you've got, the only time a rainbow ever covered up a pot"; "oh you'll wow the lady Eskimos, they don't wear bobbysox";[1] "you've got that something in your voice, so right for sellin' cheese"; "I think your jokes are great, it's just that folks are hard to please". In addition to this deployment of double meanings to disavow any hint of excessive affection between the men, *Road to Utopia* also contains a "love triangle" of the sort discussed by Gorer. In this respect, then, there is a neat "fit" between both this film and *Blue Skies* and the discourse relating to sexual anxieties provoked by the buddy relationship instantiated by Gorer. While there is nothing in the films to suggest that there is actually any element of homosexual desire in these buddy relationships, it was the *fear* of homosexuality that was sufficiently strong in American culture at the time to make these extremely close relationships between men a source of anxiety. It is certainly possible to read these elements of the films as strategies for disavowing any homosexual potential in these relationships. However, it is also possible to view them as activities that provided men with opportunities to affirm their heterosexual masculinity to themselves and other members of the male group. Of course, behaviours of these kinds will always be vulnerable to another reading—as a strategy for denying of homosexual feelings that actually did exist in these close male friendships—but the ambiguities of these behaviours ought not lead to our overlooking the straightforward possibility that these rituals of heterosexual masculinity depicted in the films, rather than registering anxieties about men's sexualities, actually simply provided a space within the culture in which the pleasures of male friendships could be examined. The fact that writers such as Gorer were so insistent on foregrounding the potentially homosexual implications of the behaviours he describes tends to support this view, since it suggests that such spaces may have been scarce elsewhere in the culture. If the scientific and quasi-scientific discourses of the period concerning men's relationships with each other could only address those relationships by regarding them as a revelation of anxieties about men's sexualities—and here Gorer's acknowledgement of the extent of the influence of psychoanalytic theory within American culture (50) may be particularly revealing of the extent to which the culture was moving towards an increasing interest in sexuality as an explanation of the motivation behind the forms of numerous cultural artefacts—then Hollywood's early postwar musicals and comedies at least afforded an opportunity for men to view images of the kind of relationship they might have enjoyed with other men during their service in the armed forces, and to imaginatively relive those relationships without experiencing sexual anxiety.

Male friendship, mature masculinity and patriarchal continuity

While *Blue Skies* and *Road to Utopia* may gain a degree of ambiguity from the "fit" between their male characters' behaviour and the type of conduct described by Gorer, other films in the group feature very close friendships between male characters which in no way resemble the sort of male relationship that Gorer discusses. *Till the Clouds Roll By*, *Night and Day*, *The Jolson Story*, *The Yearling* and *Two Years Before the Mast* all feature close friendships between an older and a younger man, which have a strongly paternalistic dynamic through which the older man helps the younger develop into a mature man. In each case these films depict a process of maturing in which the younger man benefits from the experience of the older and, in each of the musical biopics, the older man is able to enjoy a degree of success in his career that would have been impossible without the innovation and dynamism of the younger man.

In *Till the Clouds Roll By* the key relationship is that between the young and inexperienced composer, Jerome Kern, and a successful song arranger, Jim Hessler (Van Heflin). Although initially reluctant to become involved with Jerome's work, Jim soon finds himself helping the young composer with an arrangement for a song he has written. A rapport is immediately established between the men and Jerome moves into Jim's house, becoming an "uncle" to Jim's daughter and a kind of surrogate son to Jim. The two men become inseparable. When Jim moves to England to work on his symphony, Jerome follows close behind, and the men end up working late into the night, perfecting the popular songs that will make Jerome famous.

In *The Jolson Story* the relationship between the young Asa Yoelson and the veteran vaudeville performer, Steve Martin, is central to the narrative. While still a child, Asa is given permission to join Steve's act and the pair tour the country performing in numerous different cities. Early on the relationship between these male characters resembles that of father and son, since Steve assumes responsibility for Asa's well-being and education. Later, however, as Asa grows into a young man, the relationship becomes less parental and develops into a close friendship. Asa benefits from Steve's long experience in show business, but ultimately it is Asa who provides Steve with the opportunity to move away from his rather dated act, which has provided him with steady work but was clearly never destined to give him great fame or wealth, into a new position as the manager of perhaps the most successful entertainer of his time. In both *Till the Clouds Roll By* and *The Jolson Story*, then, the relationship between these male characters is a symbiotic one in which the younger man possesses enormous talent and potential, but needs the experience of the older man—whose own potential has peaked—in order to bring that talent to the fore.

Night and Day presents a variation on this relationship. In this film the key friendship is that between Cole Porter and Monty Wooley (playing himself), constructed by the film as Porter's law professor at Yale. Here it is not the older man's experience in show-business which benefits the younger men: both men begin their show-business careers at the same time and so have a similar amount of experience in this field. But the older man does provide the younger with unqualified paternalistic support, and his position as a law professor does give him a network of wealthy contacts, which are extremely valuable when the two are seeking finance for various shows they wish to stage. For his part, Monty replaces his rather stuffy career as a law professor with a more glamorous one in show-business, attaining a level of success as an actor which is likely to have evaded him if it were not for his relationship with Porter. In this respect the decision to construct Wooley as a professor of law in the film, rather than the fellow student he was in reality (see Schwartz, 1995) is particularly significant since it is this departure from the reality of the relationship between the two men that transforms it into the kind of paternalistic relationship that is such an important feature of these three films. The fact that the film should reinvent this relationship in precisely this way suggests that there was something about this type of paternalistic relationship which had a particular resonance within the culture at the time. This argument receives further support when the relationship between Al and Steve in *The Jolson Story* is considered further. The character, Steve Martin, in the film is a composite character, combining aspects of a number of vaudevillians Jolson worked with in his early career, notably Eddie Leonard—who "discovered" Jolson during an audience "singalong" in the course of Leonard's act, and with whom Jolson worked for a short time—and Aggie Beeler, better known by her stage name, "Jersey Lil", with whom Jolson toured for a time, singing from the balcony whenever Beeler's voice failed during her "bump and grind" routine (Freedland 1995: 23-25). While the collapsing of several real-life characters into a single character in this highly fictionalized film is not particularly remarkable in itself, it is noteworthy in this case because of the way the real life characters are moulded together into an older, more experienced showman in order to allow the development of a paternalistic relationship between this character and Al. The fact that one of the real people collapsed together into this fictional composite character was a woman intensifies the feeling that it is precisely the paternalistic nature of this relationship that was of particular significance rather than any other aspect of the relationship. In a similar fashion, the paternalistic figure, Jim Hessler, in *Till the Clouds Roll By* is also a fabrication of the film (see Bordman 1980). All three of these films, then, determinedly construct this kind of paternalistic relationship between major male characters.

Many a boy learns fine craftsmanship from his own father in the Studebaker plants

Plenty of staunch young exponents uphold Studebaker's ideals of quality

SOMEONE once said, "They get 'em young and train 'em right at Studebaker"—and there's a world of truth in that explanation of the consistent high quality of Studebaker workmanship.

A good many of the older men in the Studebaker factories are proud to have their own sons or younger relatives as their apprentices. In fact, not a few of the craftsmen who have grown old in Studebaker service followed fathers—and, in some cases, grandfathers—into places in these famous vehicle-building plants.

Obviously, all the fine craftsmanship that distinguishes Studebaker cars and trucks is not the work of father-and-son teams. But there's no question that most of it is the proud achievement of men who have made a lifetime career of their service under the flag of Studebaker.

A tradition nine decades strong

The story of Studebaker quality goes back over 94 years now, through generations of home-loving, home-owning craftsmen who settled in South Bend and made it one of America's strongholds of expert workmanship.

There is family pride, community pride as well as organization pride in the painstaking care which puts long-lasting performance into every car and truck that carries the trustworthy Studebaker name.

South Bend 27, Indiana, U.S.A.

BUILDER OF CARS WORTHY OF AMERICA'S HOMES

Figure 5.3 Advertisement for Studebaker cars. *Life* Magazine 18 February 1946.

In emphasizing this sort of relationship between men these films foreground a discourse of patriarchal continuity that can also be detected at other sites within the early postwar culture. This discourse is particularly prominent, for example, in a series of advertisements for *Studebaker* cars that was published in popular magazines during the mid 1940s. Departing from the familiar images of speed, luxury and hedonism which more usually characterized automobile advertising,[2] the *Studebaker* campaign focused on a number of father and son teams working in its factory. The advertisement reproduced at fig. 5.3 (published in *Life* magazine on 18 February 1946) is typical of the series. The advertisement emphasizes craftsmanship and the maintenance of quality which the transmission of skills from one generation to another guarantees. In this respect the image of the father-son relationship that the advertisements construct resembles the paternalistic relationships constructed in the three films discussed above. While the concern with this relationship in the films is limited to revealing the benefits it offers to the two men involved in it, the *Studebaker* campaign goes further, positioning the generational continuity offered by the practice of passing skills and knowledge from father to son at the heart of the ideal of community and the maintenance of American values:

> The story of Studebaker quality goes back over 94 years now, through generations of home-loving, home-owning craftsmen who settled in South Bend ...
> There is family pride, community pride ...

In the context of an advertisement for an automobile manufacturer, the rhetoric of the advertising copy strikes an odd chord: it is not clear whether the advert is aimed at selling cars or the ideological values of a patriarchally organized postwar American society. If the construction of paternalistic relationships between older and younger men in *The Jolson Story*, *Till the Clouds Roll By* and *Night and Day* is seen as an element in the same discourse of patriarchal continuity as that identified in the *Studebaker* advertising campaign, then these films can also be seen to be connected to a wider range of the most popular films of 1946 than the conventionally conceived generic classification of the films would suggest. The most obvious of these other films is *The Yearling*, which is overtly concerned with the relationship between father and son and the importance of this relationship for the intergenerational reproduction of patriarchy. While there are moments in the film where Pa Baxter adopts a stance of parental authority towards Jody, they are, for the most part, more like close friends than father and son, bound together in a exclusively masculine relationship in which Pa is consistently drawn into protecting Jody's freedom of action against Ma, who would like to see Jody take a greater degree of responsibility for domestic chores. Pa knows that only by allowing the boy to pursue "boyish" interests can Jody develop into a man who can, in turn, eventually take his central position in the patriarchal order. A similar masculine instinct can be seen behind Gordon Stewart's decision not to take any action to secure the return of his son, Charles, to shore after the latter is shanghaied aboard Gordon's ship in *Two Years Before the Mast*. Gordon's feeling that it "may do him some good" reflects a similar belief in the need for young men to develop into mature men through exclusively masculine experiences.

Although I have discussed three distinct categories of male relationships in this chapter—the all-male group, buddy relationships and paternal (or at least paternalistic) relationships—all are really interrelated dimensions of men's experiences in their friendships with other men. Relationships between men were a particularly important area of social experience in the early postwar period in America, particularly because of the opportunities which service in the armed forces during the war had presented for the development of very close friendships between men and because of the distinctively masculine dynamics these relationships possessed as a result of the almost entirely male milieu in which they developed. As I have indicated, a common response of contemporary commentators to relationships between men was anxiety about the homoerotic potential of such relationships, and this response tended to ignore entirely the non-sexual pleasures and possibilities that these friendships offered men. In contrast to this sexualization of male friendships, the utopian values promoted by the films discussed in this chapter, especially the musicals, suggest that it is more instructive to interpret these movies against the grain of this discourse; to consider how the films presented the pleasures and benefits which close male friendships offered to men. Certainly, approaching the films in this way seems more consistent with the demonstrable popularity of these films at the time, especially where, as with *Road to Utopia* and *Blue Skies*, the central male pairing is one which was repeated in numerous films in the period; it seems unlikely that audiences would continue to flock to films which consistently provoked feelings of anxiety about the sexuality of their male characters or of the enormously successful stars who played them.

This is not to say that anxiety about masculinity was not a feature of some of the movies of the early postwar period. Film noir has consistently been understood by academic film critics to provide insights into some of the period's anxieties about masculinity, as well as concerns about the family and American nationality; the three areas I have considered so far in relation to some of the most popular films of the early postwar period. In the following chapter I return to these themes in relation to some of the films released early in the postwar period that have been subsequently classed as film noir, in order to make comparisons between the treatment of these issues in film noir and in the popular films of the time.

Chapter 6

Popular films and "tough" movies

At the beginning of this book I identified one of the key issues to be addressed as being the impression, promoted by much of the existing scholarship about American films of the early post war period, that film noir represented the typical response of Hollywood filmmakers to the social disruptions experienced in that period. As I have suggested in chapter 1, numerous academics have followed the line—first promulgated by the film producer, John Houseman, in an article in *Hollywood Quarterly* in 1947—that the "tough" movie was "no lurid Hollywood invention" but in the early postwar years, presented "a fairly accurate reflection of the neurotic personality of the United States of America" (1947a: 161). Houseman's argument possesses an undeniable common-sense appeal and has passed quietly into the received wisdom of film studies, with few questions ever raised about either the typicality of film noir's characteristic representational modes or the "mood" of the wider culture that these were assumed to reflect. So pervasive is this vision of the films and culture of America after the war that my own expectation upon embarking on the research that forms the basis of this book had been that films noirs would feature significantly among the most popular films of the early postwar period, providing rich material for a discussion of anxieties about masculinity, family life and American nationality in the period. As I have indicated earlier, however, a quick scan of the rental revenues for the most popular films of the period revealed otherwise and re-directed the focus of this study.

Although Houseman's arguments were rapidly rebutted by Lester Asheim (1947)—provoking an equally swift rejoinder from Houseman (1947b)—film scholars have shown far less interest in pursuing Asheim's argument that a wider view of Hollywood's output was necessary in order to gain any insight into the mood of American society in the early postwar period, than Houseman's suggestion that films noirs or "tough" movies, as he styled them, registered the dominant mood of the postwar culture in America. It is only fairly recently that faith in the typicality of film noir's representative modes and the assumption that the mood of early postwar American society was particularly neurotic or anxious have been seriously questioned (see for example Steve Neale 2000: 156 and 158).

My naive assumptions about the popularity and ubiquity of film noir in the period following the end of World War 2 rapidly dissipated when I began to look at the rental revenues earned by films in the American market in 1946 (subject to my earlier caveats regarding the use of these figures as an index of popularity). In contrast to the easy fit that can readily be seen between film noir and common-sense assumptions about the zeitgeist of the early postwar period in America, no single mood or tone could be identified that uniformly characterized all of the most popular films, although the dominance of musicals and comedies suggested a lighter and more exuberant mood than the emphasis on film noir in academic writing would suggest. In attempting to contextualize these popular films it was necessary to take a different approach to understanding the relationship between movies and the wider culture, rejecting common-sense but empirically under-determined assumptions about the postwar cultural "mood"; an approach that attended to the popular films of the time *and* to the specificities of postwar discourses relating to the range of themes that were registered in those popular films.

Despite the inconsistency between the number of upbeat musicals and comedies among the most popular films of the early postwar period and the "mood" of that period suggested by much film noir scholarship, I do not entirely reject the suggestion that the "tough" movie represents one response to the disruptions and uncertainties of the wartime and postwar period. I do, however, take issue with the suggestion that this kind of film represented the typical response of

Hollywood filmmakers, and with the implication that the "tough" movie captured the zeitgeist of American culture in the period after the Second World War: the evidence provided by the popular films suggests otherwise, and in the contradictory impressions of the period presented by the combination of the most popular films and the "tough" movies the very notion of zeitgeist is revealed to be highly problematic.

While the common-sense equation between the "tough" films and the mood of postwar American society is challenged by the relative marginality of the "tough" movies in the early postwar period, it would be difficult to deny that these films do constitute a phenomenon that invites explanation. Although claims about the generic status of film noir are problematic, the fact that Houseman could write about "the current 'tough' movie" (161), and that Bosley Crowther could refer, in his *New York Times* review of *The Blue Dahlia* (a film produced by Houseman), to "the present expanding cycle of hard-boiled and cynical films" (9 May 1946: 3), certainly suggests that there was a distinct, if only vaguely defined, series of "tough" films produced around this time which together constituted a filmic phenomenon. Although explaining these films in vague sociological terms, as a manifestation of historically existing social anxieties, produces an inadequate account of their place within the wider culture, examination of these "tough" movies in relation to the specific themes and discourses already discussed in relation to the popular films of the period does provide a way of understanding the position of film noir within its historical setting without the need to resort to common-sense truisms about the "mood" of the culture.

In contrast to the objective approach I have adopted in identifying the popular films released within a short period after the end of World War 2, the films discussed in the present chapter have been selected specifically for their intrinsic interest as part of a genre or cycle of films. For the sake of preserving some consistency with the method used for identifying the set of popular films, I have limited this selection to those "tough" movies that registered in the listings of rental revenues discussed in chapter 1 for 1946: *Gilda*, *The Strange Love of Martha Ivers*, *The Postman Always Rings Twice*, *The Big Sleep*, *The Blue Dahlia*, *Scarlet Street* and *The Killers*. In addition, two films released in 1947 are also included because of their explicit interest in issues relating to returning veterans. *Crossfire* (Dmytryk 1947 USA) and

Boomerang! (Kazan 1947 USA) may have questionable status within the film noir canon as it is conceived today, but they are certainly good examples of the kind of "tough" films to which Houseman and Crowther refer. In addition, these films have a clear relevance to some of the discourses circulating in postwar American culture.

In discussing these "tough" films, the rest of this chapter follows a similar structure to chapters 2-5. The first section of this chapter examines issues relating to concerns about national identity in the "tough" films. In turn this is further divided into the four separate areas of concern discussed in chapter 2; the issues of status inversion experienced by veterans returning to civilian life, the American myth of classless democracy, the modernization of the American hero and, finally, the development of a sense of unified American-ness constructed from a disparate range of immigrant identities. The second section deals with the two issues relating to family life I have discussed in chapter 3, namely the figures of the absent father and the "mom". The third section addresses masculinity in the "tough" films in terms of performativity and, in the final section of this chapter, consideration is given to aspects of male friendship, namely the all-male group, the "buddy" relationship and patriarchal continuity.

Noir and Nation

Social status and the veteran experience

As I have observed earlier, the suggestion that films noirs reflect a deep concern with the character of American national identity is well rehearsed by film scholars. I have argued that "tough" movies are not unique among Hollywood's output in this respect and that issues concerning national identity are also registered in the popular films of the early postwar period. The treatment of American-ness in these two different groups of films varies considerably, with the popular films exhibiting a more optimistic stance than is typical of the "tough" movie. As I have suggested in chapter 2 the vaguely defined construct, national identity, is articulated in the popular films through a number of specific tropes concerning American society and its values. Some of these have clear connections to the particular exigencies of the historical moment while others register, in a more general sense, the myths that structure American national identity. The issue of status inversion experienced by men in the move from military to civilian life falls into the former category while the myth of American classless democracy, the modernization of the American hero and finally the presentation of America as a cultural "melting pot" exemplify the latter. These issues are not unique to the period's popular films, however, and figure in several of the early postwar "tough" films, although the ideological orientation of these movies is often at odds with that of the popular films, confirming the generally more pessimistic outlook of these "tough" films in relation to American nationality and values.

Among the "tough" movies, *Boomerang!* provides the clearest example of the inversion of social status associated with the move from military to civilian life, in its construction of the character of John Waldron (Arthur Kennedy) as an ex-serviceman who, on his return to civilian life, is unable to settle down and becomes a drifter, moving from town to town until he is arrested for the murder of a priest in a small Connecticut town. In focusing on Waldron's encounter with the machinery of civilian justice as an aspect of his post military experiences, *Boomerang!* directly examines issues concerning veterans' return to civilian life and makes an explicit link between veterans' experiences and the figure of the male drifter, a central figure in several of the "tough" movies. In *The Strange Love of Martha Ivers*, this figure is represented by Sam Masterson (Van Heflin), whose former military rank of sergeant is referenced briefly in the film. Sam drifts around America, making money here and there as a professional gambler. In *The Postman Always Rings Twice* the figure is represented by the character of Frank Chambers (John Garfield), who hitchhikes around the country with little thought to his future, and refers throughout the film to the "itchy feet" that prevent him from settling down. Similarly, the Swede (Burt Lancaster) in *The Killers* becomes a drifter after double-crossing his associates in a robbery and then being double-crossed himself by his lover, Kitty Collins (Ava Gardner). *Scarlet Street* ends showing Christopher Cross (Edward G. Robinson) roaming the streets of New York, driven insane by his guilt over the murder of his lover, Kitty March (Joan Bennett) and the State's execution of her real lover, Johnny Prince (Dan Duryea), following the latter's wrongful conviction for the killing.

The figure of the male drifter is not entirely absent from the popular films. Arguably the traveling gambler, Clint Maroon, in *Saratoga Trunk* represents a similar figure, while Fred Derry in *Best Years of Our Lives* is on the point of becoming a drifter when he is given employment by the "junkman", and Larry in *The Razor's Edge* is clearly a drifter. However, this figure is more markedly a key feature of the "tough" films. Although only *Boomerang!* and *The Strange Love of Martha Ivers* make an explicit association between this figure and ex-servicemen, the fit between this character and postwar discourses concerning the ability of veterans to readjust to civilian life implies a similar connection in each of these films. While the figure of the drifter does not register issues about status inversion in quite the same way as these issues are handled in the popular films—*Best Years of Our Lives* and *Blue Skies*—discussed in chapter 2, this aimless wandering character, unable to find a productive place in civilian society can be understood as the distillation of anxieties about the consequences that would follow should America fail to settle veterans into productive postwar roles reflecting the expectations of status that had been raised by men's military experiences. The drifter in the "tough" movies represents the ultimate degree of status inversion: not merely a move to an inferior position in the social hierarchy, but a shift from inside to outside society entirely.

There are variations in the narrative resolutions for the male drifters in the films noirs. In *Boomerang!* Waldron is eventually acquitted of the murder, as a result of the State's Prosecutor's diligence and willingness to prioritize the principles of justice over his own political ambitions. Waldron is released at the end of the film but it is unclear what becomes of him—he may just return to the life of the drifter—as the film's focus shifts towards the celebration of the just operation of America's democratic institutions. The narrative resolution for Sam in *The Strange Love of Martha Ivers* is also ambiguous. Although his departure for California with Toni (Lizabeth Scott) can be seen as an optimistic outcome—the formation of the type of heterosexual romantic couple that was so central to postwar American ideals of family life—this pairing of a gambling drifter with an ex-convict, and the backdrop of blackmail, violence and murder from which they retreat on their journey west, hardly makes them the ideal couple of American mythology.

For the remainder of the "tough" movie drifters the outcome is unambiguously pessimistic. Frank and Cora (Lana Turner) in *The Postman Always Rings Twice* are either already dead or facing inevitable death at the film's end, after becoming entangled in a sexually motivated web of murder, betrayal and blackmail. In the early part of *The Killers*, the Swede can only lie in his darkened room awaiting his own inevitable death, which will initiate the unfolding in flashback of the events—again accenting sexual desire, criminality and betrayal—that led him into his situation. Finally, by the end of *Scarlet Street*, Christopher Cross has been driven insane by guilt arising from the sexual desire, deceit and murder which propel the narrative.

In this respect there is, then, a significant difference between the "tough" movies and the popular films in their treatment of status inversion. Neither *Best Years of Our Lives* nor *Blue Skies* offers easy solutions to the problems of status inversion that are registered in the postwar experiences of Fred Derry in the former and in the song, *I've Got My Captain Working For Me Now* in the latter, but both the fact that Fred is saved from embarking on the life of a drifter by being employed by the "junkman" and can look forward to life within a normatively constructed romantic couple, and the light-hearted tone of the song-and-dance treatment of the issue of status inversion in *Blue Skies*, suggest a much more optimistic orientation toward the issue than the generally bleak treatment it receives in the "tough" films.

Class and democracy

I have argued in chapter 2 that a number of popular early postwar films reinvigorate the myth of America as a classless, democratic society. In this respect these films demonstrate that while John Belton's argument, that film noir registers a postwar crisis of national identity which is directly related to the dissolution of the myth of Jeffersonian democracy, may offer some explanation of the tone of postwar films noirs, it is not sustainable in relation to a wider range of postwar films. American society's image of itself as an egalitarian democracy (although not always exactly Jeffersonian in character) is precisely what the popular films work to promote. The issues relating to social class and the principle of democracy that receive positive treatment in the popular films are also a key feature of some of the films noirs, where they are treated rather differently.

Class and particularly class ambition are of central concern in *The Strange Love of Martha Ivers*. The upper-middle class status of the film's eponymous female protagonist is established in the opening shot of the film in which the superimposed title "1928 Iverstown" not only sets the time and place of the first scene, but also conveys a strong sense of the importance of the Ivers family in the town that bears their name. A factory sign bearing the name "E. P. Ivers" within the opening shot confirms their status as wealthy industrialists, the very embodiment of the American dream. A contrast is established between the wealthy Ivers household—Martha's only surviving family is the aunt (Judith Anderson) with whom she lives—and Martha's tutor, Mr. O'Neil (Roman Bohnen), and his son, Walter (Mickey Kuhn, younger; Kirk Douglas, elder). O'Neil has ambitions for Walter to study at Harvard and has taken the appointment as Martha's tutor in order to ingratiate himself with Mrs. Ivers in the hope of obtaining from her a scholarship for his son. The household is an unhappy one. Martha's aunt is a mean-spirited, domineering woman who maligns Martha's late mother for having married beneath her station, and her late father for being a mere worker in the Ivers family's factory. Martha frequently attempts to run away from this home, and it is her latest attempt to escape her aunt that begins the film. While the police are returning Martha to her aunt's home, O'Neil approaches Mrs. Ivers in an attempt to obtain a scholarship for Walter as a reward for information the boy has provided, which led to the apprehension of the girl. Mrs. Ivers rejects O'Neil's solicitations in a manner that indicates her disdain for the concept of class mobility: "I'm not a foundation Mr. O'Neil. I don't care whether Walter drives a truck or goes to Harvard".

O'Neil's social ambition is not so easily abated, however. When Martha kills Mrs. Ivers during a power cut shortly afterward, the tutor affects belief in the tale of a mysterious intruder in the house, which Martha concocts and which Walter verifies despite the fact he has witnessed the entire incident. Several comments by Martha later in the film confirm O'Neil's complicity in concealing the true circumstances of the killing in order to become Martha's de facto guardian and thereby gain influence over the Ivers's family fortune in order to promote his ambitions for his son.

154 HOLLYWOOD GENRES AND POSTWAR AMERICA

In contrast to the way popular films such as *Saratoga Trunk*, *The Razor's Edge* and *Two Years Before the Mast* allay social tensions arising from the reality of class stratification by having characters who symbolize the higher reaches of the class structure embrace the ideal of a classless society, *The Strange Love of Martha Ivers* preserves the function of class as an instrument of social division. Unlike these other films, *The Strange Love of Martha Ivers* does not suggest that there is any possibility of resolving antagonism between classes by the creation of a classless society, but instead constructs its main characters as having ambitions to secure advantageous positions for themselves within this inegalitarian class structure, regardless of the cost to others. Having regard to Mark Glancy's observations concerning the distinctions between Hollywood's representations of American and British societies, established by the construction of the former as egalitarian and classless and the latter as snobbish and class-ridden (1999: 129-156), it is particularly significant that *The Strange Love of Martha Ivers* should locate its distinctly un-American image of class stratification and utterly ruthless ambition for ascent through the class strata at any cost, not only within America, but in a fictional American small-town described by its own welcome sign as "America's fastest growing industrial city". In so doing, the film positions class inequality and ruthless ambition at the heart of American modernity, and so represents a pessimistic response to the revival, after the war, of the advance of America's modern, industrial age, which had been held almost in a state of suspended animation, firstly by the Great Depression and then by the war, for more than a decade and a half.

Although less concerned with class in itself, the proper functioning of America's democratic institutions, the tension between public duty and political ambition—and the threat this represents to the diligent observance of public duty within those institutions—are key issues in *Boomerang!* Waldron's trial for the murder of a priest becomes the focal point for the covert manipulations of citizens with different political interests, who are prepared to sacrifice the principles of justice in order to secure an outcome to the trial which will better serve their own political ends. In the middle of the film, when it looks certain that State's Attorney, Henry L. Harvey (Dana Andrews), will secure Waldron's conviction, a representative of one group of politically active citizens offers him, the prospect of fronting a campaign for the Governorship of the State, building on the public popularity his successful prosecution of the case will establish. Although clearly tempted by this prospect, Harvey begins to doubt the reliability of the evidence against Waldron and abandons the pursuit of his political ambitions in order to ensure that the interests of justice are served, by seeking a judicial annulment of the prosecution. In effect, State's Prosecutor Harvey sets about proving Waldron's innocence of the murder of which he stands accused. The pressures that are put on Harvey by prominent community members as the trial progresses reveal the corruption and self-interest at the core of America's political establishment. Despite this deeply cynical view of America's political elite, the film nevertheless manages to maintain some sense of faith in America's democratic institutions by individualizing both the corruption and the heroic stand against it. Only one character—Paul Harris (Ed Begley), a local businessman and influential member of the local political community—is shown to be thoroughly corrupt and although he manages to engage the support of other members of the community in the pursuit of his self-interested cause, Prosecutor Harvey is prepared to stand alone against this crowd and insist on justice. Harvey's principled stand is ultimately vindicated when he stages a dramatic demonstration in court by having Waldron's loaded gun fired at his own head. The failure of the gun to fire proves that it was faulty in such way that it was incapable of being fired at the angle at which the murder weapon must have been used. Here the coherence of the film's narrative is wholly sacrificed to its ideological imperatives—it has already been established that the fatal bullet was fired from Waldron's gun, yet Harvey's courtroom demonstration shows that the gun could not be fired at the angle necessary to inflict the fatal wound. But it is the vindication of Harvey's stand for justice against opportunistic political interests and, by extension, the overarching ideological message of continuing faith in America's democratic institutions that are the film's real points. In this respect the film's true ideological concern with persuading the viewer of the fidelity of America's political and judicial institutions is manifest. Not only does the film completely sacrifice narrative integrity to the demands of this imperative, but its use of realist, "March of Time" documentary-style aesthetics and the emphasis that is placed on the film's genesis in real events—including its closing statement that the real prosecutor upon whom Harvey's character was based went on to become the U.S. Attorney General—clearly identify the film as one with an overwhelming ideological intention of reinstating faith in America's democratic institutions.

Although the very different treatment of issues relating to class and democracy in *The Strange Love of Martha Ivers* and *Boomerang!* limits opportunities for direct comparison, it is possible to comment on the general difference in tone between the two films. In the former, class becomes the motivation for an elaborate plot to conceal a murder. This in turn becomes the cause of the systematic abuse of political power by Walter who, as a result of the social position his opportune marriage to Martha provides, has attained the office of District Attorney. This abuse of power is amply demonstrated when Walter becomes suspicious of Sam's motives in returning to Iverstown and promises to release Toni from jail if she agrees to entice Sam to a bar where Walter has arranged for a gang of private detectives to abduct Sam, give him a beating and run him out of town. Although the deaths of Walter and Martha at the film's end symbolically expunge this corruption from the system, the film hardly provides an optimistic impression of the institutions of American justice. In terms of the myth of classless democracy it is clear that *Boomerang!* is a much more affirmative film, more consistent with the expressions of faith in that myth contained in the popular films discussed in chapter 2, while *The Strange Love of Martha Ivers* demonstrates a loss of faith in the myth, which is more consistent with the claims made by academic critics, such as Belton, about the fit between these "tough" movies or films noirs and the mood of early postwar American society.

The noir hero

The modernization of the traditional western hero in a series of musical biopics released in 1946 is also considered in chapter 2. In brief, the argument I make is that certain distinct similarities between the structure of the classic western, as analyzed by Wright (1977), and these musical biopics suggest that popular early postwar films effect a transference of some of the qualities of the western hero onto a different kind of hero; one whose non-violence and emphasis on economic success may have been more resonant with the mood of postwar capitalist America. In contrast to the unambiguously affirmative heroic figures offered by these musical biopics, the "tough" noir hero is a complicated character, often possessing distinctly unheroic qualities. In some of the "tough" films—*The Postman Always Rings Twice*, *Scarlet Street* and *Gilda* are exemplary in this respect—it is difficult to identify any character as particularly heroic, wrongdoers being brought to moral justice as a result of their own character flaws, rather than the agency of a heroic figure. So far as the remainder of the "tough" films discussed here are concerned, there is a parallel between the heroic figures in these films and those in the musical biopics and, by extension, the heroes of the classic western: all are maverick figures, living outside the societal mainstream.

Henry Harvey in *Boomerang!* is the most obviously heroic character in any of these "tough" movies. Although initially at the centre of the local political establishment, his decision to seek an annulment of Waldron's trial is so strongly opposed to popular opinion and powerful local political interests that it repositions Harvey as a marginal character, a position he remains in until his decision is vindicated and popular opinion shifts into alignment with his own, thereby returning him to the social mainstream on his own terms. The presence of an unambiguously heroic character like Harvey is the exception in the "tough" films. A far more typical character is the investigator hero, such as Philip Marlowe (Humphrey Bogart) in *The Big Sleep*, Jim Reardon (Edmond O'Brien) in *The Killers*, Johnny Morrison (Alan Ladd) in *The Blue Dahlia* and Sergeant Peter Keeley (Robert Mitchum) in *Crossfire*. These investigators occupy distinctly marginal ground, being outside the official institutions of law enforcement, and routinely employing violence and intimidation in the pursuit of their inquiries. The ambiguity of the investigator hero is well illustrated by the examples of Marlowe and Reardon. Both are employed as investigators, Marlowe as a private detective and Reardon as an insurance investigator, but they pursue this activity outside the official investigative frameworks of the police and the criminal justice system. This position allows these investigators to hover between the official authorities and the underworld that they investigate, often employing the methods of the latter—which would be impermissible for the police—in the pursuit of a kind of justice that evades the official institutions of law enforcement. A similar argument can be made about Keeley in *Crossfire*, an army sergeant whose real interest lies in protecting his friend from a charge of murder, which Keeley believes to be false, but who is co-opted into assisting the police investigation of the murder in order to prove his friend's innocence. Johnny Morrison is the most marginal of all the investigator heroes in this group of films. Johnny is himself the principal suspect in the murder which he investigates, and his position on the border between legality and illegality is exaggerated by the fact that the film withholds the true identity of the killer until the very end, thereby preserving the possibility, throughout the film, that Johnny might be the murderer.

Although, at face value, the modern heroes of the musical biopics seem to have little in common with the investigator heroes of these "tough" films, they do share a common narrative direction which involves movement from marginality to the mainstream of society, which is achieved through the vindication of the hero's unwavering self-belief. Both types of heroes prioritize the individual over society in a way that reflects the pattern of the classic western and also one of the fundamental tenets of American libertarianism. Although, on the face of it, the generally bleak mood of the "tough" movies and the frequently antisocial means through which the investigator hero achieves justice do seem to imply a degree of pessimism about modern, urban America, these characters can be seen as actually rather affirmative of the deep-rooted American value of individualism when they are reinterpreted in the way I suggest here.

Noir and the melting pot

I have argued in chapter 2 that *Saratoga Trunk* and *The Jolson Story* both promote a sense of the forging of a coherent, unified American national identity from the range of immigrant identities that comprise the country's population. A sense of American national identity being comprised of a range of immigrant identities is also present in some of the "tough" movies. However, whereas the popular films celebrate the inclusiveness of America's "melting pot" culture and depict the easy assimilation of disparate immigrant identities to a unified American-ness, there is a far stronger problematization of this hybrid American identity revealed by the "tough" films.

The Killers features characters from a variety of different immigrant backgrounds. The Polish police lieutenant, Sam Lubinsky (Sam Levene) and Queenie Daugherty (Queenie Smith), the Irish hotel cleaner who is named as beneficiary of the Swede's insurance policy, contribute to a sense of the variety of immigrant identities comprising American society. But the central character, the Swede, reveals the image of easy integration of immigrants into American society to be problematic. Despite his change of name from Ole Anderson to the more American-sounding Pete Lunn, this character is most often referred to as "the Swede" throughout the film. This habit of indexing this character by reference to a pre-American national identity suggests either a failure of the character to integrate or a failure of American society to accommodate the assimilation of immigrant identities into its composite national character. While this feeling is diluted to some degree by the successful integration of immigrants such as Lubinsky and Daugherty, the centrality of the Swede to the film's narrative, in contrast to the peripheral roles played by these other characters, gives an overriding impression of the immigrants' experiences of integration and assimilation as being problematic.

Crossfire also problematizes the relationship between immigrant and American identities. The film's narrative focuses on the investigation of the killing of a Jewish man, Joseph Samuels (Sam Levene) by an anti-Semitic American soldier, Montgomery (Robert Ryan). Throughout the film, however, Montgomery's words reveal a bigotry that is far more wide-ranging than his anti-Semitism. The extent of Montgomery's bigotry problematizes the very idea of a coherent, unified American national identity by revealing, in the words of one reviewer of the film, "the secret hate or derision by one American for another" (*Crossfire* review, *Variety* 25 June 1947). Montgomery's intense anti-Semitism is readily apparent from his repeated references to Samuels as "Jew boy", his freely-expressed dislike of people with "funny names" and his open admission, late in the film, that "I don't like Jews and I don't like nobody who likes Jews". Apart from this blatant anti-Semitism, however, it is also clear that Montgomery also has little regard for other, non-ethnically marked, Americans, referring to one of his fellow soldiers as a "dumb hillbilly" and a "silly hillbilly", and making a number of derogatory comments about the supposed backwardness of Americans from the rural South: "You'll have to forgive Leroy here. Leroy's from Tennessee. He's just started wearing shoes". Although the centrality of this highly divisive bigot to the plot provides numerous opportunities for the airing of his objectionable views, the film reveals that there is no sympathy for his opinions among his fellow soldiers, and especially not from the investigating police officer, Captain Finlay (Robert Young), who is himself from an Irish Catholic, immigrant background. In this respect, although the clear ideological preference of the film endorses the image of America as a cultural "melting pot", the movie also exposes the racial and ethnic tensions that existed in postwar America.

In their ultimate endorsement of the diverse "melting pot" culture of America, *Crossfire* and *The Killers* are hardly in conflict with the inclusiveness apparent in films like *The Jolson Story* and *Saratoga Trunk*. But neither do these "tough" films have the same celebratory tone as the two more popular films. The two "tough" movies reveal a sinister undercurrent of racism and bigotry within American society,[1] running beneath the superficial optimism presented by the two popular films, and this undercurrent does represent a threat to the ideal of an American national identity formed from the merging of the country's diverse pre-American nationalities into a unified, coherent American-ness. In this respect the "tough" films do support the suggestion of Belton, and other writers on film noir, that the early postwar period saw something of a crisis of national identity. Belton's implicit assumption that this represented the dominant mood of postwar America is questionable, however, given the lower popularity of these "tough" movies compared with that of the period's higher revenue earning films.

Noir and the family

In chapter 3 I discuss two figures that came to prominence in postwar discourses about the family: the absent father and the "mom". It is difficult to simply transpose these two figures into a discussion of the "tough" movies since, as Sylvia Harvey (1998) has rightly observed, the family as a whole is largely absent from the diegetic world constructed in these films. While Harvey used the fact of this absence in a convincing and highly creative way to reconfigure the family as an absent presence in film noir, attempting to adapt her approach to the figures of the "mom" and the absent father is more problematic: it would be pushing the argument too far to make the absence of absent fathers in the "tough" films the basis for an analysis of this figure in the films. On closer examination, however, although family may remain a largely absent entity in these films, some of the "tough" movies do make fathers and father figures a key element of their narratives. So far as the "mom" is concerned, although the femme fatale does not conform to descriptions of the "mom" in contemporary literature, the anxieties about women which both of these figures articulate provide a common ground between both figures.

The absent father of film noir

General Sternwood (Charles Waldron) in *The Big Sleep* provides the most obvious image of the absent father in any of the films noirs. Although the General is not literally absent, his fragile health confines him to a peculiar existence apart from his family in an overheated glasshouse attached to the family home. Although he is effectively still resident in the same house as his two daughters, his fragility restricts his ability to exercise paternal authority in the household. As a result of this lack of paternal control his daughters, Vivian (Lauren Bacall) and particularly Carmen (Martha Vickers), have become rebellious and wayward, indulging in heavy drinking, gambling and sexual promiscuity. The result of the absence of the authority of the father is, therefore, the breakdown of the family and the women's rejection of the traditional feminine roles into which the normative, patriarchal family structure serves to acculturate them. In this respect, these representations of transgressive femininity are entirely consistent with the construction of the key female characters in *Notorious* and *Saratoga Trunk* discussed in chapter 3. As I have argued in that chapter, this way of representing women is related to a strand of postwar discourse which attributes juvenile delinquency (understood as sexual promiscuity in the case of women) to the breakdown of traditional families and, in particular, to the absence of fathers or the failure of fathers properly to perform their paternal role.

The Blue Dahlia provides the other key instance in a "tough" film of an overt expression of anxiety about the role of fathers. In this film, the use of the nickname "dad" to refer to the house detective, Newell (Will Wright), at the apartment complex where Johnny's wife lives clearly reveals the movies' interest in the paternal role. While the presence of this character called "dad" might appear to make discussion of the absent father redundant in relation to this film, the actions and behaviour of this "dad" are the opposite of the kind of behaviour expected of the caring, nurturing father anticipated by writers such as Spock in emergent postwar discourses concerning the father's role in parenting. This "dad" is an antithetical father figure; one that signifies the ideologically preferred type of father by representing his absence. So while emergent early postwar discourses on fatherhood registered an increasing acceptance of an active nurturing role for fathers, "dad" Newell is a destructive force, responsible for the murder of Helen Morrison (Doris Dowling)—one of his "children" if the use of the father and child nexus as a metaphor for the relationship between the house detective and the residents at the complex is extended—and for the blackmail of Eddie Harwood (Howard Da Silva), Johnny's ex-army buddies, Buzz and George (Hugh Beaumont), and Johnny himself.

I have argued in chapter 3 that the problematic femininities shown to arise as a result of the absence of the father are recuperated in the popular films by the involvement of women in romantic couples in which the male character assumes patriarchal authority. The same argument can also be made about *The Big Sleep*, in which Philip Marlowe becomes the romantic partner of Vivian and, throughout the film, acts as a paternalistic protector for her younger sister, Carmen. *The Blue Dahlia* is more ambiguous, however, and while the film does end with Johnny and Joyce (Veronica Lake) forming a romantic pair this is not clearly framed as an assumption of patriarchal authority by the male partner to fill a void left by an absent father. *The Blue Dahlia* frames the figure of the absent father in a rather different way from the other films, positioning him not as the cause of female promiscuity, but as the punisher of the delinquent woman. The formation of a romantic couple between two of the protagonists at the end of the film is largely incidental to this aspect of the movie, although it is the positive presence of the absent father figure, "dad" Newell, that makes this outcome possible: "dad's" killing of Helen frees Johnny from the encumbrance of his "delinquent" wife and enables him to pursue a relationship with the altogether more wholesome Joyce.

"Mom" and the femme fatale

Like the absent father, the use of the "mom" figure is less frequent in the "tough" movies than in the popular films. While Judith Anderson delivers a superb performance of domineering, "momish" womanhood as Mrs. Ivers in *The Strange Love of Martha Ivers*—replete with the sinister reverberations her star persona carries from her memorable earlier performance as Mrs. Danvers in *Rebecca* (Hitchcock, 1940 USA)—her appearance in the movie is short-lived. Christopher Cross's wife, Adele (Rosalind Ivan) provides a similar image of domineering womanhood in *Scarlet Street*. But, again, her role in the film is relatively small.

Common to all of the "tough" films examined here, however, is the key female character of the femme fatale. While the highly eroticized construction of femininity that typifies the femme fatale has no literal resemblance to the distinctly unsexy image of overweight, middle-aged, domineering motherhood painted by Wylie (1943) and others, Gorer's evaluation of the discourse about momism as being related to a "fear of ... vampire-like possession" that was "one of the components in a very strong ambivalence American men feel towards women" (1948: 45-46) does point to a link between the figures of the "mom" and the femme fatale. There may be few constructions of femininity in movies as strongly redolent of "vampire-like possession" over male desire as Gilda (Rita Hayworth), Martha Ivers, Kitty March in *Scarlet Street*, Kitty Collins in *The Killers*, Cora Smith in *The Postman Always Rings Twice* as well as some of the more peripheral characters in the "tough" films, such as Ginny Tremaine (Gloria Grahame) in *Crossfire*, Helen Morrison in *The Blue Dahlia* and Irene Nelson (Cara Williams)—a former lover of Waldron's and key witness against him at his trial—in *Boomerang!*

Although the figures of the "mom" and the femme fatale are quite distinct in their modes of construction and signification, at the core of both figures resides a deep-seated anxiety about the position and roles of women in postwar America. An assumption that has underpinned much of the academic writing on film noir—particularly that which proceeds from a psychoanalytic perspective—connects the construction of women characters in film noir to male anxieties which centre on a sexually-aggressive figure of womanhood, who represents the threat of castration. While this approach may offer an explanation of the femme fatale, it does little to explain the parallel development of the figure of the "mom" in contemporary popular films. By viewing the figures of the femme fatale and the "mom" as related to one another, however, it is possible to reconfigure this explanation of the femme fatale, freeing the understanding of this figure from its reliance on psychoanalytic film theory and placing it on a firmer historical footing. Contextual analysis that relates films to the specificities of their historical moment reveals the links between both the "mom" and the femme fatale and postwar discourses relating to women's roles in a society that, during the war, had depended on the movement of women's labour from its traditional location in the private, domestic sphere into relatively well-paid occupations in the public sphere that had previously been the almost exclusive preserve of men. The femme fatale does, then, register male anxieties—not necessarily psycho-sexual, Oedipal anxieties raised by the way the films' images of aggressive female sexuality evoke the threat of castration—but rather more mundane concerns about the gendered division of labour and the postwar reconfiguration of the traditional relationship between economically independent men and the women who, before the disruptions brought about by the shift to the war economy, would have been dependent on a male breadwinner.

Noir masculinities and performance

In a scene near the beginning of *The Big Sleep*, Philip Marlowe enters an antiquarian bookshop posing as a collector of obscure first editions; a bookworm, an intellectual. To pass in this untypical guise, however, before entering the shop he must divest himself of the toughness that—the viewer is invited to believe—is self evident from Marlowe's appearance. To achieve this he dons a pair of sunglasses, turns up the brim of his hat and adopts a fussy manner as he enters the store, peering over the upper rim of his sunglasses as he talks to the assistant. This rare instance of explicit masculine performativity in a "tough" movie turns out to be as unconvincing to the assistant—unimpressed by the esoteric knowledge of first editions that Marlowe displays, or else too absorbed by her participation in some elaborate criminal scheme to pay much attention to this curious character—as it is to the viewer. Marlowe can never be anyone but Marlowe, and his mispronunciation of "ceramics" towards the end of the scene is only the final betrayal of this shallow act. And for the viewer of the film this Marlowe is never anyone but Bogart. Steven Cohan has written about the use of a rhetoric of toughness in the construction of Bogart's star persona (1997: 79-85), and it is this coextensive quality of the actor's diegetic performances, and his extra-diegetic, transcendental performance of his star persona, which invests his screen roles with such a sense of realism and authenticity. This continuity between star and character is readily apparent from the film's advertising posters, which are dominated by the images and names of its two major stars, Bogart and Bacall, accompanied by slogans—"The picture they were born for!"; "This is the love that had to be ... this is the love team you have to see!"; "Again together! As only they can be!"—which emphasize the star characters of Bogart and Bacall, and the romantic relationship between the two actors, over the intrinsic qualities of the film and the diegetic characters they play. One poster in particular is exemplary. Dominated by two large images of the stars, seemingly "out of character", which are accompanied by a series of successively smaller images, apparently reproducing poses from the film and converging toward a final image of the two stars locked in a passionate embrace, the poster fuses diegetic and extra-diegetic levels of the stars' meanings, thereby reinforcing the sense of continuity between star and diegetic character and so the authenticity of their screen performances.

This authenticity is crucial to the realist aesthetic of the "tough" movie. So pervasive is this rhetoric of realism that Marlowe's departure from Bogart's well-established star character, when he puts on his "intellectual' act in the book shop, is only possible when the performance and the means through which it is constructed are explicitly foregrounded. As if to reassure the viewer that this momentary lapse from Bogart's/Marlowe's established star/diegetic character is temporary, this scene is mirrored by that which follows, when Marlowe enters another book shop across the street, in his "real" diegetic character this time, and begins to flirt with the attractive female assistant. The scene continues with her closing the shop in order to share "a bottle of pretty good rye" with Marlowe, in a moment "shot with sex implications", as the reviewer of the film for *Variety* observed (14 August 1946).

The rhetoric of noir realism and the contiguity between star and diegetic character is not restricted to either Bogart or to his role in this particular film. In other "tough" movies similar unbroken lines between star and diegetic character can be traced. According to the *New York Times*' review of *The Strange Love of Martha Ivers*, Van Heflin "brings to [his role] that quality of rugged integrity and certainty of action" (25 July 1946: 18). Bosley Crowther's review of *The Blue Dahlia* for the same publication referred to Alan Ladd as Paramount Pictures' "leading tough guy" (9 May 1946: 27), while the *Variety* review of the film noted that "Ladd has a cold, steel-like quality" (30 January 1946).

Not all the publicity material is as explicit about the contiguity between star and diegetic character performances. Publicity materials and contemporary reviews of the films commonly foreground the actor's skill in relation to the diegetic performance, thereby effacing the extent to which the qualities that the actor has brought to the role pre-exist the performance of the diegetic character. A publicity advance for *Boomerang!* exemplifies this separation between star and diegetic performances—remarking that "Dana Andrews has what is acknowledged to be the most challenging role of his career" (*Boomerang!* pressbook). A publicity release for *Crossfire* made a similar distinction between star and diegetic characters, emphasizing the effort involved in Robert Mitchum's performance with its assessment that, "it is one of the most exacting dramatic roles that the brilliant young star has had" (*Crossfire* pressbook). On the other hand, *Variety's* review blurred the distinction, observing that "Mitchum is the 'right' sort of cynical GI" (*Crossfire* review, 25 June 1947 – my emphasis). Reviewing the same film, Bosley Crowther commented on the performance of one of Mitchum's co-stars in terms which captured the ambiguity of the interplay between star and diegetic characters: "Robert Ryan is frighteningly real as the hard, sinewy, loud-mouthed, intolerant and vicious murderer" (*New York Times*, 23 July 1947: 19). While the phrase "Robert Ryan is..." implies a continuity between the star and his diegetic character, the way this is modified by what follows, "as the hard..." (both my emphasis), qualifies this suggestion and restores a sense of the performativity of the screen role. In its review of *Scarlet Street*, *Variety* conflated star and diegetic characters, noting that "Edward G. Robinson is the mild cashier and amateur painter" (*Scarlet Street* review 2 January 1946 – my emphasis), and in a prepared review contained in the pressbook for *Gilda*, the emphasis was firmly on the performativity of the diegetic performance: "her leading man is Glenn Ford, who turns in a most convincing performance as the tough unscrupulous gambler".

I have considered performativity in relation to popular early postwar films in chapter 4. In that chapter I argued that those films do not follow a singular representational strategy in relation to constructions of gendered identity. On the one hand a film like *The Jolson Story* positively flaunts the performativity of the central male character, while others make use of the well known qualities of star characters to ground their most explicitly performative moments in a coherent identity, and yet more frame moments of explicit performativity as comedy and thus relieve the anxiety that the foregrounding of this performance might provoke. While there are differences in the treatment of gendered identity as a performance in the "tough" films discussed in this chapter, the dominant approach places emphasis on the realism and authenticity of the films and the performances of gendered identity that they contain. In some cases this involves the use of the well-known qualities of a star character to give an authenticating ground that endows diegetic characters with a sense of masculinity as an essential condition: Humphrey Bogart is tough, Alan Ladd is "cold, steel-like". And in performing tough, cold, steel-like characters they merely reflect an underlying, essential masculinity. Even when extra-diegetic discourses surrounding the films acknowledge the effort involved in screen performances, describing roles as "challenging" or "exacting", they are hardly describing performances that are substantially in conflict with well-known star personas. But the difficulty, evident in these discourses, of consistently asserting the existence of an essential masculine identity does at least register the same tensions between these conflicting conceptions of masculinity as do the popular films discussed in chapter 4.

Noir and male companionship

In chapter 5 I have examined three different kinds of relationship between men: the all-male group, the buddy relationship and a male bond structured by a dynamic of patriarchal continuity. All three of these aspects of male experience are also relevant to the analysis of the early postwar "tough" movies, but whereas in the popular films the depiction of these relationships provides a space for representing the pleasures of male friendships; in the "tough" films, men's relationships with one another reveal deep anxieties about masculinity, anxieties that register the pessimistic outlook of certain postwar discourses concerning the return of veterans to the civilian world.

The noir male group

Three men, ex-servicemen just returned to their hometown after military service, enter a bar and take three seats at the counter. The first orders a "bourbon straight with a bourbon chaser" and the other two follow suit, the third man adding "that's two glasses, you get it?" as if wishing to further antagonize the bewildered barman. When another customer, a serviceman in uniform, starts playing a jazz record on the jukebox, the first man, disabled as a result of his war service, starts to experience a pounding in his head and complains bitterly about the "monkey music". Eventually the pounding in his head becomes too much to bear and he pulls the plug off the jukebox and almost gets into a fight with the soldier, before revealing the wartime head injury which explains his aggressive behaviour. After their drink the three men split up, two setting off to find an apartment together. The third man returns home to find his wife hosting an extravagant drinking party in their home and engaged in an affair with another man. Later that evening the wife is murdered with his gun.

In another film, a group of uniformed servicemen, biding their time between the end of the war and their final discharge from the army, are shown drinking in a bar. One accidentally knocks over a woman's drink and the group of men engages her male companion in conversation while she visits the ladies' room. Later, three of the soldiers end up at this man's apartment to continue drinking. One soldier, sick from too much drink, leaves to get some fresh air. The other two remain and one of them, driven by fierce bigotry, beats the civilian to death.

Described in general terms, these two scenes—from *The Blue Dahlia* and *Crossfire* respectively—could almost be missing scenes from *Best*

Years of Our Lives,[2] alternative versions of the tale of veterans' return home; what might have happened if, instead of insisting that he return home to his family, Fred and Al had agreed to go with Homer to "Butch's Place" for one last drink. However, while *Best Years of Our Lives* participates in a network of discourses governed by an assumption of the primacy of the family over the all-male group, and of the efficacy of the family in rehabilitating ex-servicemen to the normative behaviours of civilian life, both *Crossfire* and *The Blue Dahlia* present the dystopian concomitant of this scenario; what happens when the veteran's return to civilian life is not accompanied by a revitalized commitment to family life, when men's conduct in the postwar world remains governed by the values of the all-male group.

In the major "tough" films of 1946 the all male group is repeatedly given a negative treatment; associated with criminality and anti-sociality. In *The Killers*, a predominantly male group is assembled to commit a wages heist. Unlike the male group of some of the popular films, however, relationships between members of this group are characterized by mistrust, betrayal and violent hostility. After the robbery, a series of double-crosses pits the men against one another in a sequence of events that results in several deaths. This vision of the all-male group could hardly be further, then, from the images of supportive male friendships found in popular films such as *Two Years Before the Mast* and in particular in the montage sequence near the end of *Blue Skies* discussed in chapter 5. A similarly anti-social image of the all-male group can be found in a scene midway through *Boomerang!* in which a large crowd of men gathers outside the back entrance to the court house with the intention of exercising "mob justice" against the man accused of the priest's killing. While the crowd is deflected from its mission by the police chief and no violence actually occurs, the scene nevertheless leaves an abiding impression of the all-male group as a locus of brutal, unlawful behaviour, a source of conflict with the democratic institutions of civilian society and, therefore, as a potential threat to the American way of life. In *The Strange Love of Martha Ivers* the male group is similarly constructed as a threat to pervert the notion of American democracy: here the all-male group consists of the four private detectives hired by the district attorney to assault Sam Masterson and drive him out of town. The film provides another example of the use of a trope that identifies the all-male group as a source of violence, and of anti-democratic actions and anti-social behaviour.

Not all of the "tough" movies display such a negative stance towards the all-male group, however. The large gathering of men in the opening scenes of *Scarlet Street* provides the only setting in the film in which Christopher Cross is valued by his peers and is safe from a ruthless urban world in which his timidity and naivety leave him hopelessly vulnerable to exploitation by others. However, this gathering offers Cross only a temporary refuge from the perils of the film's dystopian vision of family life, dominated by Cross's momish wife. While the contrast between the supportive atmosphere of the all-male group and the anxieties associated with the return to family life offers a point of similarity between *Scarlet Street* and *Best Years of Our Lives*, this is short-lived since, in Wyler's film, the narrative resolution involves a reduction of the men's commitment to the all-male group and a concomitant strengthening of family bonds, whereas in *Scarlet Street* it is hard to avoid the conclusion that Cross would have been far better off if he had never ventured outside the company of other men. Scarlet Street offers a rare glimpse of a male group as a supportive environment in a "tough" movie although the overall tone of the film is so utterly pessimistic that the impact of this brief, positive interlude is considerably diluted.

Noir buddies

M: I was looking for this buddy of mine. You're cops? Has something happened?

F: Tell us about this buddy of yours.

M: Yes sir. Well, we was here. He left before we did. He wasn't feeling too good. He said he'd be right back.

F: Who's we?

M: Me and another buddy of mine.

F: Who'd you come here with?

M: With these two buddies of mine...

F: What are you doing in Washington?

M: Well I came to see a couple of my buddies.

F: Where are you staying?

M: Stewart Hotel. I used to be stationed at the
        Stewart. I'm sponging a free bunk from
        one of my buddies.
F: What was your buddy's name, this one
        who was sick, who was coming back?
M: Mitchell. Mitch we called him.

This conversation, between the murderer, Montgomery, and police captain Finlay near the beginning of *Crossfire*, provides some indication—through the insistent, repeated references to "buddies", accentuated by the rapid-fire delivery of these lines—of the significance of the buddy relationship within the value system of men in the armed forces. However, despite his repeated invocation of the buddy relationship, the fact is that Montgomery is betraying the substance of that relationship, framing Mitch for the murder he (Montgomery) actually committed, and later killing the other buddy he refers to, Floyd Bowers (Steve Brodie), when Bowers's anxieties about the killing threaten Montgomery with exposure. The relationship that actually exists between these men represents, then, a perversion of the kind of mutually supportive male friendship which characterizes representations of the buddy relationship in the popular films discussed in chapter 5; a relationship which despite the effusive espousal of buddy rhetoric is actually characterized by self-interested individualism. A brief episode in *The Blue Dahlia* casts the buddy relationship in a similar light. Following a fight, one of a pair of hoodlums is left with an injured foot. For a brief moment it seems that the film is going to offer a rare image of one man expressing his care for another, when the second hoodlum shows concern over his companion's injury and brings him a foot bath. When the uninjured man discovers evidence in Johnny's pocket that incriminates Eddie Harwood, and passes this to the other man, the facade rapidly disappears, the injured man hitting the other over the head with a cosh, revealing a return to a sinister, self-interested masculine individualism.

In the "tough" films the use of pairs of hoodlums to represent the male buddy relationship is a recurring feature. In *Crossfire*, Montgomery and Bowers (the two men who are present at the killing of Samuels) form a pair of buddies, but as in *The Blue Dahlia*, this friendship exists only as long as it continues to serve individual self-interest. In *Gilda*, the relationship between Johnny Farrell (Glenn Ford) and Ballin Munsden (George Macready) develops distinct characteristics of buddy-like friendship until the arrival of Gilda disturbs their cozy fellowship.

I have argued in the previous chapter that the buddy relationship in the popular films released after the war provides a cultural space in which the pleasures of male friendships could be represented and explored. The construction of buddy relationships in the "tough" movies, however, denies the possibility of genuine warmth between men, and any expression of warm feelings in the films is accompanied by a rapid disavowal of the possibility of any emotional bond between the men through an act of violence or betrayal between the buddies. Furthermore, in the "tough" movies the buddy relationship carries distinctly negative, anti-social connotations resulting from its association with criminality. Two characters in *The Killers* provide perhaps the clearest indication of this. Al (Charles McGraw) and Max (William Conrad), the killers referred to in the film's title, enter a diner in an early scene and engage in a dialogue with its occupants which is notable for its palpable sense of menace. A key feature of the dialogue that contributes to this sense of threat is the interaction between the two killers; each man seems to know the other's thoughts before he has expressed them. The scene gives an impression of a well-rehearsed routine between the two men, a scenario acted out by them countless times before as a precursor to the violence that will inevitably follow. Although both men are almost invulnerably tough in their speech and demeanor, the overall effect of this scene is to create a strange sense of intimacy between the two men, as if their invulnerability to the rest of the world does not exist in their relationship with each other. Unlike the other noir buddies, Max and Al do not turn on one another, but both are killed in a later scene, confirming the inevitability of destruction as the consequence of male friendships which are allowed to become too close.

Noir and patriarchal continuity

Unlike the popular postwar films, and unsurprisingly given the crisis of confidence in masculinity that is so evident in the "tough" films, these movies offer no images of patriarchal continuity. Where relationships between older and younger men are represented—such as those between Munsden and Farrell in *Gilda*; between Colfax and Swede in *The Killers*—they are generally characterized by the familiar pattern of double-crosses and violence that are distinctive features of "tough" movie masculinities generally. Only *The Big Sleep* provides an impression of a satisfactory relationship between an older and a younger man—that brief encounter between Marlowe and General Sternwood (Charles Waldron) early in the film, and the apparently paternalistic relationship between the general and Sean Regan (who is never seen in the film) which is fondly referred to by the General in that scene—but this hardly provides a sufficient basis for comparison with the more detailed narratives of patriarchal continuity contained in the popular films discussed in the previous chapter.

Overall, the ideological concerns of these "tough" films are at variance with those evident in the popular films. Although it is possible to detect areas of overlap between the two groups of films, points at which the discursive concerns identified in the popular films are registered in the films noirs, the general direction of "tough" movie narratives is more clearly pointed towards anxieties about women and the threat they represent to masculinity, than towards any of the concerns of early postwar discourse I have discussed in relation to the popular films in earlier chapters.

Reaching this conclusion, however, reveals precisely the value of the kind of broad historical study I have argued for in this book. Earlier accounts of the movie culture of America in the early postwar period—those focused exclusively on film noir and underpinned by the assumption that these represent the most emblematic type of film of that period—and the extrapolation of these accounts into general conclusions about American society at the time, have produced an impression of a tense and anxious postwar structure of feeling motivated by uncertainties about the movement of men from the army into civilian life. The account I have given in this book suggests a much more complicated situation. The existence of those anxieties is not disputed, and the "tough" movies discussed in this chapter provide ample evidence of their impact on Hollywood's filmmaking practices. However, as I have demonstrated in this chapter, even the "tough" films are not as straightforwardly homogenous as accounts of film noir suggest. The implication of this—that the social mood of the period may have been considerably more ambiguous than film noir criticism maintains; that the "zeitgeist" trumpeted by these scholars may actually have been so fragmented and contradictory as to not really be a zeitgeist at all—becomes even more convincing when the relative popularity of the two sets of films considered in this book is taken into account and when the preponderance of light-hearted films—musicals and comedies—among the popular films is also considered. The implication of this, so far as the historical study of films is concerned, is that the kind of study envisaged by Neale (2000: 252-254), in which attention is re-directed away from canonical genre categories towards inter-generic analysis and a consideration of generic hybrids and short-lived cycles of films (the musical biopics considered in an earlier chapter for example) seems to offer the far better prospects for avoiding incomplete and in some instances misleading impressions of the movies and culture of earlier times, than the highly selective accounts that have until relatively recently passed for film history. Only by pursuing this sort of agenda for future research, driven by an objective assessment of the significance of films in their moment, will film studies be able to hope to offer more reliable accounts of the film and cinematic cultures of earlier historical periods.

Chapter 7

Genre and History

Film noir is in a certain sense a fantasy...

(Cowie 1993: 121)

As a single phenomenon, *noir*, in my view, never existed. That is why no one has been able to define it, and why the contours of the larger *noir* canon in particular are so imprecise.

(Neale 2000: 173-174)

I stated near the outset of this book that one of my aims was to redress the balance between what I see as an over-emphasis on film noir in academic writing on American movies of the early postwar period and an almost total absence of attention to the contemporary films that were among the most popular at the time and which have subsequently all but disappeared from our historical consciousness of the period. In itself there is nothing objectionable about a film scholar (or even a large number of film scholars) deciding to focus on a particular group of films at the expense of giving attention to others. This becomes problematic, however, when the claims made on the basis of such a study are extended beyond the particular group of films examined and turn into general historical claims about the cinema and culture of a particular time and place. Yet this is precisely what has happened in much of the scholarly writing on film noir. Film criticism has elevated film noir to a privileged position as an expression of the cultural mood of America following the Second World War, a position which the popularity of many films noirs at the time of their release—measured in relation to the popularity of the higher-earning films of the time, such as those examined in this book—exposes as being highly questionable. At the heart of this problem is the way film scholars have approached the study of genre.

The case of film noir immediately exposes the limitations of the idea of film genre as a taxonomy that pre-exists individual genre films: noir is clearly a retrospectively constructed category which has been used to group together a set of films that would have been understood by their producers and original audiences in quite different ways. As Rick Altman convincingly argues in *Film/Genre*, however, the idea of film genre as a taxonomy that pre-exists specific instances of genre films is always misleading. Genre, Altman suggests, is a process through which the way films are understood is progressively distilled through the discursive relay—a "constant category-splitting/category-creating dialectic" (1999: 65)— between film producers and film consumers that produces a set of abstract generic qualities that, for a time, can then be said to characterize the genre and which allow the classification of individual films as part of a generic corpus. Even on this understanding of genre, however, film noir represents an unusual if not unique case, since the process through which the generic category "film noir" and the corpus of films now understood to comprise that class has evolved has not involved the sort of dialogue between producers and audiences that Altman identifies as characterizing the process of genrification; the creation of the putative generic category "film noir" is entirely the result of the discursive activities of film critics and scholars. Not only that, but the process leading to the creation of "film noir" as a generic category in critical and scholarly discourses does not involve the progressive movement through adjectival and substantive phases that Altman argues is a characteristic of the genrification process through which new genres come into being. Although the identity of the films that comprise the noir corpus may be disputed to this day, the generic surround that supposedly draws them together into a coherent corpus—the category "film noir" itself—arrived as a fully fledged, substantive generic classification from outside the industry/audience circuit that Altman sees as central to the production of new generic classes. Nothing in industry or audience discourses relating to these films prefigures the use of the term "film noir" and while it is true that Houseman's term, the "tough" movie, equally aptly describes these movies, it is hardly precise enough to amount to a prior generic identity for which "film noir" is later substituted: there were plenty of films that could be classed as "tough" (e.g. westerns) that would never be considered "noir".

"Noir" entered the discursive circuit of producers and audiences as a substantive classification and although it did arguably spawn a new cycle of American films—once called neo noir but now perhaps more accurately to be seen as generic film noir proper—this did not occur until long after the term "film noir" had crept into critical discourse about the films. The term "film noir" not only came from outside the discursive circuit of producers and audiences, but also from outside the Anglophone linguistic context, and the immediate impact of the generic category "film noir" on Hollywood producers and American audiences appears to have been negligible. As James Naremore observes of the situation in the United States in relation to the films now understood as comprising the noir canon, "reviewers had seen a vague connection between them, but no one tried to invent a new term" (1998: 16-17). In relation to what is now regarded as the classic noir period (1941-1958), Steve Neale's observation, cited at the beginning of this chapter, that noir "never existed" (2000: 173-174) is extremely persuasive. In that period film noir existed only in the discourse of a few select critics. It was, as Elizabeth Cowie suggests, "a fantasy", born out of the "desire for the very category... a wish to 'have' a certain set of films all together" (1993: 121).

As I have suggested, the contemporary impact of this critics' fantasy, outside the rarefied atmosphere of film scholarship, was negligible. There is no evidence to suggest that Hollywood filmmakers in the forties and fifties thought they were producing a "film noir" or that American audiences of the period were ever conscious that a "film noir" was what they were going to see. The problem of trying to read historical trends from this type of cultural artifact is immediately apparent: the category did not exist within the cultural context about which historical conclusions are sought and the corpus of films to which the classification later gave some coherence, did not possess that unity at the time in question. The use of a retrospectively constructed class such as "film noir" as a lens through which the cinema and culture of the past might be examined is an inherently ahistorical endeavour that offers little prospect for producing a reliable impression of the period in question.

Although the limitations of approaching cultural history through a focus on a particular movie genre are exaggerated when the genre in question is a construct that came into existence long after the period under examination, similar problems arise from any attempt to use one particular film genre as a measure of the cultural temperature of the time. Without doubt, the musical, the comedy and the romance existed as genre types in the period I have been examining in this book; indeed these genres figure large in the lists of the most popular films of the early postwar years. But any proposal to simply read off the cultural mood from one of these genres would result in an impression of that mood every bit as partial as that gained from scholars' efforts to achieve this through the lens of film noir. As Neale points out the suggestion that "socio-cultural issues can be neatly parcelled out among and between different genres" (2000: 224) is problematic, and so too is the extension of this suggestion—evident in the quotation from Fredric Jameson at the beginning of chapter 1 of this book—that historical periods can be similarly assigned a genre that expresses the deep truths of the period. The specific impediment that film noir represents to our understanding of the culture of early postwar America is, then, only a particular case of a more general problem arising from the way the relationship between genres and history has been conceived. To overcome this problem it is necessary to move away from conceptualizing the primary intertextual axis of films as being directed towards other films of a similar type, and towards the rigorous examination of the intertextual connections that flow between the films and a wide range of other contemporary texts of various different types; an investigation of syntagmatic discursive unities across a disparate textual array. As Paul Cobley conceives the role of film historians, "our task is to consider the webs of relations in which texts from the past were suspended at the moment of their first appearance" (2000: 16). Failure to attend to these intertextual relationships results in the denial of the text's "place in history, its coexistence with other generic texts and its existence as the product of contemporary readings" (24).

Earlier than Cobley, Tony Bennett invoked Pierre Macherey's suggestion that literature might not consist of literary works which can be conceived as finished products, in aid of a model for understanding textuality that comes closer to the approach proposed by Cobley, and which I also adopt in this book. According to Macherey, the study of literature entails:

> not just studying the text but perhaps also everything which has been written about it, everything which has been collected on it, become attached to it—like shells on a rock by the seashore forming a whole incrustation
>
> (cited in Bennett: 1982: 3)

More recent trends in film history have attempted to address the problem of understanding the meanings of individual films within historical reading formations by looking to some of the extra-filmic discourses that provide some sense of the original discursive context within which the film existed. In one of the most recent attempts to formulate a method for undertaking this sort of historically grounded exploration of textual meaning, Martin Barker calls for attention to be given to "how all the circulating prior information, talk, images and debates generate and shape expectations which will influence how we watch a movie" (2004: 3). While this approach certainly represents a gain over the kind of selective, canon-forming activity at the heart of the approach to film analysis that I have criticized in this book, in my opinion this does not go far enough in positioning films within their historico-social context since the types of materials Barker suggests ought to be considered along with the films—"Campaign Books, Press Books (an associated Production Stills), Electronic Press Kits, Press Releases, Teasers, Posters, Trailers, contractually-required Interviews, leaks, free give-aways, prizes of items from the set, and so on" (5)—remain too closely bound to the films themselves to provide much sense of the meanings that a film might have held when set against its historical context in the widest sense: press books will provide a sense of how producers and publicists would have wished a film to be understood but tell us little about how real cinemagoers—who, as Barker himself acknowledges (7), may have had little exposure to these publicity materials—might have understood the film. In considering what types of material help provide a contextual surround for a particular film, Barker's approach has moved forward little from that suggested by Janet Thumim (1992). I endorse Barker's argument (and by implication Thumim's) that historical study of films must involve attention to "the life of the ancillary materials, and the ways in which they constitute a discursive framework around the film" (Barker 2004: 7) but would argue that the definition of "ancillary materials" should include the widest possible range of contemporary publications, whether or not these have an immediately obvious connection with the issues presented in a particular film. Janet Staiger takes a wider view, closer to my own, of the types of extra-filmic materials that must be weighed in examining the historical meanings of particular films, arguing that these materials "ought to represent genres other than that of the text to be examined, particularly if a period's discursive organization is to be mapped" (1992: 126). Staiger includes "literary and dramatic fictions, as well as historical, political, scientific and pseudoscientific discourses" in the array of extra-filmic materials that, she argues, contribute to the construction of what Jauss terms a "horizon of expectation" ([1982] 2000: 131) for the film text, although in practice Staiger's use of extra-filmic materials to position the movies she discusses tends to focus more closely on film related or audience related materials than the wide trawl of contemporary cultural artefacts I have undertaken in this book and would advocate as a means for producing reliable historical research into films.

Staiger's deployment of Jauss's concept, "horizon of expectation" helpfully returns our focus to the central issue of the importance of genre in understanding films historically and allows us to see two separable generic dimensions that operate in the historical meaning making process that positions the popular films examined in this book firmly in their time and place. Film genre study has traditionally understood genre in terms of affiliations or similarities between films, the patterns of the genre providing the "horizon of expectation" for individual genre films; the genre itself supplying the necessary verisimilitude to each film within its corpus of works. This is the formal, diachronic operation of genre, the function that permits later generations of film viewers to engage with the particular internal "regime of verisimilitude" (Cobley, 2000: 20) of the genre: viewers today need not have knowledge of American politics or society in the early 1950s—of the cold war, McCarthyism or Alger Hiss etc.—to enjoy *Invasion of the Body Snatchers* (Seigel 1956 USA) as a Sci Fi movie. The rules of the genre—its "regime of verisimilitude" and "horizon of expectation"—are sufficiently well known that this movie is unlikely to appear as a bizarre historical oddity to today's viewer, who might even recognize thematic connections—concerns about human individualism, power over the body and the location of self-consciousness—between the film and more recent examples of the genre, such as *The Matrix* (Wachowski Brothers 1999 USA). But alongside this diachronic "horizon of expectation" provided by generic taxonomy, another equally important intertextual, synchronic "horizon of expectation" exists between films and the historical discourses instantiated in a broad range of cultural productions of their time; beside the unity of the film genre lie the historical unities of genres of discourse in which films also participate, and it is these contemporary intertextual unities that connect films to the particularity of their historical moment.[1]

Thus, for example, as this book has demonstrated, films with such diverse generic affinities as *Notorious* (romance, thriller, film noir?[2]), *Saratoga Trunk* (western, melodrama, romance), *Margie* (romance, comedy), *Blue Skies* (musical, romance), *The Big Sleep* (melodrama, romance, crime film, film noir[3]) and *The Blue Dahlia* (melodrama, crime film, film noir) are united by their deployment of the figure of the absent father, and are linked by this figure to a contemporary discourse enunciated across a wide range of sites within the culture, including (apart from the films themselves) Benjamin Spock's *Baby and Child Care*, Danziger's autobiographical articles for the *New York Times Magazine* and *Parents* magazine(1944a, 1944b), articles concerning juvenile delinquency and a range of journal articles and books relating to veterans' readjustment (e.g. Waller 1944) and/or the impact of the war on family life (Baber 1943; Overton 1945). Similarly, *Best Years of Our Lives* (prestige film, social problem film), *Two Years Before the Mast* (adventure movie, melodrama), *Saratoga Trunk* (melodrama, romance, western), *The Razor's Edge* (melodrama), *Blue Skies* (musical, romance), *Boomerang!* (social problem film) and *The Strange Love of Martha Ivers* (crime film, film noir, romance) have all been shown to have concern with America's image of itself as a classless, egalitarian democracy. And while it is true that a pessimistic, disaffected tone can be detected in those films in this group (*Boomerang!*, *The Strange Love of Martha Ivers*) that have the strongest generic affinity to that small set of films that critics—including Houseman (1947), Schatz (1981, 1999), Crowther (1988), Selby (1984), Harvey, (1998) and Belton (1994) among others—have approached as *the* film genre that most clearly resonates in tune with the wider social anxieties of the early postwar period, the same cannot be said for the majority of these films, which display a much more affirmative attitude toward these key American values (an attitude that is ultimately evident even in *Boomerang!*). And in the contradictory attitudes towards these values, evident in this group of films, begins to emerge a more complete and more materially grounded impression of an early postwar cultural milieu that was itself complicated and contradictory; an impression that challenges the commonsensical claims about the zeitgeist of that moment, which have dominated much of the film scholarship about the period.

The scope of this study has been extremely limited, looking at a small number of the most popular films, mostly released in one year just after the end of the Second World War, and as wide a range of other contemporary published materials as financial and time constraints on the research have allowed to be discovered. There is undoubtedly more work that could be done that would add to our understanding of the movies and culture of this fascinating period of American history. But the peculiar characteristics of the period examined allow the significance of the conclusions of this study to extend beyond its empirical basis to present a more general method for approaching the analysis of films; a method that is more likely than abstract theoretical approaches to movies and movie genres to produce reliable impressions of the historical significance of films and, because of its attention to the contemporary discursive horizons of expectation that surrounded the films, also to allow more reasonable speculations as to the meanings that attached to films in their original context.

I have attempted, in this book, to present a fresh impression of American films and culture as American society moved through a brief period that witnessed the seismic shift from war to peace. In examining primarily a set of popular films, among which are movies that have never been considered deserving of critical attention by film scholarship that has, explicitly or otherwise, reserved the right to critical attention to those films deemed to display sufficiently high aesthetic values, I have tried to avoid giving in to an iconoclastic impulse to decry the significance of the less popular "tough" films in order to insist on the greater significance of the popular films. As I have argued, attention to both groups of films is necessary in order to gain the fullest possible impression of the movie culture of this complicated and contradictory period. One of the gains of the approach I have adopted in this book, however, has been the opportunity to "rediscover" some of these critically neglected but historically interesting movies. Some, I will freely admit, are not films I would have chosen to study. Apart from a few good songs, *Till the Clouds Roll By* and *Night and Day* would not have passed my own test of aesthetic value, had I been choosing which films should be included in this study rather than allowing this to be determined on the basis of financial success. *Easy to Wed* lacks even the good songs. Yet when these films are considered in their wider historical context, their clear participation in key contemporary discourses makes it hard to deny the necessity of including them in a study of this type. Other films in the group—*Saratoga Trunk*, *Two Years Before the Mast* and *The Green Years* in particular—are true cinematic gems that are deserving of far more detailed attention than it is has been possible to give to them in this book. Hopefully, if this book achieves nothing else, it will at least reawaken film scholars' awareness of these films and signal that these and numerous other now forgotten but once popular films are a rich source of information about the movies and culture of the past.

Problems with "the popular"

While there are undoubtedly gains to be made through the study of the most popular films of a period, the invocation of "the popular" raises a number of problems of its own. In this book I have used several sources of financial information to produce a list of films that earned the highest revenues in 1946. Implicit in my adoption of rental revenues as a measure of popularity is an assumption that those films that earned the highest amounts were those that were seen by the greatest number of people and, therefore, enjoyed the greatest exposure to the cinema-going public at the time. However, due to the complexities of the system of theatrical exhibition in America at the time in question and to differences in the ways rentals were calculated for different classes of films, determining the quantitative popularity of movies (i.e. which films were seen by the greatest number of people) may not be quite this straightforward.

Two terms are commonly employed to talk about the amount of money earned by a film: grosses and rentals. Grosses refer to the amount of money received by movie exhibitors at the box office, rentals refer to the amount of money paid by exhibitors to film studios as payment for showing their films. While grosses provide a reliable indication of the size of the audience for a particular film, the same is not necessarily true of rentals, because the system under which rentals were calculated operated in different ways for different classes of film. Naremore gives brief account of this system, which illustrates how the distinction between 'A' and 'B' pictures is a crucial factor determining the reliability of rental figures as an index of popularity. Under this system, 'A' movies were rented on a percentage basis, with the producer/distributors of the film sometimes receiving as much as 80% of the gross amount received by exhibitors at the box office, according to Naremore's account. 'B' movies, on the other hand, were rented on the basis of a flat fee of $100 or $200 (1998: 140)[4]. It is easy to see, therefore, that several variables within this system limit the ability to predict the number of people that paid to see a movie on the basis of the rental revenue achieved by the film. The existence of variable percentage rates for 'A' movies makes comparison between movies impossible without knowledge of the exact rates applicable to different movies and so rental revenue figures for a group of 'A' movies can only be regarded as a very approximate guide to the relative popularity of those films. So far as gaining a sense of the size of the audience for a 'B' movie or making assessments of the relative sizes of audiences for 'A' and 'B' films are concerned, rental revenue figures are of no use since although rentals for 'A' movies do bear some relationship to the size of the audiences for the films the same is not true of 'B' films, because of the flat rate rentals that were charged for these films.[5] Faced with an absence of information that would clearly indicate the size of audiences for different films it is tempting to simply assume that audiences' viewing patterns would have roughly conformed to the financial picture painted by the available rental revenue figures. And there may be some merit in this approach; film studios devoted considerable resources to the marketing of their prestige 'A' grade product and this may have been highly effective in securing the largest audiences for those movies.

The anecdotal account that Naremore provides of his own experiences of watching films noirs in his local "neighbourhood" cinema during the 1950s (1998: 2) does, however, raise a question about whether such an assumption is valid. It is possible that these neighbourhood theatres were, in reality, the most regularly-attended movie venue for most people, with the more expensive first and second run venues being reserved for special occasions. If so then it is also possible that the average of 90 million weekly cinema admissions in 1946 (Schatz 1999: 462) were not evenly distributed between different types of cinemas. This makes it possible that proportionally more of the kinds of films shown in neighbourhood theatres may have been seen by a greater number of people, even though these films could never have attracted anything close to the rental revenues of the movie companies' prestige, first run, 'A' productions. Figures relating to 1945 reported by Gomery reveal that there was an almost even distribution of cinema seats between the 1,728 largest cinemas (those with a capacity in excess of 1,200 seats), which contained 30.3 per cent of all cinema seats, and the 10,818 smallest (those with a capacity up to 500 seats), which contained 30 per cent of available seats, with the remaining 41.7 per cent of seats being in intermediate cinemas with a capacity between 500 and 1,200 (1986: 13). However, this breakdown of the seating capacity of American movie houses is of little assistance in determining how many people actually saw particular grades of film, since this only indicates the size of the potential audience for any given class of cinema, not whether available seats were actually occupied.[6] Schatz's observation that in 1943 there was a surge in attendance at downtown, first run cinemas, to the detriment of attendance at neighbourhood cinemas, points to the possibility the films with the highest rental revenues, the prestige 'A' productions, may actually have also been seen by the greatest number of people (1999: 151-152). On the other hand, Schatz also notes reports in the *Wall Street Journal* in 1947 that neighbourhood cinemas were beginning to attract larger numbers of people than the large, downtown movie houses (294). This is supported by a Gallup study conducted in 1949 which noted a decline in the audience for 'A' product from 16 million in 1946 to 13 million in 1948 (cited in Schatz 1999: 294).

Determining the size and demographic make up of the audience for Hollywood's films was a matter of considerable interest to the film industry during the 1940s and it is possible to gain a sense of the scope of the research being conducted at the time from Handel's useful summary of contemporary audience research (1950). Handel's summary of research examining audience preferences for different types of story in films provides some support to one of my main conclusions in this book; that the significance of film noir has been over-rated by film studies and that contemporary audiences were more strongly drawn to other kinds of film. Handel's work is also instructive in relation to some of the assumptions that have underpinned much of the research on genre in film studies, since Handel rates story type as a much less important factor in determining audience approval for a particular film than is implicit in the focus on film genre. Handel notes that story type "ranks second to the cast in drawing power" (1950: 118) but elaborates on this conclusion, indicating, "it has been found repeatedly that it is the *particular story* rather than the *story type* which determines the interest" (119 my emphasis). Indeed, a large number of moviegoers seemed to be largely indifferent to the type of story: "they like any kind of story or type of story as long as it is made into a good motion picture" (119). This lack of audience concern about story type may be indicative of a more general indifference, among cinema audiences in the 1940s, to the films that were shown in cinemas of all classes. It is a frequently acknowledged but rarely examined truth that films are only one element in the experience of cinemagoing, but Handel's report of a study he conducted in 1941 for the Motion Picture Research Bureau, which indicated that 49 per cent of respondents had last gone to the movies because they just wanted to see any picture rather than out of their interest in a particular film or type of film (152-153) certainly suggests that studies of films and film genres need to be undertaken alongside investigations into the totality of the moviegoing experience if a sense of the cultural importance of film and cinema is to be gained.

Despite the apparent indifference of many cinemagoers to the films they went to see, where preferences for particular types of films are indicated in Handel's study, these do appear to confirm the existence of a predisposition among movie audiences in the 1940s for the types of films that I am suggesting constituted "the popular" in movies at the time. Handel's survey of two thousand respondents in forty-five towns conducted in 1942 indicates musical comedies as the most liked type of film (12.4 per cent of male and female respondents) followed by romances or love stories (11.6 per cent, with a significant disparity between male and female respondents—few men liked these films but this was the most liked type of film for female respondents and the high total figure results from the high number of women expressing a preference for these films) and, unsurprisingly, war pictures (11.2 per cent with the gender disparity noted for romances reversed—men liked these films much more than women). In contrast, the film types that may have included some of the films now classified as films noirs were not widely favoured. Gangster and G-men pictures were liked by only 3.8 per cent of the respondents and disliked by 9.3 per cent; "socially significant pictures" were liked by 2.1 per cent and disliked by 3.0 per cent. While this is undoubtedly an imprecise gauge of the tastes of moviegoers in the war and early postwar period, it does provide corroborative evidence to support the conclusions of my study of the popular films of the time and does further problematize the claim that films noirs represent the most emblematic films of the period. There is, however, much that still remains unclear about the movie culture of the period.

A further problem that inevitably follows the sort of approach to popularity I have adopted in this study arises from its tendency to produce a homogenized impression of tastes for particular types of films across the nation. As an article first published in *Fortune* magazine in 1948—*What's Playing at the Grove*, (reprinted in Waller 2002: 203-210) —indicates, these hypothetical national tastes may not have very accurately reflected regional variations. The article focuses on a 390 seat independent cinema near the centre of Galesburg, Illinois and gives a brief summary of the performance of some of the films that had been showing in the previous year. The article notes that while a film that does not feature in my list of popular films, *Anna and the King of Siam* (Cromwell 1946 USA), "did an outstanding business" (Waller 2002: 207), the same is not true of one of the films that does feature in my list; "*The Kid From Brooklyn* did only fair" (207). However, "*The Best Years of Our Lives* (second run) ran at advanced prices and we had over 300 adults the first night" while "*The Big Sleep* was no good" (207), which is consistent with the relative popularity I attribute to these two movies.

The available data does not produce a very clear picture of the tastes of 1940s audiences for particular types of films nor permit anything other than tentative conclusions to be drawn about the validity of using rental revenues as an index of the popularity of particular films. The problems inherent in this approach could be overcome by using the gross revenue for a film (the actual amount of money received by exhibitors at the box office) instead of the rental revenue (the amount paid by exhibitors to the producers and distributors of a film) as an index of its popularity. However, Thumim notes the difficulty she encountered locating a simple source of such figures in the British context (1992: 17) and similar problems have been encountered in relation to the American setting in the research for this book. Despite the importance of market research within Hollywood from the 1920s on, and the employment of the sophisticated research techniques developed by George H. Gallup and his Audience Research Institute (later Audience Research Inc.) from about 1940 on (see Schatz 1999: 68-72 on the growing importance of audience research and Handel 1950 for an example of the use of some of this data), industry publications are notably lacking in annual assessments of which films earned the highest *grosses* (as opposed to rentals) at the box office.

The lack of clear data about the size of the audience for different films and the patterns of audience attendance at various classes of cinema highlights the need for further research in this area. This research, drawing on archive materials—local newspapers, trade journals etc.—would be able to provide a better impression of what types of films were showing at different classes of cinemas, while any financial records that can be discovered for a some of those cinemas would provide valuable insights into the sizes of audiences for different kinds of films and at cinemas of different types. There are useful precedents for studies of this kind in the British context in the recent work of Jancovich, Faire and Stubbings, which paints a vivid and detailed picture of the patterns and meanings of film consumption within a well defined, localized setting. While studies of this type may lack the overarching, national scope of earlier histories of cinema exhibition such as those presented by Gomery, the sort of painstaking attention to the empirically available details of movie consumption within a limited and clearly defined setting that this research would entail could provide a much clearer impression of the patterns of consumption of films and provide a greater understanding of which films could best lay claim to the label "popular" in earlier periods.

Notes

Chapter 1 Introduction: Movies, Genre and Zeitgeist

[1] For my purposes at this point it matters little whether film noir is understood as a genre, a series or a cycle. I refer to film noir as a genre solely for convenience, not as an intervention in the debate about its status.

[2] See, for example, Maltby (1992), Krutnik (1991) and Neve (1992).

[3] An evaluation with which other critics apparently concurred. Manny Farber called the film a "horse-drawn truckload of liberal schmaltz" (1998: 15).

[4] There are frequent minor differences between the revenue figures cited by the three sources used in compiling this list. In general I attach no importance to these variations, but it is worth noting that the figure quoted by *Variety* (1955) for *Ziegfeld Follies* is $4.0m.

[5] Lyon (1989: 210-211). *Variety* gives a figure of $3.3m (1947: 63).

[6] The categories were: Performance by an actor in a leading role - James Stewart; Achievement in directing - Frank Capra; Achievement in film editing; Best picture of 1946; Sound Recording.

[7] Lyon (1989: 210-211).

[8] The categories were: Achievement in directing - Robert Siodmak; Achievement in editing; Achievement in writing (screenplay); Music.

[9] Writing (Original Screenplay) - Raymond Chandler.

[10] *The Strange Love of Martha Ivers* was the only film among the higher earning films noirs of 1946 to be nominated for an Academy Award, for Writing (Original Motion Picture Story).

[11] The precision of these figures may be questionable. Neither *Gilda* nor *The Strange Love of Martha Ivers* appears in the list of All-Time Top Grossers published by *Variety* in 1955 although the basis for inclusion in that list was domestic rentals in excess of $4 million.

Chapter 2 Re-invigorating the nation: popular films and American national identity

[1] There are numerous accounts of the history and activities of HUAC, see Kovel for example (1997).

[2] It would be inaccurate to call the film and adaptation of the book since, apart from providing names for some members of the crew and describing the hard life of merchant sailors voyaging from Boston to California, the film bears little resemblance to the book. The film's central narrative device—having the son of the ship's owner press-ganged into service—does not feature in the book. Charles's character and the narrative events that involve him are entirely creations of the film (see R.H. Dana, *Two Years Before the Mast*, publication date not specified).

[3] Contemporary critics acknowledged the lack of narrative motivation for this relationship. Bosley Crowther described it as a "phoney shipboard romance" (*New York Times* 25 September 1946: 39) while *Variety* called it "the film's only major fault" (28 August 1946).

[4] First published in *Commentary* in 1949.

[5] This performance of the role of a mulatto servant by a white English actress wearing blackface make-up deserves far more detailed consideration than I am able to give it here.

Chapter 3 The troubled postwar family: "moms" and absent fathers

[1] In this respect the finished film represents a considerable toning down of this aspect of Alicia's character from the "outright whore and drunkard" which Schatz notes in early versions of the screenplay (1998: 394).

[2] In 1954 *Life* Magazine published a humorous article entitled *The New American Domesticated Male* (4 January 1954: 42-45) and much of the debate concerning a "crisis of masculinity" during the 1950s is founded on the assumption that the increasing domesticity of men during that decade was accompanied by a concomitant decline in manliness.

[3] Michael Rogin (1984) provides an account of Wylie's celebrity as a writer in popular magazines. This exceptional influence, as well as the book's own best-

seller status, may explain the unusual importance attached to *Generation of Vipers* in the development of discourses on momism.

[4] A.J. Cronin's novel ([1944] 1949), on which the film was based, includes the fashioning of an inappropriately coloured suit from one of the great grandmother's petticoats but differs from the film in two significant respects. While the film emphasizes the rather striking image of the great grandmother removing successive layers of petticoats that she is wearing at the time in order to find a suitable fabric, the book merely refers to Grandma Leckie rummaging in her cupboard for a petticoat to use as material for the suit. Secondly, in the book, the burning of the suit is not accompanied by a new assertiveness on Robert's part and he continues to share Grandma Leckie's bed for a time after this incident. These differences between the book and film do seem to reveal the latter's greater preoccupation with momism.

Chapter 4 Performing postwar masculinities

[1] Morgan (1994) and Bourke (1999) provide vivid accounts of the role of military training as a means of producing the "soldier" as a distinct masculine type.

[2] In much the same way as Cohan (1993a) argues that the top hat and cane become so closely associated with Fred Astaire that the use of representations of these items alone came to connote Astaire, representations of a black face and white gloves become readily recognizable signifiers of Jolson.

[3] This feature of the performance deserves more attention than I am able to give it here. The adoption of this gait to signify the Chinese ethnicity of the character would seem to have a rather curious motivation, recalling western mental associations between the East and the practice of foot binding. However, since this practice was associated with women, its adoption by Astaire in the construction of a male Chinese character is perplexing. Possibly it is simply a general signifier of oriental-ness (albeit an illogical one). On the other hand the possibility that there are connotations of feminization of Astaire's diegetic character either resulting from the characters status as oriental (other) or from Astaire's position as the object of spectacle deserves further consideration.

Chapter 5 Military service and male companionship

[1] A reference to Crosby's appeal to an older female audience rather than the "bobbysoxers", a common stereotype of teenage women at the time, particularly fans of the younger Frank Sinatra. The insult contained in this line is its

suggestion of Crosby's own advancing age and his diminishing appeal for the younger audience. The sentiment is echoed elsewhere in the film in Hope's line "next time I'm gonna bring Sinatra".

[2] This rhetoric of automobile advertising is by no means a product of later times. Advertisements for Chrysler's "Airflow", during the 1930s emphasised its streamlined appearance and the pleasures of driving: "Journey's End — and you're ready for more" (see advertisement reproduced by Maltby ed. 1989: 93)

Chapter 6 Popular films and "tough" movies

[1] The repeated references to jazz as 'monkey music' by Buzz Wanchek (William Bendix) in *The Blue Dahlia* also supports this argument.
[2] James Naremore has also commented on the similarities between *The Blue Dahlia* and *The Best Years of Our Lives* (1998: 109).

Chapter 7 Genre and History

[1] This aspect also allows films to be re-inscribed in different discursive contexts, and so to take on different meanings at different historical times. To use the example of *Invasion of the Body Snatchers*, it may be speculative, but it is hardly unreasonable to suppose that a viewer encountering this movie for the first time in 2004, having no sense of the original historical location of the film, might interpret the film in the context of current media and political rhetoric concerning the so-called "war against terror" rather than the cold war, which would have provided a discursive horizon of expectation for the film's earliest audiences.

[2] Borde and Chaumeton ([1955] 2002) list the film as one of the major films noirs of 1946.

[3] Again, Borde and Chaumeton ([1955] 2002) so define the film.

[4] Other commentators provide different percentage figures. Izod puts the percentage figure for rentals at around 30 per cent before the 1948 divorcement of production from exhibition interests, rising to around 36 per cent for most films by the mid 1950s, with exceptionally popular films able to achieve between 50 and 70 per cent (1988: 124). Handel puts the percentage figure for most pictures at between 20 and 40 per cent of the box office take during the 1940s but notes that some pictures were sold under "special" arrangements where the rentals could exceed 40 per cent (1950: 7).

[5] Additionally, as Handel notes, "in the case of double features ... it is difficult to determine accurately the revenues for each attraction" (1950: 8).

[6] The situation is complicated further by the common exhibition practice at the time of allowing audience members to enter and leave the auditorium at any time irrespective of the start and end times of films, so that even gross box office receipts for a show would only provide an approximate guide to how many people actually saw a particular film included in that show (see Naremore 1998: 2; Williams 2000: 362-367).

Bibliography

Adams, S.H. *The Harvey Girls*. New York: Dell, 1946.

Agee, J. *Agee on Film: Essays and Reviews by James Agee*. Vol. 1. New York: Grossett and Dunlap, 1969.

Allen, F.L. *The Big Change 1900-1950: America Transforms Itself*. New York: Harper and Row, 1952.

Allen, R.C., and D. Gomery. *Film History: Theory and Practice*. New York, St. Louis, San Francisco, Auckland, Bogota, Caracas, Lisbon, London, Madrid, Mexico, Milan, Montreal, New Delhi, Paris, San Juan, Singapore, Sydney, Tokyo, Toronto: McGraw Hill, 1985.

Altman, R. *The American Film Musical*. London: BFI Publishing, 1987.

———. *Film/Genre*. London: BFI Publishing, 1999.

Alvarado, M., E. Buscombe, and R. Collins, eds. *The Screen Education Reader*. Basingstoke and London: Macmillan, 1993.

Anderson, P.R. "National Security in the Postwar World." *Annals of the American Academy of Political and Social Science*, no. 241 September (1945): 1-7.

Asheim, L. "The Film and the Zeitgeist." *Hollywood Quarterly* 11, no. 4, July 1947: 414-16.

Baber, R.E. "Marriage and the Family after the War." *Annals of the American Academy of Political and Social Science* September 1943 (1943): 164-75.

Babington, B., and T. Evans. *Blue Skies and Silver Linings: Aspects of the Hollywood Musical*. Manchester and Dover, New Hampshire: Manchester University Press, 1985.

Barker, M. "News, Reviews, Clues, Interviews and Other Ancillary Materials - a Critique and Research Proposal." *Scope: an online journal of film studies* February 2004 (2004).

Barthes, R. *S/Z*. London: Basil Blackwell, 1990.

Belton, J. *American Cinema/American Culture*. New York, St. Louis, San Francisco, Auckland, Bogota, Caracas, Lisbon, London, Madrid, Mexico, Milan, Montreal, New Delhi, Paris, San Juan, Singapore, Sydney, Tokyo, Toronto: McGraw-Hill,

1994.

———. *Movies and Mass Culture*. London: Athlone Press, 1996.

———. "American Cinema and Film History." In *American Cinema and Hollywood: Critical Approaches*, edited by J. Hill and P. Church-Gibson, 1-11. Oxford and New York: Oxford University Press, 2000.

Bennett, T. "Text and Social Process: The Case of James Bond." *Screen Education* 41(1982): 3-14.

Bennett, T., and J. Woollacott. *Bond and Beyond: The Politcal Career of a Popular Hero*. London: Macmillan, 1987.

Bingham, D. *Acting Male: Masculinities in the Films of James Stewart, Jack Nicholson and Clint Eastwood*. New Brunswick: Rutgers University Press, 1994.

Blake, R.A. *Screening America: Reflections on Five Classic Films*. New York and Mahwah: Paulist Press, 1991.

Bolte, C.G. "The New Veteran." *Life*, 10 December 1945, 57-66.

Boone, J.A., and M. Cadden, eds. *Engendering Men: The Question of Male Feminist Criticism*. London and New York: Routledge, 1990.

Borde, R., and E. Chaumeton. *A Panorama of American Film Noir 1941-1953*. San Francisco: City Lights Books, [1955] 2002.

Bordman, G. *Jerome Kern: His Life and Music*. Oxford and New York: Oxford University Press, 1980.

Bordwell, D. *Narration in the Fiction Film*. London: Routledge, 1986.

———. *Making Meaning: Inference and Rhetoric in the Interpretation of Cinema*. Cambridge, Massachussetts and London: Harvard University Press, 1991.

———. *On the History of Film Style*. Cambridge, Massachussetts and London: Harvard University Press, 1997.

Bordwell, D., and N. Carroll, eds. *Post-Theory: Reconstructing Film Studies*. Madison and London: University of Wisconsin Press, 1996.

Bordwell, D., J. Staiger, and K. Thompson, eds. *The Classical Hollywood Cinema: Film Style and Mode of Production to 1960*. London, Melbourne and Henley: Routledge and Kegan Paul, 1985.

Bourke, J. *An Intimate History of Killing: Face-to-Face Killing in Twentieth-Century Warfare*. London: Granta, 1999.

Brogan, D.W. *The American Character*. New York: Vintage, 1956.

Browne, N. *Refiguring American Film Genres: Theory and History*. Berkeley,

Los Angeles and London: University of California Press, 1998.

Buchsbaum, J. "Tame Wolves and Phoney Claims." In *The Movie Book of Film Noir*, edited by I Cameron, 88-97. London: Studio Vista, 1992.

Burgoyne, R. "National Identity, Gender Identity, and the 'Rescue Fantasy' in Born on the Fourth of July." *Screen* 35, no. 3 Autumn (1994): 211-34.

———. *Film Nation: Hollywood Looks at U.S. History*. Minneapolis and London: University of Minnesota Press, 1997.

Butler, J. *Gender Trouble: Feminism and the Subversion of Identity*. London and New York: Routledge, 1990.

Butsch, R. *The Making of American Audiences: From Stage to Television, 1750-1990*. Cambridge, New York, Melbourne and Madrid: Cambridge University Press, 2000.

Butterfield, R. "Van Johnson." *Life*, 5 November 1945, 114-22 & 25.

Byars, J. *All That Hollywood Allows: Re-Reading Gender in 1950s Melodrama*. Chapel Hill: University of North Carolina Press, 1991.

Cameron, I, ed. *The Movie Book of Film Noir*. London: Studio Vista, 1992.

Cameron, K.M. *America on Film: Hollywood and American History*. New York: Continuum, 1997.

Cardullo, B., ed. *Bazin at Work: Major Essays and Reviews from the Forties and Fifties*. London and New York: Routledge, 1997.

Carr, E.H. *What Is History*. London and Basingstoke: Macmillan, 1961.

Carroll, N. "Prospects for Film Theory: A Personal Assessment." In *Post-Theory: Reconstructing Film Studies*, edited by D. Bordwell and N. Carroll. Madison and London: University of Wisconsin Press, 1996.

Cassirer, E. *Language and Myth*. New York: Dover Publications, 1953.

Cawelti, J. *The Six-Gun Mystique*. Bowling Green, Ohio: Bowling Green State University Popular Press, 1984.

Chambers, J.W., and D. Culbert, eds. *World War II: Film and History*. New York and Oxford: Oxford University Press, 1996.

Chapman, R., and J. Rutherford, eds. *Male Order: Unwrapping Masculinity*. London: Lawrence and Wishart, 1988.

Cherne, L. "The Army Changes Men." *Colliers*, 27 May 1944, 23 & 69.

Christopher, N. *Somewhere in the Night: Film Noir and the American City.* New York: Free Press, 1997.

Clare, Anthony. *On Men: Masculinity in Crisis.* London: Arrow Books, 2001.

Cobley, P. *The American Thriller: Generic Innovation and Social Change in the 1970s.* Basingstoke and New York: Palgrave, 2000.

Cohan, S. *Masked Men: Masculinity and the Movies in the Fifties.* Bloomington and Indianapolis: Indiana University Press, 1997.

————. "Masquerading as the American Male in the Fifties: Picnic. William Holden and the Spectacle of Masculinity in Hollywood Film." In *Male Trouble*, edited by C. Penley and S. Willis, 203-32. Minneapolis and London: University of Minnesota Press, 1993.

————. "Feminizing the Song and Dance Man: Fred Astaire and the Spectacle of Masculinity in the Hollywood Musical." In *Screening the Male: Exploring Masculinities in Hollywood Cinema*, edited by S. Cohan and I.R. Hark, 46-69. London and New York: Routledge, 1993.

Cohan, S., and I.R. Hark. *Screening the Male: Exploring Masculinities in Hollywood Cinema.* London and New York: Routledge, 1993.

Comolli, J.L., and J. Narboni. "Cinema/Ideology/Criticism." In *Film Theory and Criticism: Introductory Readings*, edited by L. Braudy and M. Cohen, 752-59. Oxford and New York: Oxford University Press, 1999.

Cook, P., ed. *The Cinema Book.* London: BFI Publishing, 1985.

Cook, P., and P. Dodd, eds. *Women and Film: A Sight and Sound Reader.* London: Scarlet Press, 1993.

Copjec, J., ed. *Shades of Noir.* London: Verso, 1993.

Corbett, K. J. "Empty Seats: The Missing History of Movie Watching." *Journal of Film and Video* 50, no. 4 Winter 1998-1999 (1999): 34-48.

Costello, J. *Love Sex and War: Changing Values 1939-45.* London, Glasgow, Sydney, Auckland, Toronto, Johannesburg: Collins, 1985.

Couldry, N. *Inside Culture: Re-Imagining the Method of Cultural Studies.* London, Thousand Oaks, New Delhi: Sage, 2000.

Cowie, E. "Film Noir and Women." In *Shades of Noir*, edited by J. Copjec. London: Verso, 1993.

Coyne, M. *The Crowded Prairie: American National Identity in the Hollywood Western*. London and New York: I. B. Tauris, 1997.

Cranston, M.W. "The Modern Woman's Place in the Home." *Atlantic Monthly*, July 1946, 106-08.

Cripps, T. *Hollywood's High Noon: Moviemaking and Society before Television*. Baltimore and London: Johns Hopkins University Press, 1997.

Cronin, A.J. *The Green Years*. London: Victor Gollancz, [1944] 1949.

Crowther, B. "Review of *Leave Her to Heaven*." *New York Times*, 26 December 1945, 15.

———. "'Spellbound,' a Psychological Hit Starring Ingrid Bergman and Gregory Peck, Opens at Astor - Hitchcock Director." *New York Times*, 2 November 1945, 22.

———. *Film Noir: Reflections in a Dark Mirror*. London: Columbus Books, 1988.

———. "'Two Years before the Mast,' in Which Alan Ladd Turns up as Hero, Opens at Rivoli—Donlevy, Bendix Also in Cast." *New York Times*, 25 September 1946, 39.

Crowther, B. "'the Blue Dahlia,' at Paramount, with Alan Ladd and Veronica Lake in the Leading Roles, Proves an Exciting Picture." *New York Times*, 9 May 1946, 27.

———. "Review of *Crossfire*." *New York Times*, 23 July 1947, 19.

———. "The 'Ten Best'." *New York Times*, 29 December 1946, 1.

———. "'Notorious,' Hitchcock Thriller Starring Ingrid Bergman and Cary Grant, Opens at Radio City—Claude Rains Featured." *New York Times*, 16 August 1946, 19.

———. "Review of *the Yearling*." *New York Times*, 24 January 1947, 18.

———. "'Till Clouds Roll by,' Musical Biography of Life of Jerome Kern with Robert Walker in Title Role, at the Music Hall." *New York Times*, 6 December 1946, 27.

———. "'Razor's Edge,' Fox Film Based on Maugham Novel, Opens at Roxy—Tyrone Power, Gene Tierney, Anne Baxter in Cast." *New York Times*, 20 November 1946, 42.

———. "Review of *Best Years of Our Lives*." *New York Times*, 22 November 1946, 27.

———. "'Jolson Story,' Depicting the Trouper's Career, in Which Larry Parks Has the Leading Role, Is Seen at Music Hall." *New York Times*, 11 October 1946, 28.

———. "'Easy to Wed,' Second Edition of 'Libeled Lady,' with Keenan Wynn, Lucille Ball, Offers Flow of Fun at the

Capital." *New York Times*, 12 July 1946, 14.

Crowther, B. "Review of *the Green Years*." *New York Times*, 5 April 1946, 21.

———. "Review of *Ziegfeld Follies*." *New York Times*, 23 March 1946, 8.

———. "Crosby, Hope and Lamour Take 'Road to Utopia,' New Film at the Paramount, and Come up with Lightening-Like Gags." *New York Times*, 28 February 1946, 20.

———. "'Blue Skies,' with Bing Crosby and Fred Astaire, Displayed in a Highly Entertaining Fashion at the Paramount." *New York Times*, 17 October 1946, 28.

———. " 'The Harvey Girls,' Opens at Capitol—Musical Stars Judy Garland, Kenny Baker, Ray Bolger and Virginia O'brien." *New York Times*, 25 January 1946, 26.

———. "Review of *Saratoga Trunk*." *New York Times*, 22 November 1945, 39.

———. "Review of *Boomerang!*" *New York Times*, 6 March 1947, 36.

———. "Review of *Gilda*." *New York Times*, 15 March 1946, 27.

———. "'The Postman Always Rings Twice,' with Lana Turner in a Star Role, Makes Its Appearance at the Capitol." *New York Times*, 3 May 1946, 15.

———. "Review of *the Strange Love of Martha Ivers*." *New York Times*, 25 July 1946, 18.

Cyrus, D.D. "What's Wrong with the Family." *Atlantic Monthly*, November 1946, 67-73.

Damico, J. "Film Noir: A Modest Proposal." In *Perspectives on Noir*, edited by R.B. Palmer. London, Mexico City, New Delhi, Singapore, Sydney, Toronto: Prentice Hall International, 1996.

Dana, R.H. *Two Years before the Mast*. London and Glasgow: Blackie, Undated.

Danziger, J. "Life without Father." *New York Times Magazine*, 7 May 1944, 16 & 47.

———. "Daddy Comes Home on Leave." *Parents*, October 1944, 29, 70, 72 & 78.

Davies, P., and B. Neve, eds. *Cinema, Politics and Society in America*. Manchester: Manchester University Press, 1981.

deBedts, R.F. *Recent American History: Vol - 1933 through World War 2*. Homewood, London, Georgetown: Dorsey, 1973.

Deming, B. *Running Away from Myself: A Dream Portrait of America Drawn from Films of the Forties*. New York: Grossman Publishers, 1969.

Deutschman, P. "Second-Class Citizens." *Life*, 25 February 1946, 114.

Dick, B.F. "Hitchcock's Terrible Mothers." *Literature/Film Quarterly* 28, no. 4(2000): 238-49.

Doherty, T. *Projections of War: Hollywood, American Culture and World War Ii*. New York: Columbia University Press, 1993.

Durgnat, R. "Paint It Black: The Family Tree of Film Noir." In *Perspectives on Noir*, edited by R.B. Palmer. London, Mexico City, New Delhi, Singapore, Sydney, Toronto: Prentice Hall International, 1996.

Dyer, R., ed. *The Matter of Images: Essays on Representations*. London and New York: Routledge, 1993.

————. *Stars*. London: BFI Publishing, 1998.

Ehrenreich, B. *The Hearts of Men: American Dreams and the Flight from Commitment*. London: Pluto Press, 1983.

Farber, M. *Negative Space: Manny Farber on the Movies*. Expanded ed. New York: Da Capo Press, 1998.

Ferber, E. *Saratoga Trunk*. New York: Perennial Classics, 2000.

Feuer, J. *The Hollywood Musical*. London: BFI Publishing, 1982.

Filene, P. *Him/Her/Self: Gender Identities in Modern America*. 3rd ed. Baltimore and London: Johns Hopkins University Press, 1998.

Fischer, L. "Mama's Boy: Filial Hysteria in *White Heat*." In *Screening the Male: Exploring Masculinities in Hollywood Cinema*, edited by S. Cohan and I.R. Hark, 70-84. London and New York: Routledge, 1993.

Fisher, P., ed. *The New American Studies: Essays from Representations*. Berkeley, Los Angeles and London: University of California Press, 1991.

Fitzpatrick, E.A. *Universal Military Training*. New York and London: Whittlesy House, McGraw Hill, 1945.

Fortune. "What's Playing at the Grove?" In *Moviegoing in America: A Sourcebook in the History of Film Exhibition*, edited by G. A. Waller, 203-10. Oxford; Malden, Massachussets: Blackwell, 2002.

Frayling, C. "The American Western and American Society." In *Cinema, Politics and Society in America*, edited by P. Davies and B. Neve, 136-62. Manchester: University of Manchester Press, 1981.

Freedland, M. *Jolson: The Story of Al Jolson*. London: Virgin Books,

1995.

Gathorne-Hardy, J. *Sex, the Measure of All Things: A Life of Alfred C. Kinsey*. London: Chatto and Windus, 1998.

Gehring, W., ed. *Handbook of American Film Genres*. Westport and London: Greenwood Press, 1988.

Geraghty, C. "National Fictions." *Screen* 24, no. 6 November/December (1983): 94-96.

————. "Masculinity." In *National Fictions*, edited by G. Hurd, 63-67. London: BFI Publishing, 1984.

Geraghty, C. *British Cinema in the Fifties: Gender, Genre and the 'New Look'*. London and New York: Routledge, 2000.

Girgus, S.B. *Hollywood Rennaisance: The Cinema of Democracy in the Era of Ford, Capra and Kazan*. Cambridge, New York and Melbourne: Cambridge University Press, 1998.

Gledhill, C. "Pleasurable Negotiations." In *Female Spectators: Looking at Film and Television*, edited by E.D. Pribram, 64-89. London: Verso, 1988.

————, ed. *Stardom: Industry of Desire*. London and New York: Routledge, 1991.

————. "Rethinking Genre." In *Reinventing Film Studies*, edited by C. Gledhill and L. Williams, 221-43. London: Arnold, 2000.

Goffman, E. *The Presentation of Self in Everyday Life*. London: Allen Lane, The Penguin Press, 1969.

Goldman, E.F. *The Crucial Decade—and After: America 1945-1960*. New York: Vintage Books, 1960.

Gomery, D. "Movie Audiences, Urban Geography, and the History of the American Film." *Velvet Light Trap*, no. 19 Spring 1982 (1982): 23-29.

————. *Shared Pleasures: A History of Movie Presentation in the United States*. London: BFI Publishing, 1992.

————. *The Hollywood Studio System*. Basingstoke: BFI/Macmillan, 1986.

Gorer, G. *The Americans: A Study in National Character*. London: The Cresset Press, 1948.

Goulden, J.C. *The Best Years: 1945-1960*. New York: Atheneum Books, 1976.

Graebner, W. *The Age of Doubt: American Thought and Culture in the 1940s*. Boston: Twayne Publishers, 1990.

Griffith, C.R. "The Psychological Adjustment of the Returned

Servicemen and Their Families." *Journal of Home Economics* 36, no. 7 September (1944): 385-89.

Hacker, H.M. "The New Burdens of Masculinity." *Marriage and Family Living* August (1957): 227-33.

Hammett, D. *The Four Great Novels*. London: Picador, 1982.

Handel, L. A. *Hollywood Looks at Its Audience: A Report of Film Audience Research*. Urbana: University of Illinois Press, 1950.

Hark, I.R., ed. *Exhibition: The Film Reader*. London and New York: Routledge, 2002.

Harper, S., and V. Porter. "Cinema Audience Tastes in 1950s Britain." *Journal of Popular British Cinema*, no. 2(1999): 66-82.

Harvey, S. "Woman's Place: The Absent Family of Film Noir." In *Women in Film Noir*, edited by E.A. Kaplan. London: BFI Publishing, 1998.

Held, V. "Gender as an Influence on Cultural Norms Relating to War and the Environment." In *Cultural Norms, War and the Environment*, edited by A.H. Westing. Oxford and New York: Oxford University Press, 1988.

Hershey, L.B. "Procurement of Manpower in American Wars." *Annals of the American Academy of Political and Social Science*, no. 241 September (1945): 15-25.

Highham, C., and J. Greenberg. *Hollywood in the 1940s*. London and New York: A. Zwemmer Limited (USA) and A.S. Barnes and Co. (UK), 1968.

Hiley, N. ""Let's Go to the Pictures": The British Cinema Audience in the 1920s and 1930s." *Journal of Popular British Cinema*, no. 2 1999 (1999): 39-53.

Hill, J., and P. Church-Gibson, eds. *American Cinema and Hollywood*. Oxford and New York: Oxford University Press, 2000.

Houseman, J. "Today's Hero: A Review." *Hollywood Quarterly* II, no. 2, January 1947 (1947): 161-63.

———. "Houseman Replies to Asheim." *Hollywood Quarterly* III, no. 1, Fall 1947 (1947): 89-90.

Howard, K. *Sex Problems of the Returning Soldier*. Manchester: Sydney Pemberton, 1945.

Howard, S. *The Silver Cord*. New York: C. Scribner's Sons, 1927.

Hurd, G., ed. *National Fictions*. London: BFI Publishing, 1984.

Izod, J. *Hollywood and the Box Office*. Basingstoke and London: Macmillan, 1988.

Jackson, M.A. "Uncertain Peace: *The Best Years of Our Lives.*" In *American History/American Film*, edited by J. O'Connor and M.A. Jackson. New York: Ungar Publishing Co., 1988.

Jameson, F. *Postmodernism, or the Cultural Logic of Late Capitalism.* New York: Verso, 1991.

Jancovich, M., L. Faire, and S Stubbings. *The Place of the Audience: Cultural Geographies of Film Consumption.* London: BFI Publishing, 2003.

Jauss, H.R. "Theory of Genres and Medieval Literature." In *Modern Genre Theory*, edited by D. Duff. Harlow: Pearson Education, 2000.

———. *Toward an Aesthetics of Reception.* Minneapolis: University of Minnesota Press, 1982.

Jeffords, S. *Hard Bodies: Hollywood Masculinity in the Reagan Era.* New Brunswick: Rutgers University Press, 1994.

Jones, J. "Finding a Place at the Downtown Picture Palace: The Tampa Theater, Florida." In *Cinema and the City: Film and Urban Societies in a Global Context*, edited by M. Sheil and T. Fitzmaurice, 122-33. Oxford; Malden, Massachussets: Blackwell, 2001.

Ladies Home Journal. "Does War Brutalize Men?" *Ladies Home Journal*, November 1943, 120-21.

Jowett, G. *Film: The Democratic Art.* Boston: Little, Brown., 1976.

Kaminsky, S. *American Film Genres.* Chicago: Nelson Hall, 1985.

Kann, R., ed. *1951-52 International Motion Picture Almanac.* New York: Quigley Publications, 1952.

Kaplan, E.A., ed. *Women in Film Noir.* London: BFI Publishing, 1998.

———, ed. *Psychoanalysis and Cinema.* New York and London: Routledge, 1990.

———. *Looking for the Other: Feminism, Film and the Imperial Gaze.* New York and London: Routledge, 1997.

Kerr, P. "Out of What Past? Notes of the B Film Noir." In *The Hollywood Film Industry: A Reader*, edited by P. Kerr, 220-44. London and New York: Routledge and Kegan Paul, 1986.

———. *The Hollywood Film Industry: A Reader.* London and New York: Routledge and Kegan Paul, 1986.

Kinsey, A.C., W.B. Pomeroy, and C.E. Martin. *Sexual Behaviour in the Human Male.* Philadelphia and London: W.B. Saunders Company, 1948.

Kirkham, P., and J. Thumim, eds. *You Tarzan: Masculinity, Movies and Men*. London: Lawrence and Wishart, 1993.

———. *Me Jane: Masculinity, Movies and Women*. London: Lawrence and Wishart, 1995.

Kitses, J. *Horizons West*. London: Thames and Hudson, 1969.

Klapp, O.E. *Heroes, Villains and Fools: The Changing American Character*. Englewood Cliffs: Prentice Hall, 1962.

Klinger, B. "Film History Terminable and Interminable." *Screen* 38, no. 2 Summer (1997): 107-28.

Kovel, J. *Red Hunting in the Promised Land: Anticommunism and the Making of America*. London and Washington: Cassell, 1997.

Kramer, D. "What Soldiers Are Thinking About." *Harpers*, December 1943, 68-75.

Krutnick, F. *In a Lonely Street: Film Noir, Genre, Masculinity*. London and New York: Routledge, 1991.

Kuhn, A. *Women's Pictures: Feminism and Cinema*. London, Boston, Melbourne and Henley: Routledge and Kegan Paul, 1982.

Kupper, H.I. *Back to Life: The Emotional Adjustment of Our Veterans*. New York: L.B. Fischer, 1945.

La Farge, C. "Soldier into Civilian." *Harpers*, March 1945, 339-46.

Landy, M. *Cinematic Uses of the Past*. Minneapolis and London: University of Minnesota Press, 1996.

Lawrence, A. "Jimmy Stewart Is Being Beaten: *Rope* and the Postwar Crisis in American Masculinity." *Quarterly Review of Film and Video* 16, no. 1 July (1995): 41-58.

Lebergott, S. "Shall We Guarantee Full Employment." *Harpers*, February 1945, 193-202.

Lee, C. *Talking Tough: The Fight for Masculinity*. London, Sydney, Auckland and Bergvlei: Arrow Books, 1993.

Lehman, P. *Running Scared: Masculinity and the Representation of the Male Body*. Philadelphia: Temple University Press, 1993.

Lenthall, B. "Outside the Panel — Race in America's Popular Imagination: Comic Strips before and after World War Ii." *Journal of American Studies* 32, no. 1 April (1998): 39-61.

Levin, M. *Hollywood and the Great Fan Magazines*. London: Ian Allen, 1970.

Life. "Juvenile Delinquency." *Life*, 8 April 1946, 83-93.

———. "The New American Domesticated Male." *Life*, 4 January 1954, 42-45.

————. "Life Goes to Bleeck's." *Life*, 26 November 1945, 138-41.

————. "Man's Stance Declines." *Life*, 21 January 1946, 14.

Link, A.S., and R.L. Catton. *American Epoch: A History of the United States since the 1890s*. New York: Alfred A. Knopf, 1967.

Lookingbill, B. D. *Dust Bowl USA: Depression America and the Ecological Imagination 1929-1941*. Athens Ohio: Ohio University Press, 2001.

Lundberg, F., and M.F. Farnham. *Modern Woman: The Lost Sex*. New York and London: Harper and Brothers, 1947.

Lyon, R.S. *The 1990 Survival Guide to Film*. West Los Angeles: LyonHeart Publishers, 1989.

Macherey, P. *A Theory of Literary Production*. London and New York: Routledge, 1989.

Maltby, R. "Film Noir and the Politics of the Maladjusted Text." In *The Movie Book of Film Noir*, edited by I Cameron, 39-48. London: Studio Vista, 1992.

————, ed. *Dreams for Sale: Popular Culture in the 20th Century*. London: Harrap, 1989.

Maltby, R., and I. Craven. *Hollywood Cinema: An Introduction*. Oxford: Blackwell, 1995.

Maltby, R., and K. Bowles. "Hollywood: The Economics of Utopia." In *The United States in the Twentieth Century: Culture*, edited by J. Mitchell and R. Maidment. Sevenoaks: Hodder and Staughton/Open University Press, 1994.

Martin, J.B. "Anything Bothering You Soldier?" *Harpers*, July-December 1945, 453-57.

Mast, G. *A Short History of the Movies*. Oxford: Oxford University Press, 1981.

Maugham, S. *The Razor's Edge*. London, Melbourne, Toronto, Johannesburg and Auckland: William Heinemann Ltd., 1979.

May, L., ed. *Recasting America: Culture and Politics in the Age of the Cold War*. Chicago and London: University of Chicago Press, 1989.

————. *The Big Tomorrow: Hollywood and the Politics of the American Way*. Chicago and London: University of Chicago Press, 2000.

McArthur, C. *Underworld USA*. London: BFI Press, 1972.

McCann, G. *Rebel Males: Clift, Brando and Dean*. London: Hamish Hamilton, 1991.

McConnell, F. *Storytelling and Mythmaking*. Oxford and New York: Oxford University Press, 1979.

Mellen, J. *Big Bad Wolves: Masculinity in the American Film*. London: Elm Tree Books, 1978.

Menefee, S. *Assignment USA*. London: Victor Gollancz Ltd, 1944.

Milkman, R. *Gender at Work: The Dynamics of Job Segregation by Sex During World War II*. Urbana and Chicago: University of Illinois Press, 1987.

Montague Bell, H.T. *The Annual Register: A Review of Public Events at Home and Abroad for the Year 1946*. London, New York and Toronto: Longman Green and Co., 1947.

Moores, S. *Interpreting Audiences: The Ethnography of Media Consumption*. London, Thousand Oaks, New Delhi: Sage, 1993.

Morgan, D.H.J. "Theater of War: Combat, the Military, and Masculinities." In *Theorizing Masculinities: Research on Men and Masculinities*, edited by H. Brod and M. Kaufman. London, Thousand Oaks and New Delhi: Sage, 1994.

Muller, E. *Dark City: The Lost World of Film Noir*. London: Titan Books, 1998.

Mulvey, L. "Visual Pleasure and Narrative Cinema." *Screen* 16, no. 3 Autumn (1975): 6-18.

———. "Afterthoughts on 'Visual Pleasure and Narrative Cinema' Inspired by King Vidor's *Duel in the Sun* (1946)." In *Visual and Other Pleasures*, edited by L. Mulvey, 29-38. Basingstoke: Macmillan, 1989.

Munby, J. *Public Enemies Public Heroes: Screening the Gangster from Little Caesar to Touch of Evil*. Chicago and London: University of Chicago Press, 1999.

Myrdal, G. "Is American Business Deluding Itself." *Atlantic Monthly*, November 1944, 51-58.

Nachbar, J. "Film Noir." In *American Film Genres*, edited by W. Gehring. Westport and London: Greenwood Press, 1988.

Naremore, J. *More Than Night: Film Noir in Its Contexts*. Berkeley, Los Angeles, London: University of California Press, 1998.

Naremore, J. *Acting in the Cinema*. Berkeley, Los Angeles and London: University of California Press, 1990.

Neale, S. *Genre and Hollywood*. London and New York: Routledge, 2000.

———. *Genre*. London: BFI Publishing, 1980.

———. "Masculinity as Spectacle: Reflections on Men and Mainstream Cinema." *Screen* 24, no. 6 November/December

(1983): 2-16.

——. "Questions of Genre." *Screen* 31, no. 1 Spring (1990): 45-66.

——. "Aspects of Ideology and Narrative Form in the American War Film." *Screen* 32, no. 1 Spring (1991): 35-57.

Neale, S., and M. Smith, eds. *Contemporary Hollywood Cinema.* London and New York: Routledge, 1998.

Neve, B. *Film and Politics in America.* London and New York: Routledge, 1992.

Neville, R. "What's Wrong with Our Army?" *Life*, 25 February 1946, 104-12.

O'Connor, J., and M.A. Jackson, eds. *American History/American Film.* New York: Ungar Publishing Co., 1988.

O'Neill, W.L. *American High: The Years of Confidence, 1945-1960.* New York: The Free Press, 1986.

Oliver, K., and B. Trigo. *Noir Anxiety.* Minneapolis, London: University of Minnesota Press, 2003.

Overholser, W. "Effects of War on the Family." *Journal of Home Economics* 35, no. 7 September (1943): 393-95.

Overton, G.S. *Marriage in War and Peace: A Book for Parents and Counsellors of Youth.* New York, Nashville: Abingdon-Cokesbury Press, 1945.

Palahniuk, Chuck. *Fight Club.* London: Vintage, 1997.

Palmer, R.B. *Hollywood's Dark Cinema: The American Film Noir.* New York: Twayne Publishers, 1994.

——, ed. *Perspectives on Noir.* London, Mexico City, New Delhi, Singapore, Sydney, Toronto: Prentice Hall International, 1996.

Pelcovits, N.A. "Veterans Want to Be Citizens." *Harpers*, January-June 1946, 156-61.

Penley, C., and S. Willis, eds. *Male Trouble.* Minneapolis and London: University of Minnesota Press, 1993.

Perchuk, A., and H. Posner, eds. *The Masculine Masquerade: Masculinity and Representation.* Cambridge, Massachussets and London: MIT Press, 1995.

Petersen, W., ed. *American Social Patterns.* Garden City and New York: Doubleday Anchor, 1956.

Polan, D. *Power and Paranoia: History, Narrative and the American Cinema, 1940-1950.* New York: Columbia University Press, 1986.

Porfirio, R.G. "No Way Out: Existential Motifs in the Film Noir." In

Perspectives on Noir, edited by R.B. Palmer, 115-28. London, Mexico City, New Delhi, Singapore, Sydney, Toronto: Prentice Hall International, 1996.

Powers, S., D.J. Rothman, and S. Rothman. *Hollywood's America|: Social and Political Themes in Motion Pictures*. Boulder, Colo. and Oxford: Westview Press, 1996.

Pribram, E.D., ed. *Female Spectators: Looking at Film and Television*. London and New York: Verso, 1988.

Quart, L., and A. Auster. *American Film and Society since 1945*. London and Basingstoke: Macmillan, 1984.

Radway, J. "The Book-of-the-Month Club and the General Reader: On the Uses of "Serious" Fiction." *Critical Inquiry* 14 Spring (1988): 516-38.

———. *A Feeling for Books: The Book-of-the-Month Club, Literary Taste, and Middle-Class Desire*. Chapel Hill and London: University of North Carolina Press, 1997.

Radway, J. *Reading the Romance: Women, Patriarchy and Popular Literature*. Chapel Hill and London: University of North Carolina Press, 1991.

Ramsaye, T., ed. *1946-47 International Motion Picture Almanac*. New York: Quigley Publications, 1947.

———, ed. *1947-48 International Motion Picture Almanac*. New York: Quigley Publications, 1948.

———. *1948-49 International Motion Picture Almanac*. New York: Quigley Publications, 1949.

Rawlings, M.K. *The Yearling*. London: Mammoth, 1992.

Ray, R.B. *A Certain Tendency of the Hollywood Cinema, 1930-1980*. Princeton: Princeton University Press, 1985.

The New Republic. "When Twelve Million Come Home." *The New Republic*, 27 November 1944, 707-08.

Rice, T. *Sex, Marriage and the Family*. Philadelphia and New York: J.B. Lippincott and Company, 1946.

Riesman, D., N. Glazer, and R. Denney. *The Lonely Crowd: A Study of the Changing American Character*. New Haven and London: Yale University Press, 1961.

Riviere, J. "Womanliness as Masquerade." In *Formations of Fantasy*, edited by V. Burgin, J. Donald and C. Kaplan, 35-44. London and New York: Routledge, [1929] 1986.

Roffman, P., and J. Purdy. *The Hollywood Social Problem Film: Madness,*

Despair and Politics. Bloomington: Indiana University Press, 1981.

Rogers, B. *Men Only: An Investigation into Men's Organisations.* London: Pandora, 1988.

Rogin, M. "Kiss Me Deadly: Communism, Motherhood and Cold War Movies." *Representations,* no. 6 Spring (1984): 1-36.

Rollins, P.C., ed. *Hollywood as Historian: American Film in a Cultural Context.* Revised ed. Lexington: University Press of Kentucky, 1998.

Rosenstone, R.A. *Visions of the Past: The Challenge of Film to Our Idea of History.* Cambridge (USA) and London: Harvard University Press, 1995.

————. *Revisioning History: Film and the Construction of a New Past.* Princeton: Princeton University Press, 1995.

Sarris, A. *The American Cinema: Directors and Directions, 1929-1968.* New York: E.P. Dutton, 1968.

Schatz, T. *Hollywood Genres: Formulas, Filmmaking and the Studio System.* New York, St. Louis, San Francisco, Auckland, Bogota, Caracas, Lisbon, London, Madrid, Mexico, Milan, Montreal, New Delhi, Paris, San Juan, Singapore, Sydney, Tokyo, Toronto: McGraw Hill, 1981.

Schatz, T. *The Genius of the System.* London: Faber and Faber, 1998.

————. *Boom and Bust: American Cinema in the 1940s.* Berkeley, Los Angeles and London: University of California Press, 1999.

Schrader, P. "Notes on Film Noir." In *Movies and Mass Culture,* edited by J. Belton. London: Athlone, [1971] 1996.

Schwartz, C. *Cole Porter: A Biography.* New York: Da Capo Press, 1995.

Sebald, Hans. *Momism, the Silent Disease of America.* Chicago: Nelson Hall, 1976.

Selby, S. *Dark City: The Film Noir.* Jefferson, N.C. and London: McFarland, 1984.

Selig, M. "Genre, Gender and the Discourse of War: The a/Historical and Vietnam Films." *Screen* 34, no. 1 Spring (1993): 1-18.

Seward, G.H. *Sex and the Social Order.* New York and London: McGraw Hill, 1946.

Sheldon, W.H. *Varieties of Delinquent Youth.* New York: Harper and Brothers, 1949.

Silver, A., and E. Ward. *An Encyclopaedic Reference Guide to Film Noir.*

Revised and expanded ed. London: Bloomsbury, 1980.

Silverman, K. "Male Subjectivity and the Celestial Suture: *It's a Wonderful Life.*" *Framework*, no. 14 Spring (1981): 16-22.

Silverman, K. "Historical Trauma and Male Subjectivity." In *Psychoanalysis and Cinema*, edited by E.A. Kaplan, 110-27. New York and London: Routledge, 1990.

———. *Male Subjectivity at the Margins.* London and New York: Routledge, 1992.

Simons, J.D., ed. *Literature and Film in the Historical Dimension: Selected Papers from the 15th Florida State University Conference on Literature and Film.* Gainesville: University Press of Florida, 1994.

Sklar, R. *Movie Made America: A Cultural History of American Movies.* New York: Vintage Books, 1975.

Slichter, S.H. "Jobs after the War." *Atlantic Monthly*, October 1944, 87-91.

Slotkin, R. *Gunfighter Nation: The Myth of the Frontier in Twentieth-Century America.* Norman: University of Oklahoma Press, 1998.

Sobchak, V., ed. *The Persistence of History: Cinema, Television and the Modern Event.* New York and London: Routledge, 1996.

———. "Lounge Time: Postwar Crises and the Chronotope of Film Noir." In *Refiguring American Film Genres: Theory and History*, edited by N. Browne. Berkeley, Los Angeles and London: University of California Press, 1998.

Sparrow, J.C. *History of Personnel Demobilization in the United States Army.* Washington DC: Office of the Chief of Military History, Department of the Army, 1951.

Spicer, A. *Film Noir.* Harlow, London, New York, Reading, San Francisco, Toronto, Don Mills, Ontario, Sydney, Tokyo, Singapore, Hong Kong, Seoul, Taipei, Cape Town, Madrid, Mexico City, Amsterdam, Munich, Paris, Milan: Longman, 2002.

Spock, B. *The Pocket Book of Baby and Child Care.* New York: Pocket Books, 1946.

———. *Problems of Parents.* London: The Bodley Head, 1963.

Staiger, J. *Interpreting Films: Studies in the Historical Reception of American Cinema.* Princeton: Princeton University Press, 1992.

———. *Perverse Spectators: The Practices of Film Reception.* New York: New York University Press, 2000.

Stanford, N. "From Foxhole to Main Street - Part 1." *Christian Science*

Monitor, 9 September 1944, 3 & 15.

————. "From Foxhole to Main Street - Part 2." *Christian Science Monitor*, 16 September 1944, 3.

Stassen, H.E. "Jobs and Freedom." *Atlantic monthly*, March 1946, 48-52.

Steinberg, C.S. *Reel Facts: The Movie Book of Records*. New York: Vintage Books, 1982.

Stephens, M.L. *Film Noir: A Comprehensive Illustrated Reference to Movies*. Jefferson NC and London: McFarland and Co., 1995.

Stewart, G.R. *American Ways of Life*. Garden City and New York: Dolphin Books, 1954.

Stokes, M., and R. Maltby. *Identifying Hollywood's Audiences: Cultural Identity and the Movies*. London: BFI Publishing, 1999.

Strecker, E.A. *Their Mother's Sons: The Psychiatrist Examines an American Problem*. Philadelphia and New York: J.B. Lippincott Co., 1946.

Studlar, G. *This Mad Masquerade: Stardom and Masculinity in the Jazz Age*. New York: Columbia University Press, 1996.

Terkel, S. *The Good War: An Oral History of World War Two*. Harmondsworth, New York, Victoria, Markham, Auckland: Penguin, 1986.

Thomas, D. *Reading Hollywood: Spaces and Meanings in American Film*. London and New York: Wallflower Press, 2001.

————. "How Hollywood Deals with the Deviant Male." In *The Movie Book of Film Noir*, edited by I. Cameron, 59-70. London: Studio Vista, 1992.

Thompson, K., and D. Bordwell. *Film History: An Introduction*. New York: McGraw Hill, 1994.

Thumim, J. *Celluloid Sisters: Women and Popular Cinema*. Basingstoke and London: Macmillan, 1992.

Time. "Crime Wave Coming." *Time*, 3 April 1944, 6.

Times, The New York. "Review of *the Strange Love of Martha Ivers*." *New York Times*, 25 July 1946, 18.

Todorov, T. *The Poetics of Prose*. Ithaca: Cornell University Press, 1977.

————. *Genres in Discourse*. Cambridge, New York, Port Chester, Melbourne, Sydney: Cambridge University Press, 1990.

Trilling, L. "Sex and Science: The Kinsey Report." In *The Scene before You: A New Approach to American Culture*, edited by C. Brossard. New York and Toronto: Rinehart and Co., 1955.

Turner, B., and T. Rennell. *When Daddy Came Home: How Family Life Changed Forever in 1945*. London, Sydney, Auckland, Bergvlei: Hutchinson, 1995.

Turner, G. *Film as a Social Practice*. London: Routledge, 1988.

Tuska, J. *Dark Cinema*. Westport CT and London: Greenwood Press, 1984.

Variety. "All-Time Top Grossers." *Variety*, 5 January 1955, 59 & 63.

———. "Review of *Notorious*." *Variety*, 24 July 1946.

Variety. "60 Top Grossers of 1946." *Variety*, 8 January 1947, 8.

———. "Top Grossers of 1947." *Variety*, 7 January 1948, 63.

———. "Top Grossers of 1948." *Variety*, 5 January 1949, 46.

———. "Top-Grossers of 1949." *Variety*, 4 January 1950, 59.

———. "Top-Grossers of 1950." *Variety*, 3 January 1951, 58.

———. "Review of *Leave Her to Heaven*." *Variety*, 2 January 1946.

———. "Review of *Spellbound*." *Variety*, 31 October 1945.

———. "Review of Best Years of Our Lives." *Variety*, 27 November 1946.

———. "Review of Two Years before the Mast." *Variety*, 28 August 1946.

———. "Review of *the Big Sleep*." *Variety*, 14 August 1946.

Variety. "Review of *the Blue Dahlia*." *Variety*, 30 January 1946.

———. "Review of *Crossfire*." *Variety*, 25 July 1947.

———. "Review of Scarlet Street." *Variety*, 2 January 1946.

———. "Review of *the Yearling*." *Variety*, 27 November 1946.

———. "Review of *the Razor's Edge*." *Variety*, 20 November 1946.

———. "Review of *Till the Clouds Roll By*." *Variety*, 13 November 1946.

———. "Review of *the Jolson Story*." *Variety*, 18 September 1946.

———. "Review of *the Green Years*." *Variety*, 13 March 1946.

———. "Review of *the Strange Love of Martha Ivers*." *Variety*, 13 March 1946.

———. "Review of *Road to Utopia*." *Variety*, 5 December 1945.

Variety. "Review of Saratoga Trunk." *Variety*, 21 November 1945.

———. "Review of *Easy to Wed*." *Variety*, 10 April 1946.

———. "Review of *Notorious*." *Variety*, 24 July 1946.

———. "Review of *Two Years before the Mast*." *Variety*, 28 August 1946.

———. "Review of *Blue Skies*." *Variety*, 25 September 1946.

———. "Review of *Margie*." *Variety*, 16 October 1946.

———. "Review of *Ziegfeld Follies*." *Variety*, 15 August 1945.

———. "Review of *the Harvey Girls*." *Variety*, 2 January 1946.

———. "Review of *Boomerang!*" *Variety*, 29 January 1947.

———. "Review of the Kid from Brooklyn." *Variety*, 20 March 1946.

Variety. "Review of *the Postman Always Rings Twice*." *Variety*, 20 March 1946.

———. "Review of *Gilda*." *Variety*, 20 March 1946.

———. "Review of *the Killers*." *Variety*, 7 August 1946.

———. "Review of *the Strange Love of Martha Ivers*." *Variety*, 13 March 1946.

Vernet, M. "Film Noir on the Edge of Doom." In *Shades of Noir*, edited by J. Copjec. London: Verso, 1993.

Viser, V.J. "Winning the Peace: American Planning for a Profitable Post-War World." *Journal of American Studies*, no. 35 April 2001 (2001): 111-26.

Volosinov, V. *Marxism and the Philosophy of Language*. New York and London: Seminar Press, 1973.

Walker, M. "Film Noir: Introduction." In *The Movie Book of Film Noir*, edited by I. Cameron. London: Studio Vista, 1992.

Waller, G. A., ed. *Moviegoing in America: A Sourcebook in the History of Film Exhibition*. Oxford; Malden, Massachussets: Blackwell, 2002.

Waller, W. *The Veteran Comes Back*. New York: The Dryden Press, 1944.

———. "The Veteran's Attitudes." *Annals of the American Academy of Political and Social Science*, no. 238 March (1945): 174-77.

———. "A Sociologist Looks at Conscription." *Annals of the American Academy of Political and Social Science*, no. 241 September (1945): 95-101.

Warshow, R. *The Immediate Experience: Movies, Comics, Theatre and Other Aspects of Popular Culture*. Cambridge, Massachussets and London, England: Harvard University Press, 2001.

Weaver, S.L. "Blasts 'Intellectual' Critics: 'the Public Makes the Hits'." *Variety* 3 January (1951): 101.

Wetta, F.J., and S.J. Curley. *Celluloid Wars: A Guide to Film and the American Experience of War*. New York, Westport CT and London: Greenwood Press, 1992.

Wexman, V.W. *Creating the Couple: Love. Marriage and Hollywood Performance*. Princeton: Princeton University Press, 1993.

Willett, R. "The Nation in Crisis: Hollywood's Response to the 1940s." In *Cinema, Politics and Society in America*, edited by P.

Davies and B. Neve. Manchester: Manchester University Press, 1981.

Williams, R. *The Long Revolution*. London: Chatto and Windus, 1961.

———. *Marxism and Literature*. Oxford: Oxford University Press, 1977.

Williams, L. "Discipline and Fun: *Psycho* and Postmodern Cinema." In *Reinventing Film Studies*, edited by C. Gledhill and L. Williams. London: Arnold, 2000.

Wolfe, B. "Ecstatic in Blackface: The Negro as Song-and-Dance Man." In *The Scene before You: A New Approach to American Culture*, edited by C. Brossard. New York and Toronto: Rinehart and Company, 1955.

Wood, M. *America in the Movies or, "Santa Maria It Had Slipped My Mind!"* London: Secker and Warburg, 1975.

Wright, W. *Sixguns and Society: A Structural Study of the Western*. Berkeley, Los Angeles and London: University of California Press, 1977.

Wylie, P. *Generation of Vipers*. New York and Toronto: Farrar and Rhinehart, 1942.

Index

Absent father, 24, 64, 66-69, 71, 73-81, 93, 149, 160, 161, 162, 163
Allen, Frederick Lewis, 29
All-male group, 24, 40, 121-133, 139, 144, 149, 167, 168, 169, 170
Altman, Rick, 12, 21, 22, 23, 176
Alexander, John, 50
Anderson, Judith, 153, 163
Anderson, Paul, 130
Andrews, Dana, 31, 34, 154, 165
Anna and the King of Siam, 187
Anti-semitism, 159
Asheim, Lester, 3, 16, 147
Astaire, Fred, 112, 113, 136, 191 Ch4 n2, n3
Atlantic, The, 54
Audience Research Institute, 188
Austin, Jerry, 60
Baber, R. E., 68, 181
Baby and Child Care, 65, 181
Babbington, B. and Evans, T., 108
Bacall, Lauren, 160, 165
Back to Life: The Emotional Adjustment of Our Veterans, 30
Barker, Martin, 179, 180
Barthes, Roland, 61
Beaumont, Hugh, 162
Beeler, Aggie ("Jersey Lil"), 141
Begley, Ed, 155
Bells of St Mary's, The, 18
Belton, John, 26, 28, 152, 156, 160, 182
Benchley, Robert, 115
Bendix, William, 106, 192 Ch6 n1
Bennett, Joan, 150
Bennett, Tony, 179,
Bergman, Ingrid, 19, 41, 42, 68
Best Years of Our Lives, 9, 12, 13, 15, 18, 28, 31-36, 47, 97, 103-107, 111, 113, 119, 123, 126, 127, 133, 151, 152, 168-169, 170, 181, 187, 192 Ch6 n2
Big Sleep, The, 14, 15, 148, 157, 160, 162, 164, 173, 181, 187
Blackface, 52, 53, 58, 59, 60, 108
Blue Dahlia, The, 14, 15, 148, 157, 161, 162, 163, 165, 168, 169, 171, 181, 192 Ch6 n2
Blue Skies, 13, 18, 28, 29, 80, 81, 82, 93, 131-133, 135, 136, 138, 139, 145, 151, 152, 169, 181
Bogart, Humphrey, 157, 165, 166, 167
Bohnen, Roman, 153
Boomerang!, 149, 150, 151, 154, 156, 157, 163, 165, 169, 181, 182
Borde, Raymond and Chaumeton, Etienne, 12, 192 Ch7 n2, n3
Bordman, G.,142
Bremer, Lucille, 113
Brodie, Steve, 171
Brown, C., 13
"Buddy" relationship, 122, 133-136, 144, 149, 167, 170, 171, 172
Butler, Judith, 24, 96, 97
Buzzell, Edward, 13
Cagney, James, 89
Capra, Frank, 14, 189 Ch1 n6
Caulfield, Joan, 80, 135
Chandler, Raymond, 189 Ch1 n9
Cherne, Leo, 95, 100, 101
Christian Science Monitor, 31
"Cinderellas" of the services, 30, 31, 63
Class, 27, 31-46, 48, 51, 60, 130, 153, 154
Classlessness, 27- 29, 33-41, 44- 47, 49, 62, 63, 149, 150, 152, 154, 156, 181
Cobley, Paul, 178, 179, 180
Coburn, Charles, 89

Cohan, Steven, 24, 82, 112, 165, 191
Ch4 n2
Collier's, 100
Commentary, 190 Ch2 n4
Conrad, William, 172
Cook, Pam, 3
Cooper, Gary, 40, 41
Cooper, Gladys, 89, 90
Couldry, Nick, 9
Cowie, Elizabeth, 175, 177
Crain, Jeanne, 76
Cromwell, John, 187
Cronin, A. J., 191 Ch3 n4
Cronyn, Hume, 90
Crosby, Bing, 29, 114, 116, 132, 136
191/2 Ch5 n1
Crossfire, 148, 157, 159, 160, 163,
165, 168, 169, 171
Crowther, Bosley, 13, 19, 20, 148,
149, 165, 190 Ch2 n3
Crowther, Bruce, 26, 182
Curtiz, Michael, 13
Dale, Esther, 76
Dana, Richard, H. 38, 190 Ch2 n2
Danziger, Juliet, 79, 181
Da Silva, Howard, 37, 162
Dean, James, 89
De Bedts, R. F., 95, 98
Delinquency, 71, 72, 73, 75, 76, 79,
162
   - Juvenile, 67, 68, 78, 80, 161
Demarest, William, 50
De Mille, Cecil B., 17
De Wolfe, Billy, 29
Dmytryk, Edward, 148
Donath, Ludwig, 48
Donlevy, Brian, 38
Douglas, Kirk, 153
Dowling, Doris, 162
Drake, Tom, 62
Duel in the Sun, 18, 21
Duryea, Dan, 150
Easy to Wed, 13, 14, 16, 113, 116,
118, 119, 136, 183
Egg and I, The, 18
Family, 11, 17, 24, 65-67, 74, 78-83,
93, 122-127, 129-131, 133, 145, 146,
151, 160, 161, 169, 170
Farber, Manny, 189 Ch1 n3

Farrow, John, 13
Femme fatale, 66, 89, 92, 161, 163,
164
Fernandez, Esther, 38
Filene, P., 66, 98
Film noir, 2-4, 6, 8, 9-16, 19, 20, 21,
23-27, 53, 64, 66, 89, 92, 93, 145-
149, 152, 153, 156-158, 160, 161,
163, 166-168, 170, 172, 173, 175-
178, 181, 186, 187, 189 Ch1 n1
Fischer, L., 82
Fitzpatrick, Edward, 131
Ford, Glenn, 167, 172
Forever Amber, 18
Foster, Preston, 57
Freedland, Michael, 58, 109, 141
Gallup, George, H., 188
Gardner, Ava, 150
Garfield, John, 150
Garland, Judy, 57
Garnett, Tay, 14
Generation of Vipers, 82, 86, 191 Ch3
n3
Genre, 2, 6, 12, 14, 15, 16, 19, 20-26,
40, 49, 50, 52, 57, 65, 93, 97, 98,
107, 113, 114, 119, 120, 127, 148,
174, 175-178, 180, 181, 182, 186,
189 Ch1 n1
Gilda, 14, 15, 148, 157, 167, 172,
173, 189 Ch1 n11
Glancy, H. Mark, 154
Goffman, Erving, 102
Gomery, Douglas, 185, 188
Goodwin, Bill, 52
Gorer, Geoffrey, 57, 82, 89, 91, 134,
135, 136, 138, 139, 163
Goulden, Joseph C., 4
Goulding, Edmund, 13
Graebner, William, 5
Grahame, Gloria, 163
Grant, Cary, 47, 69, 72
Great Depression, 62, 66, 154
Green, Alfred E.,13
Green Dolphin Street, 18
Green Years, The, 13, 14, 18, 28, 62,
84, 89, 90, 93, 183
Griffith, Coleman, R., 102
Grines, Karolyn, Kay, 80
Hall, Michael, 124

Hammerstein, Oscar, 52
Handel, L. A., 186, 188, 192 Ch7 n4, 193 Ch7 n5
Hard-boiled, 148
Harpers, 30, 31
Harvey Girls, The, 13, 14, 57
Harvey, Sylvia, 3, 160, 182
Hawks, Howard, 14
Hayworth, Rita, 163
Heflin, Van, 140, 150, 165
Heisler, S., 13
Hitchcock, Alfred, 13, 19, 163
Hiss, Alger, 180
Hodiak, John, 57
Hollywood Quarterly, 2, 3, 146
Hope, Bob, 114, 116, 192 Ch5 n1
"Horizon of expectation", 180, 181, 182
Houseman, John, 2, 3, 13,16, 146, 147, 148, 149, 177, 182
Howard, Sidney, 82
HUAC, 17, 27, 190 Ch2 n1
Hucksters, The, 18
Invasion of the Body Snatchers, 181, 192 Ch7 n1
It's a Wonderful Life, 14, 15, 66
Ivan, Rosalind, 163
I've Got My Captain Working For Me Now, 29, 152
Jameson, Fredric, 1, 2, 21, 22, 178
Jauss, H. R., 180
Jefferson, Thomas, 28, 152
Johnson, Van, 116, 117, 118
Jolson, Al, 47, 48, 49, 50, 51, 52, 53, 55, 58, 59, 60, 107-112, 141, 191 Ch4 n2
Jolson Sings Again, 17, 18, 47
Jolson Story, The, 13, 15, 18, 28, 47, 48, 51, 57, 58, 60, 62, 107, 109, 111-114, 119, 139-141, 143, 158, 160, 167
Journal of Home Economics, 102
Kaye, Danny, 118
Kazan, Elia, 149
Kelly, Gene, 113, 136
Kennedy, Arthur, 150
Kern, Jerome, 140
Kid From Brooklyn, The, 13, 14, 113, 116, 118, 119, 187

King, Henry, 13
Killers, The, 15, 148, 150, 151, 157, 158, 160, 163, 169, 172, 173
Kern, Jerome, 47, 51, 55, 62
Keyes, Evelyn, 108, 109
Kinsey, Alfred, 134
Konstantin, Leopoldine, 72, 84, 85, 86, 87
Krutnik, Frank, 189 Ch1 n2
Kuhn, Mickey, 153
Kupper, H. I., 30, 31, 95, 101, 123, 133, 134
Ladd, Alan, 37, 106, 157, 166, 167
Ladies Home Journal, 95
Lake, Veronica, 162
Lamour, Dorothy, 114
Lang, Fritz, 14
Langan, Glen, 76
Lancaster, Burt
Leave Her to Heaven, 18, 19, 20
Lebergott, Stanley, 30
Leonard, Eddie, 141
Levene, Sam, 158, 159
Levin, Henry, 17, 47
Life, 29, 30, 67, 96, 118, 125, 142, 143, 190 Ch3 n2
Life With Father, 18
Lundberg, F. and Farnham, M. F., 66, 93
Lyon, R. S.,12, 15, 189 Ch1 n5, n7
Macherey, Pierre, 179
Macready, George, 172
Maltby, Richard, 3, 23, 189 Ch1 n2, 192 Ch5 n2
March, Fredric, 32, 34, 104
"March of Time", 155
Margie, 13, 14, 75, 76, 77, 81, 93, 181
Marshall, George, 14
Marshall, Herbert, 46
Masculinity, 11, 17, 24, 39, 40, 42, 43, 121, 126, 145, 146, 168, 172, 173
- as performance of gender, 24, 96-107, 111-120, 149, 164, 167
Matrix, The, 181
Maugham, Somerset, 46, 47
May, Lary, 7, 8
McCarthyism, 180
McGraw, Charles, 172
McLeod, Norman Z., 13

"Melting pot", 28, 57, 60, 64, 150, 158, 160
Milestone, Lewis, 14
Minnelli, Vincente, 13
Mitchum, Robert, 157, 166
Momism, 24, 64, 66, 82-89, 91, 92, 93, 149, 160, 161, 163, 164, 170
Motion Picture Research Bureau, 186
Myrdal, Gunnar, 54
Myth, 25-28, 33, 36, 56, 60, 62-64, 149, 150, 151, 152, 156
Naremore, James, 177, 184, 185, 192 Ch6 n2, 193 Ch7n6
National Identity, 11, 17, 24-28, 36, 40, 46, 51, 54, 56-58, 60-63, 145, 146, 149, 150, 152, 158, 159
Neale, Steve, 4, 22, 23, 147, 174, 175, 177, 178
Neo-noir, 177
Neve, Brian, 189 Ch1 n2
New American Domesticated Male, The, 190 Ch3 n2
New Republic, The, 102
New York Times, 13, 19, 20, 79, 148, 166, 181, 190 Ch2 n3
Night and Day, 13, 14, 28, 47, 51, 57, 139, 140, 143, 183
Notorious, 12, 13, 14, 19, 20, 68, 71, 72, 74-76, 77, 81, 84, 85, 88, 89, 93, 161, 181
O'Brien, Edmond, 157
O'Neill, William L., 4, 5, 6
Overton, Grace Sloan, 66, 68, 93, 181
Palmer, R. Barton, 10
Paramount Decree, 17
Paramount Pictures, 115, 166
Parents, 79, 181
Parks, Larry, 107, 108, 109
Peck, Gregory, 19, 127
Pelcovits, N. A., 31
Phillips, Norman, Jr., 33
Porter, Cole, 47, 51, 55, 140, 141
Postman Always Rings Twice, The, 14, 15, 148, 150, 152, 157, 163
Powell, William, 112
Power, Tyrone, 44
Rains, Claude, 69, 72

Ray, Nicholas, 89
Razor's Edge, The, 13, 18, 28, 44, 46, 47, 151, 154, 181
Rebecca, 163
Rebel Without a Cause, 89
"Regime of verisimilitude", 180
Road to Utopia, 13, 18, 113-116, 118, 119, 136-139, 145
Robinson, Edward G., 150, 166
Robson, Flora, 60
Rogers and Hart, 47
Ryan, Robert, 159, 166
Samson and Delilah, 17, 18
Saratoga Trunk, 13, 14, 28, 41, 44, 47, 60-62, 64, 68, 73, 75-77, 81, 92, 93, 151, 154, 158, 160, 161, 181, 183
Sarris, Andrew, 8
Saville, Victor, 13
Scarlet Street, 14, 15, 148, 150, 152, 163, 166, 170
Schatz, Thomas, 3, 47, 182, 185, 188, 190 Ch3 n1
Schwartz, C., 141
Scott, Lizabeth, 151
Sebald, Hans, 83
Seigel, Don, 181
Selby, Spencer, 3, 182
Shayne, Tamara, 48
Sidney, George, 13
Silver Cord, The, 82
Sinatra, Frank, 191/2 Ch5 n1
Siodmak, Robert, 15, 189 Ch1 n8
Slichter, Sumner, H., 54
Small town, 66, 154
Smith, Ethel, 118
Smith, Queenie, 158
Spellbound, 18, 19
Spock, Dr. Benjamin, 65, 66, 71, 72, 78, 79, 81, 93, 162, 181
Stahl, John M., 19
Staiger, Janet, 180
Stanford, Neal, 31, 32
Stassen, Harold, E., 54
Status inversion, 27, 28, 31, 32, 33, 149, 150, 151, 152
Steinberg, C. S., 12
Stewart, George, R., 134
Stewart, James, 189 Ch1 n6
Stockwell, Dean, 62, 90

Strange Love of Martha Ivers, The, 14, 15, 148, 150, 151, 153, 154, 156, 163, 166, 181, 189 Ch1 n10, n11
Strecker, Edward A., 82, 83, 89, 91
Studebaker, 142, 143
Taurog, Norman, 47
Thomas, Deborah, 7, 16
Thumim, Janet, 60, 180, 188
Tierney, Gene, 20, 45
Till the Clouds Roll By, 13, 14, 28, 47, 51, 57, 62, 139-141, 143, 183
Time, 95
Turner, Lana, 152
Twentieth Century Fox, 20
Two Years Before the Mast, 13, 14, 28, 37, 41, 44, 97, 103, 106, 107, 111, 113, 119, 129-131, 133, 139, 144, 154, 169, 181, 183
Unconquered, 18
Variety, 8, 12, 13, 17, 18, 19, 20, 32, 159, 165, 166, 189 Ch1 n4, n5, n11, 190 Ch2 n3
Veteran Comes Back, The, 30
Vickers, Martha, 161
Vidor, King, 14, 21
Viser, Victor J., 4, 6
Wachowski Brothers, 181
Waldron, Charles, 161, 173
Walker, Hal, 13
Walker, Robert, 51
Waller, Willard, 30, 31, 67, 95, 99, 100, 101, 122, 123, 131, 181
Wall Street Crash, 46
Wall Street Journal, 185
Walsh, Raoul, 89
Warburton, John, 75
Warshow, Robert, 5, 6, 8, 9
Weaver, Sylvester L., 8
Webb, Clifton, 44
Welcome Stranger, 18
White Christmas, 132
White Heat, 89
Whorf, Richard, 13
Wilde, Cornell, 20
Williams, Cara, 163
Williams, Esther, 117
Williams, Linda, 193 Ch7n6
Wolfe, Bernard, 59
Wood, Sam, 13

Wooley, Monty, 140, 141
Words and Music, 47
Wright, Will (Academic), 55, 56, 156
Wright, Will (Actor), 161
Wyler, William, 9, 13, 170
Wylie, Philip, 82, 83, 86, 87, 89, 91, 92, 163, 190 Ch3 n3
Wynn, Keenan, 136
Yearling, The, 13, 18, 92, 93, 127, 133, 139, 143
Yoelson, Asa, 48, 58, 108-111, 140
Young, James Webb,
Young, Robert, 160
Zeitgeist, 2, 3, 4, 6, 10, 11, 12, 15, 16, 20, 23, 25, 26, 147, 148, 174, 182
Ziegfeld Follies, 13, 14, 112, 113, 136, 189 Ch1 n4